LOW-FAT
VEGETARIAN
100 STEP-BY-STEP RECIPES

LOW-FAT
VEGETARIAN
100 STEP-BY-STEP RECIPES

Healthy and delicious low-fat ideas for any occasion, all shown step-by-step and illustrated with over 400 colour photographs

Consultant editor: Anne Sheasby

southwater

This edition is published by Southwater, an imprint of
Anness Publishing Ltd, Hermes House, 88–89 Blackfriars Road,
London SE1 8HA; tel. 020 7401 2077; fax 020 7633 9499

www.southwaterbooks.com; www.annesspublishing.com

If you like the images in this book and would like to investigate
using them for publishing, promotions or advertising, please visit
our website www.practicalpictures.com for more information.

UK agent: The Manning Partnership Ltd
  tel. 01225 478444; fax 01225 478440;
  sales@manning-partnership.co.uk
UK distributor: Grantham Book Services Ltd
  tel. 01476 541080; fax 01476 541061; orders@gbs.tbs-ltd.co.uk
North American agent/distributor: National Book Network
  tel. 301 459 3366; fax 301 429 5746; www.nbnbooks.com
Australian agent/distributor: Pan Macmillan Australia
  tel. 1300 135 113; fax 1300 135 103
  customer.service@macmillan.com.au
New Zealand agent/distributor: David Bateman Ltd
  tel. (09) 415 7664; fax (09) 415 8892

Publisher: Joanna Lorenz
Editorial Director: Helen Sudell
Editors: James Harrison and Elizabeth Woodland
Recipes: Pepita Aris, Catherine Atkinson, Mary Banks, Alex Barker,
  Ghillie Basan, Judy Bastyra, Angela Boggiano, Jacqueline Clark,
  Maxine Clark, Trish Davies, Roz Denny, Joanna Farrow, Jennie
  Fleetwood, Brian Glover, Nicola Graimes, Carole Handslip,
  Christine Ingram, Becky Johnson, Lucy Knox, Sally Mansfield,
  Christine McFadden, Jane Milton, Sallie Morris, Rena Salaman,
  Jenni Shapter, Marlena Spieler, Liz Trigg, Jenny White, Kate
  Whiteman, Lucy Whiteman, Jeni Wright.
Home economists: Eliza Baird, Alex Barker, Caroline Barty, Joanna
  Farrow, Annabel Ford, Christine France, Carole Handslip, Kate Jay,
  Becky Johnson, Jill Jones, Bridget Sargeson, Jennie Shapter,
  Carol Tennant, Sunil Vijayakar, Jenny White.
Photographers: Frank Adam, Tim Auty, Martin Brigdale, Louisa Dare,
  Nicki Dowey, Gus Filgate, Ian Garlick, Michelle Garrett,
  John Heseltine, Amanda Heywood, Janine Hosegood,
  Dave Jordan, Dave King, William Lingwood, Thomas Odulate,
  Craig Roberson, Simon Smith, Sam Stowell.
Designer: Graham Webb, Design Principals
Cover Designer: Nigel Partridge
Production Manager: Claire Rae

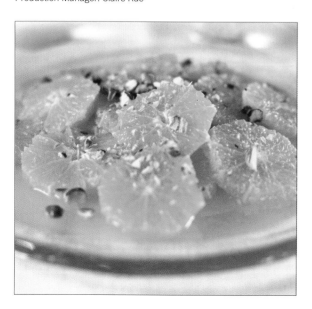

Ethical Trading Policy

At Anness Publishing we believe that business should be conducted in an ethical and
ecologically sustainable way, with respect for the environment and a proper regard to the
replacement of the natural resources we employ.

As a publisher, we use a lot of wood pulp to make high-quality paper for printing,
and that wood commonly comes from spruce trees. We are therefore currently growing
more than 500,000 trees in two Scottish forest plantations near Aberdeen – Berrymoss
(130 hectares/320 acres) and West Touxhill (125 hectares/305 acres). The forests we
manage contain twice the number of trees employed each year in paper-making for
our books.

Because of this ongoing ecological investment programme, you, as our customer, can
have the pleasure and reassurance of knowing that a tree is being cultivated on your
behalf to naturally replace the materials used to make the book you are holding.

Our forestry programme is run in accordance with the UK Woodland Assurance
Scheme (UKWAS) and will be certified by the internationally recognized Forest
Stewardship Council (FSC). The FSC is a non-government organization dedicated to
promoting responsible management of the world's forests. Certification ensures forests
are managed in an environmentally sustainable and socially responsible way. For further
information about this scheme, go to www.annesspublishing.com/trees

Notes

Bracketed terms are intended for American readers.

For all recipes, quantities are given in both metric and imperial measures and, where
appropriate, in standard cups and spoons. Follow one set, but not a mixture, because
they are not interchangeable.

Standard spoon and cup measures are level. 1 tsp = 5ml, 1 tbsp = 15ml,
1 cup = 250ml/8fl oz. Australian standard tablespoons are 20ml. Australian readers
should use 3 tsp in place of 1 tbsp for measuring small quantities of flour, salt, etc.

American pints are 16fl oz/2 cups. American readers should use 20fl oz/2.5 cups in
place of 1 pint when measuring liquids.

The nutritional analysis given for each recipe is calculated per portion (i.e. serving or
item), unless otherwise stated. If the recipe gives a range, such as Serves 4–6, then the
nutritional analysis will be for the smaller portion size, i.e. 6 servings. The nutritional
analysis of recipes also excludes all optional ingredients (where the word 'optional'
appears in brackets after an ingredient), serving suggestions, foods/ingredients 'to
serve', croûtons (in a couple of the soup recipes), garnishes and decorations, as well as
variations and cook's tips. Measurements for sodium do not include salt added to taste.

Each recipe title in this book is followed by a symbol that indicates the following:
★ = 5g of fat or less per serving ★★ = 10g of fat or less per serving

We have included cooking temperatures for electric and gas ovens. If you have a
fan-assisted oven, remember that you need to reduce the oven temperature slightly
(usually by around 20°C/40°F) and/or adjust the cooking times. Please refer to
manufacturer's guidelines for more specific information on adjusting the temperature
and time for your oven.

Some of the recipes in this book may contain raw or lightly cooked eggs – these
recipes are not recommended for babies and young children, pregnant women,
the elderly and those convalescing. Medium (US large) eggs are used unless
otherwise stated.

Ideally, home-made low-fat vegetable stock should be used for all relevant recipes in
this book. Alternatively, good quality stock cubes or bouillon powder can be used.

While every care has been taken in compiling and testing the recipes in this book, the
publisher or any other persons who have been involved in working on this publication
cannot accept responsibility for any errors or omissions, inadvertent or not, that may be
found in the recipes or text, nor for any problems that may arise as a result of preparing
one of these recipes.

Previously published as part of a larger volume, *Low-Fat, No-Fat Vegetarian*

Main cover image shows Cassava Sweet, for recipe see page 141

CONTENTS

THE LOW-FAT VEGETARIAN

Many people think that vegetarianism is a relatively new trend, but in many countries around the globe, vegetarianism, in one form or another, has been the natural way to eat for many hundreds, if not thousands, of years. Today, there are millions of people who are vegetarians.

Although some vegetarian dishes are high in calories and fat, many can be enjoyed as part of a healthy low-fat eating regime, and with a few basic guidelines, a low-fat vegetarian diet is simple to achieve.

Defining vegetarianism

There are various forms of vegetarianism: you might be a vegan, a lacto-vegetarian, a fruitarian or on a macrobiotic diet. According to the Vegetarian Society, the definition of a vegetarian is "someone living on a diet of grains, pulses, nuts, seeds, vegetables and fruits with or without the use of dairy products and eggs (preferably free-range)".

A vegetarian does not eat any meat, poultry, game, fish, shellfish or crustacea, or meat by-products such as gelatine or animal fats.

A typical vegetarian diet includes a wide range of different food groups such as cereals/grains, pulses, nuts, seeds, fruit and vegetables, as well as dairy or soya products, eggs and vegetable oils and fats. These form the basis of a healthy and nutritious eating regime.

There are several different kinds of vegetarian diets. The most common vegetarians are Lacto-ovo-vegetarians who avoid meat, poultry and fish, etc, but include dairy products and eggs in their diet. Lacto-vegetarians are the same as Lacto-ovo-vegetarians, but they do not eat eggs.

Vegans, on the other hand, follow a much stricter eating regime and do not eat meat, poultry and fish, dairy products, eggs, or any other animal product. Fruitarians eat a diet which consists mainly of raw fruit, grains and nuts. Very few processed or cooked foods are eaten. Finally, some people choose a macrobiotic diet, which is a diet followed for spiritual and philosophical reasons. This specific diet progresses through ten levels, becoming increasingly restrictive. Although not all levels are vegetarian, each level gradually eliminates animal products until the highest level eventually reaches a brown rice diet.

As long as you eat a wide variety of foods, life never need be dull if you choose to follow a vegetarian diet. By its very nature, a balanced vegetarian diet tends to be naturally low in saturated and total fat, high in dietary fibre and complex carbohydrates, and high in many protective vitamins and minerals. A well-balanced vegetarian diet should provide all the nutrients, vitamins and minerals your body needs.

Through vegetarian cooking, you can mix and match the vibrant colours, textures and flavours of vegetables, fruits, pulses and grains with many other exciting ingredients, and experiment with a wide variety of interesting and unusual foods to create all kinds of delicious and tempting dishes from many parts of the world.

Choosing vegetarian food

Many vegetarian foods available in shops and supermarkets are clearly marked on their packaging as being 'suitable for vegetarians'. Some food products also carry the 'V' (vegetarian) symbol and others carry vegetarian symbols familiar to particular countries such as the 'two green leaves' symbol. Some vegetarian foods carry a Vegetarian Society symbol, which indicates that they are approved and meet specific criteria that ensures the foods are absolutely suitable for vegetarians. Other food products,

Left: Rice is perfect for experimenting with many different vegetarian options.

such as cheese, may also include additional useful information, for example advice that the cheese is made using 'non-animal rennet'.

Nutrition and the vegetarian diet

In a vegetarian diet, protein, which is made up of amino acids, is needed for the growth and repair of all body cells. Protein is provided by foods such as eggs, milk, yogurt, cheese and soya bean products, such as tofu and tempeh, all of which contain many of the essential amino acids we need.

Other foods such as beans, peas, lentils, grains, nuts and seeds also provide a valuable source of protein.

Carbohydrates, which divide into simple and complex carbohydrates, supply the body with energy. Simple carbohydrates tend to be found in sugars and sweet foods, which should only be eaten in moderation. Complex carbohydrates on the other hand are a vital part of a healthy diet and these are provided by foods such as rice, pasta, bread, potatoes and other vegetables, as well as many fruits. Many of these complex carbohydrate foods also provide fibre, vitamins and minerals.

Vitamins and minerals have many vital functions and important roles, such as keeping the nervous system

Below: Onions have excellent culinary and medicinal values for the vegetarian.

Above: Tomatoes on the vine contain vitamin C, folic acid, potassium and lycopene – an antioxidant that is thought to help prevent cancer.

and other tissues healthy, helping to maintain healthy eyes, skin and hair, and to protect against disease. A balanced vegetarian diet should supply many of these, although some vegetarians choose to increase their intake of vitamins and minerals with supplements such as vitamin B12, calcium, iron and zinc.

How to use this book

Here are 100 delicious and easy-to-follow low-fat vegetarian recipes for all the family to enjoy. Our tempting selection of recipes ranges from soups, appetizers, side dishes and accompaniments, to light meals and main course dishes. It also includes a tasty collection of delicious sweet treats and bakes and breads.

The following pages give lots of useful and informative advice, including helpful hints and tips on low-fat and fat-free vegetarian ingredients and low-fat or fat-free cooking techniques. You will find practical tips on how to reduce fat and saturated fat in your diet and an interesting and useful insight

Above: Reconstituted dried mushrooms are great for adding intense flavour to rice and pasta dishes. Sweat mushrooms in a little stock rather than butter.

into many of the different ingredients typically found in the vegetarian kitchen and used widely in vegetarian cooking.

Each recipe gives a nutritional breakdown, providing at-a-glance calorie and fat contents, as well as other key nutrients such as protein, carbohydrate, cholesterol, calcium, fibre and sodium.

As its title suggest, all the recipes in this cookbook are low in fat – the majority containing five grams or less of fat per serving, and some containing less than one gram. The only exceptions are in the Light Meals and Main Courses chapters, where the more substantial of the recipes contain ten grams of fat or less per serving.

For ease of reference, throughout the recipe section, all recipes with a single ★ following the recipe name contain five grams of fat or fewer, and those with ★★ contain ten grams of fat or fewer. All the recipes contain even less fat than typical vegetarian recipes yet they are still full of delicious flavour and appeal.

A HEALTHY VEGETARIAN DIET

A healthy vegetarian diet is one that provides you with all the nutrients you need. By eating the right types, balance and proportions of foods, you are more likely to feel healthy, have plenty of energy and have a higher resistance to disease. You will be less likely to develop illnesses such as heart disease, cancers, bowel disorders and obesity.

By choosing a variety of foods every day, you will ensure that you are supplying your body with all the essential nutrients, including vitamins and minerals, it needs. To get the balance right, it is important to know just how much of each type of food you should be eating.

It is recommended that you eat plenty of fruits and vegetables (at least five portions a day, not including potatoes) and foods such as cereals, pasta, rice and potatoes; moderate amounts of dairy products (and meat, fish and poultry if you follow a non-vegetarian diet), and only small amounts of foods containing fat or sugar.

By choosing a good balance of foods from these groups every day, and by choosing lower-fat, lower-sugar and lower-salt alternatives, we will be supplying our bodies with all the nutrients they need for optimum health.

THE ROLE OF FAT IN THE DIET

Most people eat fats in some form or other every day. We all need a small amount of fat in our diet to maintain a healthy, balanced eating plan. However, many of us eat far too much fat and you should be looking to reduce your overall fat intake, especially of saturated fats (as in butter, cream, milk, etc), as this contributes to a rise in blood cholesterol levels and may lead to coronary heart disease. Instead you should choose unsaturated fats such as olive and sunflower oils, which are high in

Above: Broad (fava) beans provide potassium and iron for the vegetarian diet.

monounsaturated and polyunsaturated fat and low in saturated fat, as these are healthier types of fat and are thought actually to help lower cholesterol levels. If you use these types of fat in moderation, they can be enjoyed as part of a low-fat diet – especially if combined with regular exercise.

Some other ingredients typically used in vegetarian cooking, such as cheese and yogurt, can be high in fat, but they can be substituted with lower-fat versions such as reduced-fat cheeses or low-fat yogurts. In many recipes, the quantity of the high-fat food can often simply be reduced to lower the fat content of the dish. When preparing recipes, you will be surprised at how small an amount of oil you need, for example when sautéing vegetables. Foods such as pasta and rice are also ideal for a low-fat diet as they are naturally high in carbohydrates and low in fat. By cutting down on the amount of fat you eat and making simple changes to your diet, you will soon be reducing your overall fat intake and enjoying a much healthier lifestyle, and you'll hardly notice the difference.

Left: Vegetables such as cauliflower and broccoli should be staples of a vegetarian diet and are best steamed or stir-fried or added washed and raw in salads.

The daily intake of fat should be limited to no more than 30–35 per cent of the total number of calories. Since each gram of fat provides nine calories, for anyone eating 2,000 calories a day, the total daily intake should be no more than around 70g fat.

As a general rule, the total intake of saturated fats should be no more than approximately ten per cent of the total number of calories.

TYPES OF FAT

All fats in our foods are made up of building blocks of fatty acids and glycerol, and their properties vary according to the way they are combined.

There are two main types of fat, which are referred to as saturated and unsaturated. The unsaturated group of fats is divided into two further types – polyunsaturated and monounsaturated fats. There is usually a combination of these types of unsaturated fat in foods that contain fat, but the amount of each type varies from one kind of food to another.

Saturated fats

These fats are usually hard at room temperature. They are not essential in the diet, and should be limited, as they are linked to increasing the level of blood cholesterol, which can increase the likelihood of heart disease.

The main sources of saturated fats are animal products, such as fatty cuts of meat and meat products, spreading

Above: With a deep green skin and firm, pale flesh, courgettes (zucchini) provide perfect bulk for vegetable stews. They are low in calories with a high water content.

fats, such as butter, lard and margarine, that are solid at room temperature, and full-fat dairy products such as cream and cheese. However, there are also saturated fats of vegetable origin, notably coconut and palm oils, and some margarines and oils, which, when processed, change the nature of the fat from unsaturated fatty acids to saturated ones. These fats are labelled "hydrogenated" (for example hydrogenated vegetable oil), and should be limited. Saturated fats are also found in many processed foods, such as chips (French fries), savoury snacks and crisps (US potato chips), as well as cookies, and cakes.

Polyunsaturated fats

There are two types of polyunsaturated fats: that of vegetable or plant origin (known as omega 6), which is found in sunflower oil, soft margarine and seeds, and that from oily fish (known as omega 3), such as salmon, herring, mackerel and sardines. Both fats are usually liquid at room temperature. Small amounts of polyunsaturated fats are essential for good health and are thought to help reduce the blood cholesterol level. It is generally agreed that polyunsaturated fats are healthier than saturated fats, but like all fats they

LOW-FAT AND VERY LOW-FAT SNACKS

Instead of reaching for a packet of crisps (US potato chips), a high-fat cookie or a chocolate bar when hunger strikes, choose one of these tasty low-fat snacks to fill that hole.
• A piece of fresh fruit or vegetable such as an apple, banana or carrot – keep chunks or sticks wrapped in a polythene bag in the fridge.
• Fresh fruit or vegetable chunks – skewer them on to cocktail sticks (toothpicks) or short bamboo skewers to make them into mini kebabs.
• A handful of dried fruit such as raisins, apricots or sultanas. These also make a perfect addition to children's packed lunches or school break snacks.
• A portion of canned fruit in natural fruit juice – serve with a spoonful or two of fat-free yogurt.
• One or two crisp rice cakes – delicious on their own, or topped with honey or reduced-fat cheese.
• Crackers, such as water biscuits or crisp breads, spread with reduced-sugar jam or marmalade.
• A bowl of wholemeal (whole-wheat) breakfast cereal or no-added-sugar muesli with a little skimmed milk.
• Very low-fat natural (plain) or fruit yogurt or fromage frais.
• A toasted teacake spread with reduced-sugar jam or marmalade.
• Toasted crumpet spread with yeast extract.

are high in calories and should be eaten sparingly. They also provide essential fatty acids for healthy skin and the development of body cells.

Monounsaturated fats

Foods such as rapeseed oil, olive oil, some nuts, including almonds and pecans, olives and avocados all contain monounsaturated fats. These fats are generally thought to have the beneficial effect of reducing the blood cholesterol level, so it's fine to include them in moderation in the diet.

PLANNING A LOW-FAT DIET

You can still cut down on sources of fat even in a vegetarian diet, by reducing your intake of butter, oils, margarine, cream, full cream (whole) milk and full-fat cheese. Low-fat calcium-fortified soya-based beverages, for example, can provide calcium in amounts similar to milk. Also try to build meals around protein sources that are naturally low in fat, such as beans, rice and lentils, and don't overload meals with high-fat cheeses to replace the meat. Basically, aim to limit the intake of saturated fats, cholesterol, added sugars and salt. For example it's natural to add dressings, sauces, marinades and relishes for moistness and flavour, but there are low-fat versions you can make yourself (see page 14) or purchase off the shelf.

By educating yourself and being aware of which foods are high in fats, particularly saturated fats, and by making simple changes to your diet, you can reduce the total fat content of your diet quite considerably.

Fill up on very low-fat foods, such as fruits and vegetables, as well as foods that are high in carbohydrates, such as pasta, rice, bread and potatoes.

Cutting down on fat doesn't mean sacrificing taste. It's easy and enjoyable to follow a sensible healthy eating plan without forgoing all your favourite foods.

THE CHOLESTEROL QUESTION

Cholesterol is a fat-like substance that plays a vital role in the body. It's the material from which many essential hormones and vitamin D are made. Too much saturated fat encourages the body to make more cholesterol than it uses or can rid itself of. Cholesterol is carried around the body, attached to proteins called high-density lipoproteins (HDL), low-density lipoproteins (LDL), and very low-density lipoproteins (VLDL or triglycerides).

After a meal the LDLs carry the fat in the blood to the cells where it's required. Any surplus should be excreted from the body, however, if there is too much LDL in the blood, some of the fat will be deposited on the walls of the arteries. This furring up gradually narrows the arteries and is one of the most common

Above: Fresh, organic vegetables are well worth the extra cost for taste and health.

causes of heart attacks and strokes. In contrast, HDLs appear to protect against heart disease. Whether high triglyceride levels are risk factors remains unknown.

For some people, an excess of cholesterol is a hereditary trait; in others, it's mainly the result of consumption of too much saturated fat. In both cases it can be reduced by a low-fat diet.

CUTTING DOWN ON FAT IN THE VEGETARIAN DIET

Most of us eat about 115g/4oz of fat every day. Yet just 10g/¼oz, about the amount in a single packet of crisps (US potato chips) or a thin slice of Cheddar cheese, is all we actually need.

Follow the simple "eat less, try instead" suggestions below to discover how to reduce the fat in your diet.
• Eat less butter or hard margarine.
• Try reduced-fat, low-fat or fat-free spreads. Try low-fat cream cheese or low-fat soft cheese for sandwiches and toast.
• Eat fewer full-fat dairy products such as full cream (whole) milk, cream, butter, hard margarine, crème fraîche, whole-milk yogurts and hard cheese.
• Try instead semi-skimmed (low-fat) or skimmed milk, low-fat or reduced-fat milk products, low-fat yogurts, low-fat fromage frais and low-fat soft and low-fat cream cheeses, reduced-fat hard

cheeses such as Cheddar, and reduced-fat crème fraîche.
• Use lots of low-fat protein products such as peas, beans, lentils or tofu.
• Do not cook with hard cooking fats, such as hard margarine.
• Try instead polyunsaturated or mono-unsaturated oils, such as sunflower, corn or olive oil for cooking (but don't use too much).
• Eat fewer rich salad dressings, and less full-fat mayonnaise.
• Try instead reduced-fat or fat-free mayonnaise or dressings. Make your own salad dressings at home with low-fat yogurt or fromage frais.
• Eat less fried food.
• Try instead fat-free cooking methods such as grilling (broiling), baking, microwaving or steaming whenever possible. Try cooking in non-stick pans with only a very small amount of oil.
• Eat fewer deep-fried and sautéed potatoes.
• Try instead low-fat starchy foods such as pasta, couscous and rice. Choose baked or boiled potatoes.
• Eat less added fat in cooking.
• Try instead to cook with little or no fat. Use heavy, good-quality non-stick pans so that the food doesn't stick. Try using a small amount of spray oil in cooking to control how much fat you are using.

HOW <u>TO</u> COOK <u>A</u> LOW-FAT MEAL

Once you get into the habit, it's easy to cook without fat. For example, whenever possible, grill (broil), bake, microwave and steam foods without the addition of fat, or try stir-frying with little or no fat. Alternatively, try using a low-fat or fat-free stock, wine or fruit juice for cooking, instead of fat.

• By choosing good-quality, non-stick cookware, you'll find that the amount of fat needed for cooking foods can be kept to an absolute minimum. If you do need a little fat for cooking, choose an oil that is high in unsaturates, such as olive or sunflower oil, and use as little as possible, or try an unsaturated spray oil.

• When baking low-fat cookies and cakes, use good-quality non-stick bakeware that doesn't need greasing before use, or use baking parchment and only lightly grease before lining.
• Look for non-stick coated fabric sheets. This re-usable non-stick material is amazingly versatile, as it can be cut to size and used to line cake tins (pans), baking sheets or frying pans. Heat-resistant up to 290°C/550°F and microwave-safe, it will last for up to five years.
• Sauté vegetables in low-fat or fat-free stock, wine or fruit juice instead of oil.
• Try a low-fat type of oil or just vinegar or lemon juice for salad dressings.
• Parcel-cooking vegetables and fruit allows the food to cook in its own juices.

The steam created holds in all the flavour and nutrient value and eliminates the need for oil or fats. Enclose food in individual foil or greaseproof parcels, add extra flavourings such as wine, herbs and spices, if liked, twist or fold parcel ends to secure and ensure juices can't run out, then bake, steam or cook on a barbecue.

• When grilling (broiling) foods, the addition of fat is often unnecessary. If the food shows signs of drying, lightly brush with a small amount of unsaturated oil, such as olive, sunflower or corn oil.
• Microwaved foods rarely need the addition of fat, so add herbs or spices for extra flavour and colour.

• Steaming and boiling are easy, fat-free ways of cooking many foods. Cook vegetables in a covered pan over a low heat with a little water so they cook in their own juices.
• Try poaching foods such as fruit in a fat-free stock or syrup.

• Try braising vegetables in the oven in low-fat or fat-free stock, wine or simply water with the addition of some chopped fresh or dried herbs.
• When serving vegetables resist the temptation to add a knob (pat) of butter or margarine. Instead, sprinkle with chopped fresh herbs or ground spices.

• Don't pan-fry vegetables, such as onions, mushrooms, carrots and celery, in oil or butter. Instead, put the sliced vegetables into a non-stick saucepan or frying pan with about 150ml/¼ pint/⅔ cup low-fat stock. Cover and cook for 5 minutes or until the vegetables are tender and the stock has reduced. If you like, add 15ml/1 tbsp dry wine or wine vinegar for a little piquancy and continue cooking for a further few minutes until the vegetables are dry and appear lightly browned.

LOW-FAT SPREADS IN COOKING

There is a huge variety of low-fat and reduced-fat spreads available in stores. Generally speaking, any very low-fat spreads with a fat content of around 20 per cent or less have a high water content. These are unsuitable for cooking and can only be used for spreading.

STOCKS, SAUCES AND FLAVOURINGS

Using ingredients like vinegar, lemon juice, herbs, tomato and garlic means you needn't worry about giving up on taste and flavour to achieve satisfying low-fat sauces.

LOW-FAT VEGETABLE STOCK

A good home-made vegetable stock is invaluable in the kitchen, forming the basis for many vegetarian soups, appetizers and main course dishes. Below is a low-fat vegetable stock recipe which is economical and easy to make. You could vary the ingredients in the vegetable stock according to taste and availability.

MAKES ABOUT 2.4 LITRES/4 PINTS/10 CUPS

INGREDIENTS
2 large onions, coarsely chopped
2 leeks, sliced
3 garlic cloves, crushed
3 carrots, coarsely chopped
4 celery sticks, sliced
a large strip of pared lemon rind
12 fresh parsley stalks
a few fresh thyme sprigs
2 bay leaves
2.4 litres/4 pints/10 cups water

1 Put the prepared vegetables in a large pan. Add the lemon rind, with the parsley, thyme and bay leaves. Pour in the water and bring to the boil. Skim off the foam that rises to the surface.

2 Lower the heat and simmer, uncovered, for 30 minutes. Strain, season to taste and leave to cool.

BOUQUET GARNI

A little bundle of herbs is perfect for adding flavour to vegetable stocks, soups and stews. Tying the herbs in a bundle means that the bouquet garni is easy to remove after cooking. A traditional bouquet garni comprises sprigs of parsley, thyme and a bay leaf, but you can vary the herbs according to the dish and/or main ingredients. Rosemary and oregano are a good combination, while mint, chervil, basil, chives and tarragon go well together.

1 Using a short length of string about 15 cm (6 in) in length, tie together a bay leaf with sprigs of thyme and parsley. Work from the thickest part.

2 Alternatively, you can place the herbs in the centre of a square of muslin (cheesecloth) and then tie them into a neat bundle using a short length of string to close the opening.

3 Use the bouquet garni immediately or freeze. (Herbs tied in muslin are better suited for freezing than string-tied herbs.)

LOW-FAT TOMATO SAUCE

MAKES ABOUT 350ML/12FL OZ/1½ CUPS

INGREDIENTS
10ml/2 tsp olive oil
1 onion, finely chopped
1 garlic clove, crushed
400g/14oz can chopped tomatoes
15ml/1 tbsp tomato purée (paste)
15ml/1 tbsp chopped fresh mixed
  herbs (parsley, thyme, oregano, basil)
pinch of granulated sugar
salt and ground black pepper

1 Heat the oil in a non-stick pan and cook the onion and garlic gently until softened. Stir in the tomatoes, tomato purée, herbs, sugar, salt and pepper.

2 Simmer, uncovered, for 15–20 minutes, stirring occasionally, until the mixture has reduced and is thick. Use immediately or store in the refrigerator.

COOK'S TIP
Use this sauce on pizzas or pasta. It also tastes excellent with vegetables. Spoon it over cooked cauliflower, top with a little grated reduced-fat cheese and grill.

Stock Energy 5Kcal/21kJ; Protein 0.3g; Carbohydrate 0.2g, of which sugars 0g; Fat 0.3g, of which saturates 0g; Cholesterol 0mg; Calcium 1mg; Fibre 0g; Sodium 336mg.
Sauce Energy 160Kcal/673kJ; Protein 4.7g; Carbohydrate 19.7g, of which sugars 18.2g; Fat 7.6g, of which saturates 1.3g; Cholesterol 0mg; Calcium 78mg; Fibre 6g; Sodium 79mg.

LOW-FAT SAUCES AND STOCKS

Adding sauces can mean introducing an unwelcome amount of fat into a recipe, so that dishes which start out low in fat may end up being served in a rich, high-fat coating. Unfortunately, it is not possible simply to introduce a low-fat spread into most sauce recipes. The traditional roux method for making a sauce won't work successfully using low-fat spreads because of their high water content, which evaporates on heating, leaving insufficient fat to blend with the flour. Below are three quick and easy low-fat cooking methods to try out, plus some low-fat vegetarian alternatives to classic richer sauces.

• The All-in-One Method: Place 25g/1oz/2 tbsp each of low-fat spread and plain flour in a saucepan with 300ml/½ pint/1¼ cups skimmed milk. Bring to the boil, stirring continuously until the sauce is thickened and smooth.

• Using Cornflour to Thicken: Blend 15ml/1 tbsp cornflour with 15–30ml/1–2 tbsp cold water, then whisk into 300ml/½ pint/1¼ cups simmering stock or milk, bring to the boil and cook for 1 minute, stirring continuously.

• Using Stock to Replace Fat: Sweat your vegetables, such as onions, mushrooms and leeks, in a pan using a small amount of vegetable stock rather than frying in fat. This will help reduce fat intake.

LOW-FAT VARIATIONS OF CLASSIC SAUCES

• **Mayonnaise** You can buy commercially made reduced-calorie mayonnaise or, to make further fat and calorie savings, substitute half the stated quantity with low-fat natural yogurt or low-fat fromage frais. This works well for mayonnaise-based dips or sauces like Thousand Island, which have tomato purée or ketchup added.

• **Hollandaise** This sauce is classically made with egg yolks, butter and vinegar and can't be made with low-fat spreads. However, some fat saving can be made by using less butter and including buttermilk.

1 Place 3 egg yolks in a bowl with the grated rind and 15ml/1 tbsp juice from 1 lemon.

2 Heat gently over a pan of water, stirring until thickened.

3 Gradually whisk in 75g/3oz/6 tbsp softened butter, in small pieces, until smooth.

4 Whisk in 45ml/3 tbsp buttermilk and season. Reserve for special occasions.

• **Vinaigrette Dressings** Buy reduced-calorie and oil-free dressings and check the labels carefully. Or, if you like the real thing, simply use less.

• **Vegetable Purées** Many recipes are traditionally thickened by adding cream, beurre manié (a butter and flour paste) or egg yolks, all of which add unwanted fat to the sauce. If cooked vegetables are included in the recipe, blend some down in a food processor to make a purée, then stir back into the juices to produce this low-fat version of a thickened vegetable sauce.

Above: if you use olive oil, portion it out using tablespoons to keep tabs on the calories. Low-fat butter contains about half the fat of butter. Consume in moderation.

DRESSINGS, MARINADES AND RELISHES

Fortunately today there is a very good choice of ready-made low-fat sauces to give your meals a bit of zing, but it's also easy to experiment with your own selection of ingredients. Try these.

LOW-FAT FRENCH DRESSING

Serve this tasty low-fat French-style dressing drizzled over mixed salad leaves, tomato salads, or chargrilled vegetables.

MAKES ABOUT 200ML/7FL OZ/SCANT 1 CUP

INGREDIENTS
    105ml/7 tbsp white grape juice
    60ml/4 tbsp extra-virgin olive oil
    30ml/2 tbsp red wine vinegar or
        tarragon vinegar
    5–7.5ml/1–1½ tsp Dijon or
        wholegrain mustard
    5–10ml/1–2 tsp chopped mixed fresh
        herbs (such as parsley, thyme,
        oregano and basil or chives)
    a pinch of caster (superfine) sugar
    salt and ground black pepper

1 Put the grape juice, olive oil, vinegar, mustard, chopped herbs, sugar, salt and pepper into a small bowl. Whisk the ingredients together thoroughly.

2 Alternatively, put all the ingredients into a clean screw-top jar, seal.

3 Shake well until thoroughly mixed and adjust the seasoning to taste. Serve immediately, or keep in a screw-top jar in the refrigerator for up to 3 days.

LOW-FAT TOMATO SALAD DRESSING

Drizzle this flavourful low-fat salad dressing over roast vegetables such as peppers and courgettes, or simply serve it with a mixed green or baby leaf salad.

MAKES ABOUT 200ML/7FL OZ/SCANT 1 CUP

INGREDIENTS
    105ml/7 tbsp tomato juice
    60ml/4 tbsp extra-virgin olive oil
    30ml/2 tbsp cider vinegar
    15ml/1 tbsp tomato ketchup
    5ml/1 tsp Dijon mustard
    2.5ml/½ tsp caster (superfine) sugar
    1 clove garlic, crushed (optional)
    a few drops of Tabasco
        sauce (optional)
    salt and ground black pepper

1 Put the tomato juice, olive oil, vinegar, tomato ketchup, mustard, sugar, garlic and Tabasco sauce, if using, and salt and pepper into a small bowl. Whisk the ingredients together until thoroughly mixed.

2 As an alternative, you can put the ingredients into a pre-cleaned screw-top jar, seal and shake well.

3 The dressing is immediately ready to serve or to save in the jar in the refrigerator for a few days.

QUICK-FIX OIL-FREE DRESSING

1 Whisk together 90ml/6 tbsp low-fat natural (plain) yogurt and 30ml/2 tbsp freshly squeezed lemon juice. Season to taste with freshly ground black pepper. If you prefer, wine, cider or even orange juice could be used in place of the lemon juice.

2 Add chopped fresh herbs, crushed garlic, mustard, honey, grated horseradish or other flavourings. Mix well, or shake thoroughly in a pre-washed screw-top jar. Adjust to taste. It's ready to serve immediately, or to store.

Above: Try adding honey, mustard, garlic, herbs, shallots, or chillies to add flavour and body to low-fat dressings.

GRAPEFRUIT AND YOGURT DRESSING

This oil-free dressing makes a healthy change from vinaigrette.

MAKES ABOUT 250ML/8FL OZ/1 CUP

INGREDIENTS
    30ml/2 tbsp pink grapefruit juice
    15ml/1 tbsp sherry vinegar
    1 garlic clove, crushed
    5ml/1 tsp wholegrain mustard
    150ml/¼ pint/⅔ cup low-fat natural
        (plain) yogurt
    15ml/1 tbsp chopped fresh herbs

Mix the juice and vinegar in a bowl. Add garlic and mustard, whisk in the yogurt and herbs. Serve with mixed salad leaves or drizzle over cold cooked vegetables.

COOK'S TIP

For vinaigrette dressings, the usual ratio of oil to vinegar is 3 to 1. Try to reverse it so you have 3 parts vinegar to 1 part oil. Or simply replace some of the oil with water, juice or fat-free broth.

French Energy 480Kcal/1981kJ; Protein 2.4g; Carbohydrate 15.1g, of which sugars 12.3g; Fat 46.7g, of which saturates 6.4g; Cholesterol 0mg; Calcium 119mg; Fibre 0g; Sodium 12mg.

Tomato Energy 451Kcal/1863kJ; Protein 2g; Carbohydrate 10.7g, of which sugars 9.9g; Fat 45.3g, of which saturates 6.3g; Cholesterol 0mg; Calcium 24mg; Fibre 0.8g; Sodium 486mg.

Grapefruit Energy 113Kcal/474kJ; Protein 9.1g; Carbohydrate 14.8g, of which sugars 14.1g; Fat 3.1g, of which saturates 0.8g; Cholesterol 2mg; Calcium 329mg; Fibre 0.8g; Sodium 132mg.

FRESH TARRAGON DRESSING

Serve this light and tasty dressing with cooked cold or warm asparagus, or with mixed salad leaves.

MAKES ABOUT 325ML/11FL OZ/
GENEROUS 1¼ CUPS

INGREDIENTS
    175g/6oz low-fat soft cheese
    150ml/¼ pint/⅔ cup reduced-fat
      single (light) cream or low-fat
      natural (plain) yogurt
    15–30ml/1–2 tbsp chopped
      fresh tarragon
    10–15ml/2–3 tsp tarragon vinegar
    salt and ground black pepper

1 Put the soft cheese into a small bowl and stir or mash until smooth, then stir in the cream or yogurt until well blended.

2 Stir in the tarragon and vinegar to taste, mixing well, then season to taste with salt and pepper.

3 Cover and leave to stand in a cool place for 30 minutes before serving, to allow the flavours to develop. Taste and adjust the seasoning before serving.

QUICK IDEAS FOR MARINADES

• Mix olive oil with chopped fresh herbs such as parsley, chives, garlic, chervil and basil. Add a splash or two of lemon juice and season with salt and pepper.
• Combine groundnut oil, toasted sesame oil, dark soy sauce, sweet sherry, rice vinegar and crushed garlic. Use as a marinade for tofu or tempeh.
• Mix together olive oil, lemon juice, sherry, honey and crushed garlic and use as a marinade for vegetable kebabs.

CUCUMBER RELISH

A cool, refreshing relish, this can be used as a dip, or as a sauce with vegetable kebabs. Serve when still fresh, so that the pieces are still crunchy. As cucumber is very refreshing add some ice cubes for extra chill.

INGREDIENTS
    ½ cucumber
    2 celery sticks, chopped
    1 green (bell) pepper, seeded
      and chopped
    1 garlic clove, crushed
    300ml/½ pint/1¼ cups low-fat
      natural (plain) yogurt
    15ml/1 tbsp chopped fresh
      coriander (cilantro)
    ground black pepper

1 Dice the cucumber and place in a large bowl.

2 Add the celery, green pepper and crushed garlic.

3 Stir in the yogurt and fresh coriander. Season with the pepper. Cover and chill.

CHILLI RELISH

This warm and spicy relish is ideal served with vegetarian snacks. If you prefer a slightly milder flavour, remove the seeds from the chilli before serving.

INGREDIENTS
    2 large tomatoes
    1 red onion
    10ml/2 tsp chilli sauce
    15ml/1 tbsp chopped fresh basil
    1 fresh green chilli, finely chopped
    pinch of salt
    pinch of granulated sugar

1 Finely chop the tomatoes and place in a mixing bowl.

2 Finely chop the onion and add to the tomatoes with the chilli sauce.

3 Stir in the fresh basil, chilli, salt and sugar.

TOMATO RELISH

This cooked relish may be served hot or cold. It has a concentrated flavour, making it ideal with pasta or vegetable kebabs.

INGREDIENTS
    10ml/2 tsp olive oil
    1 onion, chopped
    1 garlic clove, crushed
    25g/1oz/2 tbsp plain
      (all-purpose) flour
    30ml/2 tbsp tomato ketchup
    300ml/½ pint/1¼ cups passata
      (bottled strained tomatoes)
    5ml/1 tsp granulated sugar
    15ml/1 tbsp chopped fresh parsley

1 Heat the oil in a non-stick pan. Add the onion and garlic clove and sauté for 5 minutes, stirring from time to time.

2 Stir in the flour and cook for a further minute.

3 Stir in the tomato ketchup, passata, sugar and fresh parsley. Bring to the boil. Chill and use as required.

COOK'S TIP
•Passata is a smooth liquid made from sieved tomatoes. It is used as a base for recipes such as soups and sauces.
• All these relishes should be used as quickly as possible for optimum flavour. They will keep in the fridge for 3–4 days.

Tarragon Energy 330Kcal/1378kJ; Protein 35.1g; Carbohydrate 18.6g, of which sugars 18.4g; Fat 16.1g, of which saturates 9.8g; Cholesterol 44mg; Calcium 578mg; Fibre 2.3g; Sodium 906mg.

VEGETABLES

Naturally low in fat and bursting with vitamins and minerals, vegetables are one food group that should ideally make up the bulk of our daily diet. The most common vegetables contain less than 1g fat, although the humble pea ranks 1.5g per 100g/3½oz portion. Vegetables have always played an essential role in vegetarian cooking. They are sometimes served as dishes in their own right, and sometimes as accompaniments. Either way, there is a vast range of imaginative low-fat recipes from all over the world, incorporating vegetables, from salads to hearty vegetable stews. A whole variety of flavourings, such as herbs, can bring out the best flavour in vegetables.

ROOTS AND TUBERS

Vegetables such as carrots, swedes, parsnips and potatoes are a comforting and nourishing food, and it is not surprising that they should be popular in the winter. Their sweet, dense flesh provides sustained energy, valuable fibre, vitamins and minerals.

Carrots

The best carrots are not restricted to cold winter months. Summer welcomes the slender sweet new crop, often sold with their green, feathery tops, which are best removed after buying as they rob the root of moisture and nutrients. Buy organic carrots if you can because high pesticide residues have been found in non-organic ones. As an added bonus, organic carrots do not need peeling. Look for firm, smooth carrots – the smaller they are, the sweeter they are. Carrots should be prepared just before use to preserve their valuable nutrients. They are delicious raw, and can be steamed, stir-fried, roasted or puréed.

Beetroot (Beet)

Deep, ruby-red in colour, beetroot adds a vibrant hue and flavour to all sorts of dishes. It is often pickled in vinegar, but is much better roasted, as this emphasizes its sweet earthy flavour. Raw beetroot can be grated into salads or used to make relishes. It can also be added to vegetarian risottos or

delicious soups. If cooking beetroot whole, wash carefully, taking care not to damage the skin or the nutrients and colour will leach out. Trim the stalks to about 2.5cm/1in above the root. Small beetroots tend to be sweeter and more tender than the larger ones.

Parsnips

This vegetable has a sweet, creamy flavour and is delicious roasted, puréed or steamed. Parsnips are best purchased after the first frost of the year as the cold converts their starches into sugar, enhancing their sweetness. Scrub before use and only peel if tough. Avoid large roots, which can be woody.

Celeriac

This knobbly root is closely related to celery, which explains its flavour – a cross between aniseed, celery and parsley. Similar in size to a small swede (rutabaga), it has ivory flesh and is one of the few root vegetables that must be peeled before use. When grated and eaten raw in salads, celeriac has a crunchy texture. It can also be steamed, baked in gratins or combined with potatoes and mashed with butter or margarine and grainy mustard. Celeriac can also be used in vegetarian soups and broths.

Swedes

The globe-shaped swede (rutabaga) has pale orange flesh with a delicate sweet but earthy flavour. Trim off the thick peel, then treat in the same way as other root vegetables: grate raw into salads; dice and cook in vegetable casseroles and soups; steam, then mash, season to taste, and serve as an accompaniment.

Turnips

The humble root vegetable has many health-giving qualities, and small turnips with their green tops intact are especially nutritious. Their crisp, ivory flesh, which is enclosed in white, green

Above: Parsnips are very low in saturated fat, cholesterol and sodium. The vegetables also contain plenty of dietary fibre and Vitamin C. Above all they are a tasty and versatile addition to many quite different dishes.

and pink-tinged skin, has a pleasant, slightly peppery flavour, the intensity of which depends on their size and the time of harvesting. Small turnips can be eaten raw. Alternatively, steam, bake or use in vegetable casseroles and soups.

Potatoes

There are thousands of potato varieties, and many lend themselves to particular cooking methods. Small potatoes, such as Pink Fir Apple and Charlotte, and new potatoes, such as Jersey Royals, are best steamed. They have a waxy texture, which retains its shape after cooking, making them ideal for salads. Main crop potatoes, such as Estima and Maris Piper, are more suited to roasting, baking or mashing, and can be used to make chips (French fries). Discard any potatoes with green patches as these indicate the presence of toxic alkaloids called solanines.

Vitamins and minerals are stored in, or just below, the skin, so it is best to use potatoes unpeeled. New potatoes and special salad potatoes need only be scrubbed.

Potatoes are not in themselves fattening – it is added ingredients such as cheese and butter and the cooking method that can bump up the calories. Steam rather than boil and bake instead of frying to retain valuable nutrients and to keep fat levels down.

Jerusalem artichokes

The Jerusalem artichoke is an entirely different vegetable to the globe artichoke. It is, in fact, a tuber belonging to the sunflower family. Jerusalem artichokes look rather like knobbly potatoes, and can be treated as such. They have a lovely distinctive flavour and are good in vegetarian soups. They are also delicious baked, braised, lightly sautéed or puréed.

Radishes

There are several types of this peppery-flavoured vegetable, which is a member of the cruciferous family. The round ruby red variety is most familiar; the longer, white-tipped type has a milder taste. Mooli or daikon radishes are white and very long; they can weigh up to several kilos or pounds. Radishes can be used to add flavour and a crunchy texture to salads and stir-fries.

BRASSICAS AND GREEN LEAFY VEGETABLES

This large group of vegetables boasts an extraordinary number of health-giving properties especially for some cancers and cardiovascular diseases. Brassicas range from the crinkly-leafed Savoy cabbage to the small, walnut-sized Brussels sprout. Green, leafy vegetables include spinach, spring greens and Swiss chard.

Broccoli

This nutritious vegetable should be a regular part of everyone's diet. Two types are commonly available: purple-sprouting, which has fine, leafy stems and a delicate head, and

Below: Potatoes for baking or boiling.

calabrese, the more substantial variety with a tightly budded top and thick stalk. Choose broccoli that has bright, compact florets. Yellowing florets, a limp woody stalk and a pungent smell are an indication of overmaturity. Trim stalks before cooking, though young stems can be eaten, too. Serve raw in salads or with a dip. If you cook broccoli, steam or stir-fry it to preserve the nutrients and keep the cooking time brief to retain the vivid green colour and crisp texture.

Cauliflowers

The cream-coloured compact florets should be encased in large, bright green leaves. To get the most nutrients from a cauliflower, eat it raw, or bake or steam lightly. Cauliflower has a mild flavour and is delicious tossed in a light vinaigrette dressing or combined with tomatoes and spices.

Cabbages

Frequently overcooked, cabbage is best eaten raw, or cooked until only just

Above: Broccoli is versatile, offers a superb source of vitamin C and calcium, and a great taste.

tender. There are several different varieties: Savoy cabbage has substantial, crinkly leaves with a strong flavour and is perfect for stuffing; firm white and red cabbages can be shredded and used raw in salads (as can Chinese leaves (Chinese cabbage)); while pak choi (bok choy) is best cooked in stir-fries or with noodles.

Brussels sprouts

These are basically miniature cabbages that grow on a long tough stalk. They have a strong nutty flavour. The best are small with tightly packed leaves – avoid any that are very large or turning yellow or brown. Sprouts are sweeter when picked after the first frost. They are best cooked very lightly, so either steam or, better still, stir-fry to keep their green colour and crisp texture, as well as to retain the vitamins and minerals.

Spinach

For years we have been told to eat up our greens. Research into their health benefits now indicates that eating dark green leafy vegetables, such as spinach, spring greens, chard and kale on a regular basis may protect us against certain forms of cancer as well as supplying vitamins and iron to the vegetarian diet. Spinach is rich in fibre which can help to lower harmful levels of LDL cholesterol. Young, tender spinach leaves can be eaten raw and need little preparation, but older leaves should be washed well, then picked over and the tough stalks removed. Spinach is delicious combined with eggs.

Above: Spinach wilts dramatically when cooked so allow at least 250g/9oz raw weight per person.

Swiss chard

A member of the beet family, Swiss chard has large, dark leaves and thick, white, orange or red edible ribs. It can be used in the same way as spinach, or the stems may be cooked on their own. Swiss chard is rich in vitamins and minerals although, like spinach, it contains oxalic acid.

Spring greens (collard)

These leafy, dark green young cabbages are full of flavour and are rich in vitamin C and beta carotene.

PUMPKINS AND SQUASHES

Widely popular in the USA, Africa, Australia and the Caribbean, pumpkins and squashes come in a tremendous range of shapes, colours and sizes. Squashes are broadly divided into summer and winter types: cucumbers, courgettes and marrows fall into the summer category, while pumpkins, butternut and acorn squashes are winter varieties.

Acorn squash

This small to medium-size squash has an attractive, fluted shape and looks rather like a large acorn – hence its name. The orange flesh has a sweet flavour and slightly dry texture, and the skin colour ranges from golden to dark green. Its large seed cavity is perfect for stuffing.

Butternut squash

A large, pear-shaped squash with a golden brown skin and vibrant orange flesh. The skin is inedible and should be removed along with the seeds. Roast, bake, mash or use in soups or vegetable casseroles. The flesh has a rich, sweet,

creamy flavour when cooked and makes a good substitute for pumpkin.

Pumpkins

Small pumpkins have sweeter, less fibrous flesh than the larger ones, which are perhaps best kept for making into lanterns. Deep orange in colour, pumpkin can be used in both sweet and savoury dishes, such as pies, soups, vegetable casseroles, soufflés and even ice cream. Avoid boiling pumpkin as it can become waterlogged and soggy. The seeds are edible and highly nutritious.

Winter squashes

These have tough inedible skins, dense, fibrous flesh and large seeds. Most winter squashes can be used in both sweet and savoury dishes.

Summer squashes

Picked when still young, summer squash have thin edible skins and tender, edible seeds. Their delicate flesh cooks quickly.

Pattypan squash

These pretty, baby squash resemble mini flying saucers. They are similar in taste to a courgette and are best steamed or roasted. They may be yellow or bright green, and although they can be expensive to buy, there is no waste. Pattypan squash will only keep for a few days in the fridge.

Courgettes (zucchini)

These summer squash typically have shiny green skin, a sweet delicate flavour and a crisp texture. They are at their best when they are small. The green variety is most common, but yellow ones are sometimes available.

Left: Butternut squash is delicious baked in an oven for 30 minutes or until the flesh is soft. Cut in half, scoop out the seeds and bake cut-side down. Serve in the skin, or remove the flesh and mash with a low-fat spread or yogurt.

Above: Marrows

Courgettes can be sliced or grated and eaten raw, or they can be cooked, combining well with other vegetables such as peppers, tomatoes and aubergines (eggplant). The larger courgettes become, the less flavour they have. When buying, choose firm, shiny specimens. Do not buy flabby courgettes or those with blemished skins. In countries such as Italy and France, the golden courgette flowers are also highly prized for eating. Courgettes are available almost all year round, but are best in spring and summer. They are perhaps best known as a key ingredient with tomatoes and onions in the popular vegetarian dish ratatouille.

Marrows

The 'grown-up' courgettes (zucchini), marrows have a pleasant, mild flavour and are best baked either plain or with a stuffing. Spices, chillies and tomatoes are particularly good flavourings.

Cucumbers

Probably cultivated as long ago as 10,000 BC, cucumbers were popular vegetables with the Greeks and the Romans. The long, thin, smooth-skinned variety is most familiar. Their refreshing, mild flavour makes cucumbers perfect to use raw in salads or thinly sliced as a sandwich filling. However, they can also be pickled and cooked in other ways, such as steaming, baking or stir-frying.

SHOOT VEGETABLES

This highly prized collection of vegetables, each honoured with a distinctive flavour and appearance, ranges from the aristocratic asparagus to the flowerbud-like globe artichoke.

Above: Fennel bulb, when cooked, has a subtle aniseed flavour.

Fennel bulb/Florence fennel

So called to distinguish it from the feathery green herb, fennel bulb or Florence fennel resembles a fat white root with overlapping leaves and green, wispy fronds. It has a delicate but distinctive flavour of aniseed and a crisp, refreshing texture. It can be eaten raw, dressed with a low-fat vinaigrette or served in a mixed salad. It can also be lightly sautéed, baked or braised. When cooked, the aniseed flavour becomes

more subtle and the texture resembles cooked celery. Choose firm, rounded bulbs, in which the outer layers are crisp and white, and if possible, buy those with the feathery green fronds intact.

Asparagus

Highly prized as a luxury vegetable all over Europe, asparagus has a very short growing season, from spring to early summer, and is really only worth eating during this period. Both green and white asparagus are cultivated. The green variety is grown above ground, so that the entire spear is bright green, and is harvested when it is about 15cm/6in high. The fat white spears with their pale yellow tips are grown under mounds of soil to protect them from the light.

Asparagus spears can be boiled, steamed, grilled (broiled) or roasted in a little olive oil, and served as a first course with a light sprinkling of freshly grated Parmesan cheese, or served with a light vinaigrette. Asparagus spears make an ideal accompaniment to low-fat vegetarian meals and asparagus tips also make a luxury addition to risottos.

Celery

Like asparagus, celery was once grown primarily for medicinal reasons. Serve raw, steam or braise. Celery leaves have a tangy taste and are also useful for adding flavour to stocks. Low in calories, but rich in vitamin C and potassium, celery is a recognized diuretic and sedative.

Left: Although they are both artichokes, the tightly packed heads of the green leafy globe artichoke (left) are not to be confused with the root vegetable Jerusalem artichoke (right).

Right: Jerusalem artichokes have a very distinctive flavour and are delicious baked, braised, lightly sautéed or puréed.

Above: If you're trying to eat five portions of fruit and vegetables a day then about five or six asparagus spears counts as one portion. Asparagus is a great source for B vitamin folate.

Globe artichokes

Tall vegetables that grow a round head (hence the name globe) on a long stem and are visibly striking when cultivated, globe artichokes produce edible, slightly nutty-flavoured heads (flower buds). Look for artichoke heads with tightly packed leaves, as open leaves indicate that the vegetable is too mature. When an artichoke is old, the tops of the leaves will turn brown. If possible, buy artichokes that are attached to their stems, as they will stay fresh for longer. Artichokes will keep fresh for several days if you place the stalks in water. Otherwise wrap them in clear film (plastic wrap) and keep in the vegetable drawer of the refrigerator for a day or two.

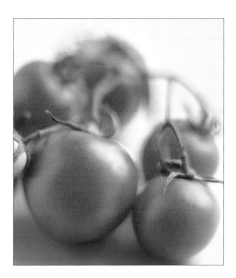

Above: Tomatoes form the basis of many healthy vegetarian dishes, especially soups and sauces.

VEGETABLE FRUITS

By cultivation and use, tomatoes, aubergines and peppers are all vegetables, but botanically they are classified as fruit. Part of the nightshade family, they have only relatively recently become appreciated for their health-giving qualities.

Tomatoes

Sun-ripened and full of flavour, tomatoes form an essential ingredient for many healthy vegetarian recipes. The smallest tomatoes are cherry tomatoes, which are sweet and tasty. Medium tomatoes are also delicious and good for slicing. Plum tomatoes have thick walls and fewer seeds and so are ideal for tomato-based sauces. Beefsteaks are the largest type of tomato and are the best for stuffing or for slicing for salads. Bright red fruits literally bursting with aroma and flavour, tomatoes are essential ingredients in low-fat, no-fat dishes.

They can be eaten raw, sliced and served with a trickle of extra virgin olive oil and some torn fresh basil leaves. Raw ripe tomatoes can be chopped with herbs and garlic to make a fresh-tasting pasta sauce. Tomatoes can be grilled (broiled), lightly fried, baked, stuffed or stewed and made into tasty low-fat sauces and soups. Tomatoes are at their best when they have ripened naturally in the sun.

Choose your tomatoes according to the way you wish to use them. As well as fresh tomatoes, canned and sun-dried tomatoes are invaluable store cupboard (pantry) items, together with passata (bottled strained tomatoes) and tomato purée (paste). Remember, dry-packed sun-dried tomatoes are lower in fat than the oil-packed ones.

Aubergines (eggplant)

Originating in Asia, aubergines today feature in vegetarian dishes from many other countries. The plump purple variety is the most common. Look for firm, shiny-skinned specimens with green stalks, that are heavy for their size. A light aubergine may have a dry, spongy inside and could contain a lot of seeds. Do not buy those with wrinkled or damaged skins. Aubergines will keep in the refrigerator for up to a week and are a very versatile vegetable. They can be grilled (broiled), baked, stuffed, stewed or lightly sautéed, either on their own or with other vegetables, and since they absorb flavours well, they can be used with most seasonings.

Peppers

Capsicums, or bell peppers as they are also known, come in a range of colours including green, red, yellow, orange and even a purplish-black, though they all have the same sweetish flavour and crunchy texture. Peppers are commonly used in vegetarian dishes. They can be eaten raw or lightly roasted in salads or as an antipasto, and can be cooked in a variety of ways – roasted and dressed with a light olive oil or vinaigrette dressing, grilled (broiled) or stuffed and baked. To make the most of their flavour, grill (broil) peppers until charred, then rub off and discard the skins. Peppers have a great affinity with other ingredients such as olives, capers, aubergines (eggplants), courgettes (zucchini) and tomatoes.

BEANS AND PEAS

Most of these vegetables are delicious eaten fresh, but can also be bought frozen. High in nutritional value, these popular vegetables are available all year.

Above: (Bell) peppers are a very healthy food, being naturally low in fat and rich in vitamin C.

Other types of pea include mangetouts (snow peas) and sugar snap peas, which can be eaten whole, including the pod.

Broad (fava) beans

These beans are at their best in late spring or early summer when they are small and tender, or cooked and skinned later in the season. When young they can be cooked and eaten, pods and all. Cooked broad beans have a milder flavour than raw. Dried broad beans are popular in the Middle East where they are cooked with spices or added to vegetable stews.

Green beans

French, runner and dwarf beans are eaten whole. They should be bright green and crisp textured. Simply top and tail and lightly cook or steam them. Serve green beans hot, or leave to cool slightly and serve as a warm salad with a squeeze of fresh lemon juice or a vinaigrette dressing.

Corn

Corn cobs are best eaten soon after picking, before their natural sugars start to convert into starch when the flavour fades and the kernels toughen. Remove the green outer leaves and cook whole or slice off the kernels with a sharp knife. Baby corn cobs can be eaten raw, and are good in stir-fries.

Above: Garlic is available fresh, dried powdered and in liquid form.

THE ONION FAMILY

Both onions and garlic contain allicin, which stimulates the body's antioxidant mechanisms, raising levels of beneficial HDL cholesterol and combating the formation of clogged arteries. They are an absolute must in cooking and add flavour to a huge range of savoury dishes. Delicate leeks, sweet shallots and tangy spring onions (scallions) are members of the onion family.

Onions

These strongly flavoured vegetables are an essential component of virtually all savoury low-fat vegetarian dishes. Red- or white-skinned onion varieties have a sweet, mild flavour and are good used raw in salads. Large, Spanish (Bermuda) onions are also mild and a good choice when a large quantity of onions is called for in a recipe.

Leeks

With a sweeter, less overpowering flavour than onions, leeks should be a mainstay of the vegetarian diet. They have a very small bulb and a long whitish cylindrical stalk of superimposed layers that flows into green, tightly wrapped, flat leaves. Cultivated leeks are usually about 30cm (1ft) long. Leeks make a perfect base for soups and stews. They are excellent braised and served with a tasty sauce.

Garlic

Used crushed, sliced or even whole, garlic develops a smooth, gentle flavour with long, slow cooking. Used raw in salads, light sauces, dressings and marindades, garlic adds a delicious, strong flavour. Garlic also has a medicinal value, being a decongestant and helping to lower blood pressure and blood cholesterol.

MUSHROOMS

Button (white), open cup and flat mushrooms are used in vegetarian dishes all year round. Regional wild species such as ceps, chanterelles and oyster mushrooms are to be found in the markets during autumn. Mushrooms can be sliced and eaten raw, dressed with a dash of extra virgin olive oil, or they can be lightly brushed with olive oil and grilled (broiled).

LETTUCES

Nutritionally, lettuce is best eaten raw, but it can be braised, steamed or made into a soup. Large-leafed varieties can be used to wrap around a filling.

Cos lettuce

The cos or romaine lettuce has long, sturdy leaves and a strong flavour. Little Gem (Bibb) is a baby version of cos and has firm, densely packed leaves.

Iceberg lettuce

Crisp lettuce with a round, firm head of pale green leaves. It has a mild, slightly bitter flavour and is perfect in salads.

Oak leaf

Red tinged and soft textured with a slightly bitter flavour.

Lollo rosso

The pretty, frilly leaves of lollo rosso are green at the base and a deep, autumn-red around the edge. Its imposing shape means it is best mixed with other leaves if used in a salad or as a base for roasted vegetables.

Frisée lettuce

Also known as curly endive, frisée has spiky, ragged leaves that are dark green on the outside and fade to an attractive pale yellow-green towards its centre. It has a distinctive bitter flavour that is enhanced by a robust low-fat dressing.

Radicchio

The crisp leaves of radicchio taste slightly bitter and can be eaten raw or cooked. Radicchio is delicious grilled (broiled) and drizzled with a little olive oil and sprinkled with black pepper, or shredded and stirred into risotto or spaghetti. The raw leaves look pretty in salads.

Rocket (arugula)

Classified as a herb, rocket is popular in salads, or as a starter with thin shavings of Parmesan cheese. It has a strong, peppery flavour, which is more robust in wild rocket. Lightly steamed rocket has a milder flavour than the raw leaves but it is equally delicious.

Sorrel

The long pointed leaves of sorrel have a refreshing, sharp flavour that is best when mixed with milder tasting leaves.

Watercress

The hot, peppery flavour of watercress complements milder tasting leaves and is classically combined with fresh orange. It does not keep well and is best used within two days of purchase. Watercress is a member of the cruciferous family and shares its cancer-fighting properties.

Above, clockwise from left: frisée lettuce, oak leaf, cos, butterhead and iceberg lettuces.

FRUIT

Fruit is used extensively in vegetarian cuisine. It is used in both sweet and savoury dishes and complements both flavours well. Raw fruit may also be eaten on its own as a simple dessert. Many fruits are naturally low in calories and fat and provide plenty of vitamin C.

ORCHARD FRUITS

Soft fruit from cultivated fruit trees grown mostly in temperate climates, these include apples, plums and pears.

Apples

There are thousands of varieties of apple, though the choice in supermakets is somewhat limited. Some of the most well-liked eating varieties are harvested in the UK, North America, Canada, Australia, New Zealand and South Africa. Popular varieties include Golden and Red Delicious, Braeburn, Jonagold, Fuji, Cox's Orange Pippin, Granny Smith, Gala, and Pink Lady. The Bramley Seedling, with its thick, shiny, green skin and tart flesh, is the most familiar cooking apple and is perfect for baking, or as the basis of apple sauce. Some less well-known varieties, many of which have a short season, are often available from farm shops.

Apples are delicious when they are eaten raw with their skin on. However, this versatile fruit is often used in vegetarian breakfast dishes, main meals, salads, desserts, pies and even soups. Large cooking apples are ideal puréed, stewed or baked, but their tartness means that sugar has to be added. Some varieties of eating apple are just as good

Below: A selection of larger cooking apples on the left and eating apples to the right.

cooked and don't need any added sugar. When buying apples, choose bright, firm fruits without any bruises. Store apples in a cool place, away from direct sunlight.

Apricots

The best apricots are sunshine gold in colour and full of juice. They are delicious baked or used raw in salads. An apricot is at its best when truly ripe. Immature fruits are hard and tasteless and never seem to attain the right level of sweetness.

Cherries

There are two types of cherry: sweet and sour. Some are best eaten raw like the popular Bing, while others, such as Morello, are best cooked.

Choose firm, bright, glossy fruits that have fresh, green stems. Discard any that are soft, or have split or damaged skin.

Peaches and nectarines

Among the most delicious summer fruits, peaches and nectarines need plenty of sun to ripen them and are grown in China, Japan, and neighbouring Asian countries, as well as the Mediterranean and North America. Peaches may be yellow-, pink- or white-fleshed, with a velvety, fuzzy skin. Nectarines are smooth-skinned, with all the luscious flavour of peaches. They also come in yellow and white varieties and, like peaches, the white nectarines have a finer flavour. Look for bruise-free specimens that just give when squeezed gently and choose fruits with an intense, sweet scent. Peaches and nectarines are interchangeable in recipes, whether cooked or raw. They can both be macerated in fortified wine or spirits, or poached in white wine and syrup. Peaches and nectarines are also delicious served with raspberries or made into fruit drinks and smoothies, low-fat ice creams and sorbets.

Pears

Succulent pears have been popular for thousands of years and were extensively cultivated by the Greeks and the Romans. Pears come into their own in the late summer and

Above: Look for peaches that have a background of yellow or cream colour plus a rosy blush on their cheeks.

autumn with the arrival of the new season's crops. Particular favourites are green and brown-skinned Conference; Williams, with its thin, yellow skin and sweet, soft flesh; plump Comice, which has a pale yellow skin with a green tinge; and Packham, an excellent cooking pear.

Pears can be used in both sweet and savoury vegetarian dishes; they are excellent in salads, and can be baked, poached in syrup, and used in low-fat crumbles and bakes.

Choose firm, plump fruits that are just slightly underripe. Pears can ripen in a day or so and then they pass their peak very quickly and become woolly or squashy. To tell if a pear is ripe, feel around the base of the stalk, where it should give slightly when gently pressed, but the pear itself should remain firm.

Plums

Ranging in colour from pale yellow to dark, rich purple, plums come in many different varieties, although only a few are available in shops. They can be sweet and juicy or slightly tart; the latter are best cooked in low-fat desserts, or made into a delicious jam. Sweet plums can be eaten as they are, and are good in fruit salads, or they can be puréed and combined with low-fat custard or low-fat yogurt to make a fruit fool.

Plums should be just firm, and not too soft, with shiny, smooth skin that has a slight "bloom". Store ripe plums in the fridge. Unripe fruits can be kept at room temperature for a few days to ripen.

Quince

Fragrant, knobbly fruits, with a thin, yellow or green skin, quinces can be either apple- or pear-shaped. They are too hard and sour to eat raw and the seeds are poisonous and should not be consumed. Their high pectin content makes for good jellies and, in Spain and France, quinces are used to make a fruit paste that is served with soft cheeses.

CITRUS FRUITS

Juicy, acidic and brightly coloured, citrus fruits such as oranges, grapefruit, lemons and limes are best known for their slightly bitter taste and high vitamin C content.

Oranges

Varieties of this popular fruit include seedless navel oranges, red-fleshed blood oranges and Seville oranges.

NUTRITIONAL CITRUS

Eating an orange a day will generally supply an adult's requirement for vitamin C, but citrus fruits also contain phosphorus, potassium, calcium, beta carotene and fibre. Pectin, a soluble fibre that is found in the flesh and particularly in the membranes of citrus fruit, has been shown to reduce cholesterol levels. The membranes also contain bioflavonoids, which have powerful antioxidant properties. Drink fresh fruit juice when you can, as bottled, canned and concentrated citrus juices have reduced levels of vitamin C.

Seville (Temple) oranges, the bitter marmalade variety, have a very short season, just after Christmas. Oranges should have unblemished shiny skins and feel heavy for their size, which indicates that they contain plenty of juice and that the flesh is not dry. Orange varieties vary in levels of sweetness. Choose unwaxed oranges if you intend to use the rind in recipes.

Grapefruit

The flesh of the grapefruit ranges in colour from vivid pink and ruby red to white; the pink and red varieties are sweeter. Heavier fruits are likely to be juicier. Served juiced, halved or cut into slices, grapefruit can provide a refreshing start to the day. The fruit also adds a refreshing tang to vegetarian salads. Cooking or grilling (broiling) mellows the tartness, but keep cooking times brief to preserve the nutrients. A glass of grapefruit juice before bed is said to promote sleep.

Lemons

These bright yellow citrus fruits are low in calories and fat and rich in vitamin C. They have an aromatic flavour which enhances many dishes and they are very versatile. Depending on the variety, lemons may have a thick indented skin or be perfectly smooth. Their appearance does not affect the flavour, but they should feel heavy for their size. Buy unwaxed lemons if you intend to use the rind in recipes. The rind also imparts a wonderful flavour to savoury vegetarian dishes, light salad dressings and low-fat desserts.

The juice can be squeezed to make a drink, or it can be added to tea, low-fat dressings and sauces. Lemons are also antioxidants, and prevent discoloration when brushed over fruits and vegetables that tend to turn brown when cut.

Limes

Once considered to be rather exotic, limes are now widely available. Avoid fruits with a yellowing skin as this is a sign of deterioration. The juice has a sharper flavour than that of lemons and if you substitute limes for lemons in a

Above: Lemons have an aromatic flavour, which enhances many vegetarian dishes. Try to choose organic, unwaxed ones but keep in the fridge as they go mouldy.

recipe, you will need to use less juice. Limes are used a great deal in Asian cooking and the rind can be used to flavour low-fat vegetarian curries, marinades and dips. Coriander, chillies, garlic and ginger are all natural partners.

BERRIES AND CURRANTS

These baubles of vivid red, purple and black are the epitome of summer and autumn, although they are now likely to be available all year round.

Strawberries

These are the favourite summer fruits and do not need any embellishment. Serve ripe (avoid those with white or green tips) and raw, on their own, or with a little low-fat natural yogurt. Wash only if absolutely necessary and just before serving.

Raspberries

Soft and fragrant, raspberries are best served simply and unadulterated – maybe with a spoonful of low-fat natural (plain) yogurt. Those grown in Scotland are regarded as the best in the world. Raspberries are very fragile and require the minimum of handling, so wash only if really necessary.

They are best eaten raw as cooking spoils their flavour and vitamin C content.

Blueberries

Dark purple in colour, blueberries come from the family which includes cranberries and bilberries. When ripe, the berries are plump and slightly firm, with a natural "bloom". Avoid any that are soft and dull-skinned, and wash and dry carefully to avoid bruising. Cultivated blueberries are larger than the wild variety. Both types are sweet enough to be eaten raw (though they can be tart) but are also good cooked in low-fat muffins, used for jellies and jams, or made into a sauce to serve with nut or vegetable roasts. Unwashed blueberries will keep for up to a week in the refrigerator.

Blackberries

These are a familiar sight in early autumn, growing wild in hedgerows. Cultivated blackberries are generally much larger than the wild fruits. Juicy and plump, blackberries can vary in sweetness, which is why they are so often cooked. Wash them carefully to prevent bruising the fruits, then pat dry with kitchen paper. Use in low-fat fruit desserts, or make into jams and jellies. The berries can also be lightly cooked, then puréed and sieved to make a sauce to serve with other fruits or low-fat ice cream.

Look for firm, glossy berries and currants. Make sure that they are not squashed or mouldy. Ripe fruits generally do not keep well and are best eaten on the day of purchase – store in the refrigerator. Unripe fruits can be kept for longer.

Gooseberries

A favourite fruit of Northern Europe, gooseberries are relatively rare in other parts of the world. They range from the hard and sour green type to the sweeter, softer purple variety. The skin can vary from smooth and silky to fuzzy and spiky. Slightly unripe, tart gooseberries make wonderful low-fat crumbles or jams and jellies. Ripe, softer fruits can be puréed and mixed with low-fat yogurt or custard, to make a delicious fruit fool. Gooseberries are a good source of vitamin A.

Right: Blackcurrants go well with apples and pears.

Blackcurrants and redcurrants

These small, pretty fruits are usually sold in bunches on the stem. To remove the currants from the stalk, run the prongs of a fork down through the clusters, taking care not to damage the fruit. Wash the fruits carefully. Raw blackcurrants are quite tart, but this makes them ideal for cooking in fruit desserts such as low-fat crumbles or pies. They make delicious jams and jellies, and are especially good in summer pudding when they are partnered by other berries. Sweeter whitecurrants make a delightful addition to fruit salads.

GRAPES, MELONS, DATES, OLIVES AND FIGS

These fruits were some of the first ever to be cultivated and are therefore steeped in history. They are available in an immense variety of shapes, colours and sizes, and with the exception of melons, they can also be bought dried.

Grapes

Fresh grapes are naturally low in fat while being rich in potassium and vitamins. Grapes tends to be heavily sprayed so you should always wash them thoroughly after purchase. Beneath the skin the flesh is always pale green and juicy. Buy bunches of grapes with fruit of equal size and not too densely packed on the stalk.

Right: Melons come in many different varieties, sizes, shapes and colours. The riper the melon, the sweeter the flavour. Melons can be served for breakfast, as an appetizer, dessert or snack.

Melons

This fruit comes in many different varieties, sizes, shapes and colours, including cantaloupe, Charentais, Galia, honeydew and Ogen, which are orange- and green-fleshed varieties, and also the wonderful pink-fleshed watermelon. Melons are often served in slices and decorated with other fresh fruits, simply as dessert fruit on their own. Ripe melons should yield to gentle pressure from your thumbs at the stalk end and have a fragrant, slightly sweet scent. If they smell highly perfumed and musky, they will probably be overripe. Melons contain mostly water, are naturally low in calories and fat, and provide some vitamin C.

Figs

Fresh figs are delicious served simply on their own either raw or lightly cooked. They vary in colour, from dark purple to green to a golden yellow, but all are made up of hundreds of tiny seeds, surrounded by soft pink flesh, which is perfectly edible. Choose firm, unblemished fruit that just yields to the touch. Figs are highly perishable so use quickly. Fresh figs can also be served with low-fat Greek (US strained plain) yogurt and honey, or stuffed with raspberry coulis and served as a dessert. Poached in a little water or wine flavoured with cinnamon or nutmeg, they make an excellent appetizer or accompaniment.

Above: Dates go particularly well with oranges and make a good addition to fruit salads.

Dates

When plump and slightly wrinkled, fresh dates have a rich honey-like flavour and dense, slightly chewy texture. They are delicious stoned (pitted) and served with low-fat Greek (US strained plain) yogurt. Dried dates can be used in the same way, but fewer are needed as the flavour is concentrated.

Olives

The fruit of one of the earliest known trees native to the Mediterranean, olives are popular in vegetarian cooking. There are many varieties, differing in size and taste. Colour depends purely on ripeness – the fruit changes from yellow to green, purple, brown and finally black when fully ripened. Fresh olives are picked at the desired stage, then soaked in water, bruised and immersed in brine to produce the familiar-tasting result. Olives are available loose, bottled or canned and may be

whole or pitted. They are sometimes stuffed with pimientos or nuts, or bottled with flavourings such as garlic and chilli. Olives are quite high in monounsaturated fat and low in saturated fat, and should be used in moderation.

TROPICAL FRUIT

This exotic collection of fruits ranges from the familiar bananas and pineapples to the more unusual papayas and passion fruit.

Pineapples

These distinctive looking fruits have a sweet, exceedingly juicy and golden flesh. Unlike most other fruits, pineapples do not ripen after picking, although leaving a slightly unripe fruit for a few days at room temperature may reduce its acidity. Choose pineapples that have fresh green spiky leaves, are heavy for their size, and are slightly soft to the touch.

Papaya

Also known as pawpaw, these pear-shaped fruits come from tropical regions. When ripe, the green skin turns a speckled yellow and the pulp is a glorious orange-pink colour. The numerous edible, small black seeds taste peppery when dried. Peel off the skin using a sharp knife or a vegetable peeler before enjoying the creamy flesh which has a lovely perfumed aroma and sweet flavour. Ripe papaya is best eaten raw, while unripe green fruit can be used in cooking.

Mangoes

The skin of these luscious, fragrant fruits can range in colour from green to yellow, orange or red. Their shape varies tremendously, too. An entirely green skin is a sign of an unripe fruit, although in Asia, these are often used in salads. Ripe fruit should yield

Left: Sweet, red-skinned bananas and the more familiar large and small yellow-skinned varieties.

to gentle pressure and, when cut, it should reveal a juicy, orange flesh. Preparing a mango can be fiddly. Serve sliced, or purée and use as a base for low-fat ice creams and sorbets.

Bananas

A concentrated bundle of energy, bananas are also full of valuable nutrients. The soft and creamy flesh can be blended into smooth, sweet drinks, mashed and mixed with yogurt, or the fruits can be baked and barbecued whole. Bananas also make an ideal weaning food for babies as they rarely cause an allergic reaction.

If you wish to buy ripe bananas, choose yellow (or red) fruits that are patched with brown. Bananas with patches of green can be ripened at room temperature. Completely green bananas rarely ripen properly. Store bananas at cool room temperature.

Pomegranates

Golden, apple-shaped fruits with a tough skin, pomegranates contain hundreds of seeds covered with a deep pink flesh that has a delicate, slightly tart flavour. Try sprinkling over sweet dishes such as fruit salads. A good source of vitamin C.

OTHER TROPICAL FRUIT

Kiwi fruit, which is also known as the Chinese gooseberry, has a brown, downy skin and vivid green flesh that is peppered with tiny black seeds. It is extremely rich in vitamin C.

Passion fruit is a dark purple, wrinkly, egg-shaped fruit, which hides a pulpy, golden flesh with edible black seeds. Cut in half and scoop out the inside with a spoon. Passion fruit is rich in vitamins A and C.

LOW-FAT DAIRY PRODUCE

Skimmed and semi-skimmed (low-fat) milk, half-fat and reduced-fat hard cheeses, cottage cheese, mozzarella light, feta and ricotta are all medium- to low-fat options when it comes to cooking with dairy produce.

MILK

Skimmed milk contains half the calories of full-fat milk and only a fraction of the fat, but nutritionally it is on a par, retaining the same vitamins, calcium and other minerals. Semi-skimmed (low-fat) milk has a fat content of only 1.5-1.8 per cent. In baking try using buttermilk which contains only 0.1 per cent fat. Avoid cream, but if you want to use it, choose half-fat single (light) cream with 12 per cent fat – still a quarter that of double (heavy) cream.

Soya milk

The most widely used alternative to milk is soya milk made from pulverized soya beans. It is suitable for both cooking and drinking and is used to make yogurt, cream and cheese. Soya milk is interchangeable with cow's milk, although it has a slightly thicker consistency and a nutty flavour. It is a valuable source of protein, calcium, iron, magnesium, phosphorus and vitamin E. It's also low in calories and contains no cholesterol.

Rice milk (with fewer nutrients) and goat's milk (with 20 per cent less cholesterol) are other milk alternatives.

Below: Choose reduced-fat or low-fat varieties of cheese.

MARGARINE

Vegetable margarine contains the same amount of fat as butter, which contains 80 per cent saturated fat, but the fat in margarine is polyunsaturated. This was once considered to give margarine greater health benefits. But margarine manufacturing processes change the fats into trans fats, or hydrogenated fats. Studies have shown that trans fats may be more likely than the saturated fat in butter to damage the heart and blood vessels.

SPREADS

Lower fat margarines are called spreads. They contain less than 80 per cent fat and those that are under 65 per cent fat can be classified as reduced fat. When the fat content falls below 41 per cent, a spread can be called low fat or half fat. Very low-fat spreads may contain gelatine (from animal tissues) and therefore are unsuitable for vegetarians. Olive oil based spreads are rich in monounsaturated fats and are said to reduce cholesterol levels. They can be used for cooking. When buying margarine and spreads always choose good-quality brands that contain no hydrogenated fats. Margarines and spreads absorb other flavours, so keep well-wrapped. Always store these products in the fridge; unsalted butters will keep for up to two weeks, other butters for up to a month, and margarines and spreads will keep for about two months.

CHEESE

Many low-fat varieties of cheese including Gruyère, Cheddar, Red Leicester, Danish blue, Dolcelatte, Parmesan, mozzarella, feta and many goat's cheeses are readily available and are suitable for vegetarians. Full-fat cheeses such as Parmesan can also be used sparingly to add extra flavour, but because of their high-fat content, they should only be used in small amounts. Look out for vegetarian Parmesan cheese, which goes a long way to adding delicious flavour to many vegetarian dishes, from pasta and polenta to risotto and pizzas.

Cottage cheese

Lower in fat than most other cheeses (between 2 and 5 per cent), cottage cheese is not usually used for cooking but is good in salads and dips. It makes a fine accompaniment to soft fruits and is best eaten as fresh as possible.

Quark

A soft, white cheese made from fermented skimmed milk, quark is virtually fat free, but check the label as some varieties are enriched with cream.

YOGURT

The fat content of this valuable health food ranges from 0.5g per 100g for very low-fat to virtually fat-free yogurts to 4g per 100g and above. Yogurt is used as a marinade, a dip and to enrich vegetarian soups and stews. Choose low-fat, reduced-fat or fat-free varieties, to keep the fat content of your vegetarian dishes down. Lower-fat yogurts can also be used instead of cream, but are best used in uncooked dishes.

Crème fraîche and fromage frais

These are excellent alternatives to cream. Crème fraîche is a thick, sour cream with a milky, lemony taste. The half-fat version has a fat content of 15 per cent. Fromage frais is a fresh, soft cheese available as virtually fat-free (0.4 per cent fat) and in a more creamy variety, which contains 7.9 per cent fat.

Below: Reduced-fat or low-fat Greek (US strained plain) yogurt is ideal for use in low-fat desserts, dips and marinades.

SOYA PRODUCE

Soya beans are incredibly versatile and are used to produce an extensive array of by-products that can be used in cooking – tofu, tempeh, textured vegetable protein, flour, miso, and a variety of sauces. The soya bean is the most nutritious of all beans. Rich in high-quality protein, it is one of the few vegetarian foods that contains all eight essential amino acids that cannot be synthesized in the body and are vital for the renewal of cells and tissues.

Tofu

Also known as beancurd, tofu is made in a similar way to soft cheese. The beans are boiled, mashed and sieved to make soya "milk", and the "milk" is then curdled using a coagulant. The resulting curds are drained and pressed to make tofu, and there are several different types to choose from.

Firm tofu

This type of tofu is sold in blocks and can be cubed or sliced and used in vegetable stir-fries, kebabs, salads, soups and casseroles. Alternatively, firm tofu can be mashed and used in bakes and burgers. The bland flavour of firm tofu is improved by marinating, because its porous texture readily absorbs flavours and seasonings.

Silken tofu

Soft with a silky, smooth texture, this type of tofu is ideal for use in sauces, dressings, dips and soups. It is a useful dairy-free alternative to cream, soft cheese or yogurt, and can be used to make creamy desserts.

Other forms of tofu

Smoked, marinated and deep-fried tofu are also available in health food stores as well as Oriental and other supermarkets.

Deep-fried tofu is fairly tasteless, but it has an interesting texture. It puffs up during cooking and, underneath the golden, crisp coating, the tofu is white and soft, easily absorbing the flavour of other ingredients. It can be used in much the same way as firm tofu and, as it has been fried in vegetable oil, it is suitable for vegetarian cooking.

Tempeh

This Indonesian speciality is made by fermenting cooked soya beans with a cultured starter. Tempeh is similar to tofu but has a nuttier, more savoury flavour. It can be used in the same way as firm tofu and also benefits from marinating. While some types of tofu are regarded as a dairy replacement, the firmer texture of tempeh means that it can be used instead of meat in pies and casseroles.

Beancurd skins and sticks

Made from soya "milk", dried beancurd skins and sticks, like fresh beancurd, have neither aroma nor flavour until they are cooked, when they will rapidly absorb the flavour of seasonings and other ingredients. Beancurd skins and sticks are used in Chinese cooking and need to be soaked until pliable before use. Beancurd skins should be soaked in cold water for an hour or two and can be used to wrap a variety of fillings.

Beancurd sticks need to be soaked for several hours or overnight. They can be chopped and added to soups, stir-fries and casseroles.

TVP

Textured vegetable protein, or TVP, is a useful meat replacement and is usually bought in dry chunks or as mince. Made from processed soya beans, TVP is very versatile and readily absorbs the strong

flavours of ingredients such as herbs, spices and vegetable stock. It is inexpensive and is a convenient store-cupboard item. TVP needs to be rehydrated in boiling water or vegetable stock, and can be used in stews and curries, or as a filling for pies.

TOFU FRUIT FOOL

1 Place a packet of silken tofu in the bowl of a food processor. Add some soft fruit or berries – for example, strawberries, raspberries or blackberries.

2 Process the mixture to form a smooth purée, then sweeten to taste with a little honey, maple syrup or maize malt syrup.

Above, clockwise from left: Silken bean curd, bean curd skins, firm bean curd, and marinated bean curd. Tofu is a soya bean curd made from coagulated soya milk. It can be bought as silken tofu which is soft and creamy, or firm tofu which also comes smoked and marinated.

PASTA, RICE, GRAINS AND PULSES

These important staple ingredients are used as the basis of many healthy vegetarian meals. They may be added to hearty soups or vegetable stews such as tagines, used in salads such as tabbouleh, or served as accompaniments to vegetarian dishes. They are versatile, healthy, nutritious and delicious – and above all naturally low in fat.

PASTA

Once considered a fattening food, pasta is now recognized as an important part of a healthy diet. The variety of shapes is almost endless, from the myriad tiny soup pastas to huge shells used for stuffing. Low in fat and high in complex carbohydrates, pasta provides plenty of long-term energy.

Durum wheat pasta

This is the most readily available type of pasta and can be made with or without egg. Plain wheat pasta is used for straight long shapes such as spaghetti, while long shapes made with egg pasta, because it is more delicate, are traditionally packed in nests or compressed into waves. Lasagne can be made with either plain or egg pasta. At one time, almost all short pasta shapes were made from plain pasta, but shapes made with egg pasta are becoming increasingly available. Pasta made with egg has several advantages over plain pasta: it is more nutritious, many people consider it to have a superior flavour, and it is more difficult to overcook.

Wholemeal (whole-wheat) pasta

This substantial pasta is made using wholemeal flour and it contains more fibre than plain durum wheat pasta. It has a slightly chewy texture and nutty flavour and it does takes longer to cook. Wholemeal (whole-wheat) spaghetti, called bigoli, is a traditional Italian variety that comes from the area around Venice known as the Veneto and can be found in good Italian delicatessens, as well as in health food shops and supermarkets. There is a growing range of tempting wholemeal shapes, from tiny soup pastas to rotelle (wheels) and lasagne.

Buckwheat pasta

Pasta made from buckwheat flour has a nutty taste and is darker in colour than wholemeal (whole-wheat) pasta. Pizzoccheri from Lombardy is the classic shape. These thin, flat noodles are traditionally sold in nests like tagliatelle (although pizzoccheri are about half the length), but they are also available cut into short strips.

Corn pasta

This pasta is made with corn or maize flour, is gluten-free and is a good alternative pasta for people who cannot tolerate gluten or wheat. It is made in a wide range of shapes, including spaghetti, fusilli (spirals) and conchiglie (shells), as well as more unusual varieties. Plain corn pasta is a sunshine-yellow colour, and may be flavoured with spinach or tomato.

PASTA SHAPES

From capellini (meaning 'angel hair') to thicker pasta shapes, such as fettucine, pasta comes in all sorts of shapes and sizes. As a general rule thin spaghetti goes well with light, thin sauces, while heavier sauces mix well with the thicker tagliatelles.

Long pasta

Dried long pasta in the form of spaghetti is probably the best known, but there are many other varieties, from fine vermicelli to pappardelle – broad ribbon noodles. Tagliatelle, the most common form of ribbon noodles, is usually sold coiled into nests. Long pasta is best served with a thin sauce, made with olive oil, butter, cream, eggs, grated cheese or chopped fresh herbs. When vegetables are added to the sauce, they should be finely chopped. Fresh spaghetti, tagliatelle and fettucine are widely available.

Short pasta

There are hundreds of different short dried pasta shapes, which may be made with plain pasta dough or the more nutritious yellow, egg pasta. Short pasta isn't often sold fresh because most shapes are difficult to produce.

Above: Pasta has very little fat but plenty of "complex" carbohydrates to keep one feeling satisfied after a meal.

Conchiglie (shells) are one of the most useful shapes because they are concave and trap the sauce. Fusilli (spirals) are good with thick tomato-based sauces and farfalle (butterflies) can be served with creamy sauces, but are very versatile and work equally well with tomato- or olive oil-based sauces. Macaroni used to be the most common short shape, and being hollow, it is good for most sauces and baked dishes. However, penne (quills) have become more popular, perhaps because the hollow tubes with diagonally cut ends go particularly well with chunky vegetable sauces.

Flat pasta

Lasagne is designed to be baked between layers of sauce, or cooked in boiling water, then layered, or rolled around a filling to make cannelloni. Lasagne is made from plain or egg pasta and both fresh and dried versions are available. The pasta sheets may be flavoured with tomato or spinach, or made with wholemeal (whole-wheat) flour.

Stuffed pasta

The most common stuffed pasta shapes are ravioli, tortellini (little pies) and cappelletti (little hats). Plain, spinach and tomato doughs are the most usual, and there is a wide range of vegetarian fillings.

RICE

For over half the world's population rice is a staple food. In Italy, there are at least four different short-grained types such as arborio and carnaroli, used for risotto. In Spain, Valencia rice is the preferred variety for paella. In Thailand fragrant jasmine rice is often used. This valuable low-fat food provides a good source of vitamins and minerals, and creates an ideal basis for a wide variety of nutritious, low-fat vegetarian dishes.

Long grain rice

The most widely used type of rice is long grain rice, where the grain is five times as long as it is wide. Long grain brown rice has had its outer husk removed, leaving the bran and germ intact, which gives it a chewy nutty flavour. It takes longer to cook than white rice but contains more fibre, vitamins and minerals. Long grain white rice has had its husk, bran and germ removed, taking most of the nutrients with them and leaving a bland-flavoured rice that is light and fluffy when cooked. It is often whitened with chalk, talc or other preservatives, so rinsing is essential. Easy-cook long grain white rice, sometimes called parboiled or converted rice, has been steamed under pressure. This process hardens the grain and makes it difficult to overcook, and some nutrients are transferred from the bran and germ into the kernel during this process. Easy-cook brown rice cooks more quickly than normal brown rice.

Basmati rice

This is a slender, long grain rice, which is grown in the foothills of the Himalayas. It is aged for a year after harvest, giving it a characteristic light, fluffy texture and aromatic flavour. Its name means "fragrant".

Both white and brown types of basmati rice are available. Brown basmati contains more nutrients, and has a slightly nuttier flavour than the white variety. Widely used in Indian cooking, basmati rice has a cooling effect on hot and spicy curries. It is also excellent for biryanis and rice salads.

Wild rice

This is not a true rice but an aquatic grass grown in North America. It has dramatic, long, slender brown-black grains that have a nutty flavour and chewy texture. It takes longer to cook than most types of rice – from 35–60 minutes, depending on whether you like it chewy or tender – but you can reduce the cooking time by soaking it in water overnight. Wild rice is extremely nutritious. It contains all eight essential amino acids and is particularly rich in lysine. It is a good source of fibre, low in calories and gluten free. Use in stuffings, serve plain or mix with other rices in pilaffs and rice salads.

Risotto rice

To make Italian risotto, it is essential that you use a special, fat, short grain rice. Arborio rice, which originates from the Po Valley region in Italy, is the most widely sold variety. When cooked, most rice absorbs around three times its weight in water, but risotto rice can absorb nearly five times its weight, and the result is a creamy grain that still retains a slight bite.

OTHER GRAINS

There are other grains besides wheat and rice that provide variety in our diet and are packed with nutrients. Amongst them are oats, rye, corn, barley, quinoa

Above: Basmati makes an excellent long grain rice. Boil, steam or bake for healthiest results and fuller flavour. It stores well in sealed containers.

(originally from the high Andes this ivory coloured nutrient-rich grain cooks like regular rice but takes half the time), and spelt (an ancient wheat variety useful for those with wheat allergies). Grains come in many forms, from wholegrains to flour and are used for baking, breakfast cereals and cooked dishes.

Oats

Available rolled, flaked, as oatmeal or oatbran, oats are warming and sustaining when cooked. Like rye, oats are a popular grain in northern Europe, particularly Scotland, where they are turned into porridge and oatcakes.

Whole oats are unprocessed with the nutritious bran and germ remaining intact. Oat groats are the hulled, whole kernel, while rolled oats are made from groats that have been heated and pressed flat. Quick cooking rolled oats have been pre-cooked in water and then dried, which diminishes their nutritional value. Medium oatmeal is best in cakes and breads, while fine is ideal in pancakes and fruit and milk drinks. Oat bran can be sprinkled over breakfast cereals and mixed into natural (plain) or fruit yogurt.

Rye

The most popular grain for bread-making in Eastern Europe, Scandinavia and Russia, rye flour produces a dark, dense and dry loaf that keeps well. The wholegrain can be soaked overnight, then cooked in boiling water until tender, but the flour, with its robust, full flavour and greyish colour, is the most commonly used form. The flour ranges from dark to light, depending on whether the bran and germ have been removed. Rye is low in gluten and is a good source of vitamin E and some B vitamins, as well as protein, calcium, iron, phosphorus and potassium. It is also high in fibre.

Corn

We are most familiar with yellow corn or maize and in its ground form it remains an essential store-cupboard ingredient in the USA, the Caribbean and Italy.

Cornmeal

The main culinary uses for cornmeal are cornbread, a classic, southern American bread, and polenta, which confusingly is both the Italian name for cornmeal as well as a dish made with the grain. Polenta (the cooked dish) is a thick, golden porridge, which is often flavoured with butter and cheese or chopped herbs. Once cooked, polenta can also be left to cool, then cut into slabs and fried, barbecued or griddled until golden brown. It is delicious with roasted vegetables.

Cornflour (cornstarch)

This fine white powder is a useful thickening agent for sauces, soups and casseroles. It can also be added to cakes.

Above: Cornmeal, a grainy yellow flour, comes in many forms, such as polenta.

Barley

Believed to be the oldest cultivated grain, barley is a fundamental part of everyday Eastern and Asian cooking. Pearl barley, the most usual form, is husked, steamed and then polished to give it its characteristic ivory-coloured appearance. It has a mild, sweet flavour and chewy texture, and can be added to soups, stews and bakes. It is also used to make old-fashioned barley water. Barley flakes make a satisfying porridge, and barley flour is also available.

Buckwheat

In spite of its name, buckwheat is not a type of wheat, but is actually related to the rhubarb family. Available plain or toasted, it has a nutty, earthy flavour. It is a staple food in Eastern Europe where it is milled to make blini. The flour is also used in Japan for soba noodles and in Italy for pasta.

Couscous

This tiny yellowish grain is a form of pasta made from semolina. It is a staple of North African cooking and widely available in packaged form in most supermarkets. Couscous is a good low-fat source of complex carbohydrates. The grains are rolled, dampened and cooked with fine wheat flour. Couscous simply needs soaking, although it can also be steamed or baked. It has a light and fluffy texture and a fairly bland flavour, which makes it a good foil for spicy dishes, such as low-fat vegetable stews. Couscous is also ideal for salads.

Quinoa

From the ancient Incas, this amazing grain has protein at least equivalent to that in milk and is stuffed full of potassium and riboflavin, as well as vitamin B6. Among other uses quinoa can be used in soups, salads and desserts or in pilaff recipes.

PULSES

Pulses are the edible seeds from plants belonging to the legume family. They include chickpeas and a vast range of beans and are packed with protein, vitamins, minerals and fibre. They are extremely low in fat. For the cook, their ability to absorb the flavours of other foods means that pulses can be used as the base for an infinite number of dishes. Dried pulses require soaking overnight in cold water before use.

Lentils

These low-fat nutritious pulses come in different sizes and can be yellow, red, brown or green. The tiny green Puy lentils are favoured in France, whereas the brown and red ones are more popular in the Middle East, where they are often cooked with spices. They do not need soaking before cooking.

Aduki beans

Also known as adzuki beans, these tiny, deep-red beans have a sweet, nutty flavour and are popular in Oriental dishes. In Chinese cooking, they form the base of red bean paste. Known as the "king of beans" in Japan, the aduki bean is reputed to be good for the liver and kidneys. They cook quickly and can be used in casseroles and bakes.

Black beans

These shiny, black, kidney-shaped beans are often used in Caribbean cooking. They have a sweetish flavour, and their distinctive colour adds a dramatic touch to soups, mixed bean salads or casseroles.

Black-eyed beans (peas)

Known as black-eyed peas or cow peas in the USA, black-eyed beans are an essential ingredient in Creole cooking and some spicy Indian curries. The small, creamy-coloured bean is characterized by the black spot on its side where it was once attached to the

Above: Red lentils become very soft when cooked and are ideal for purées. Green or brown lentils are firmer and retain more texture. The finest flavoured are Puy lentils.

PREPARING PULSES

1 Rinse well, pick out any small stones, then put the pulses in a bowl of cold water. Soak for 4–8 hours.

2 Drain the pulses, rinse them under cold water and drain them again. Tip them into a pan. Add plenty of cold water but no salt. Bring to boil, boil hard for 10 minutes, then simmer until tender. Drain and season.

pod. Good in soups and salads, they can also be added to savoury bakes and casseroles, and can be used in place of haricot (navy) or flageolet or cannellini beans in a wide variety of dishes.

Borlotti beans

These oval beans have red-streaked, pinkish-brown skin and a bitter-sweet flavour. When cooked, they have a tender, moist texture, which is good in Italian bean and pasta soups, as well as hearty vegetable stews. In most recipes, they are interchangeable with red kidney beans.

Broad (fava) beans

These large beans were first cultivated by the ancient Egyptians. Usually eaten in their fresh form, broad beans change in colour from green to brown when dried, making them difficult to recognize in their dried state. The outer skin can be very tough and chewy, and some people prefer to remove it after cooking. They can also be bought ready-skinned.

Butter (wax) beans and lima beans

Similar in flavour and appearance, both butter beans and lima beans are characterized by their flattish, kidney shape and soft, floury texture. Cream-coloured butter beans are familiar in Britain and Greece, while lima beans are popular in the USA. Butter and lima beans are good with creamy herb sauces. Care should be taken not to overcook butter and lima beans as they tend to become pulpy and mushy in texture.

Cannellini beans

These small, white, kidney-shaped beans have a soft, creamy texture when cooked and are popular in Italian cooking. They can be used in place of haricot (navy) beans and, when dressed with olive oil, lemon juice, crushed garlic and fresh chopped parsley, make an excellent warm salad.

Chickpeas

Also known as garbanzo beans, robust and hearty chickpeas resemble shelled hazelnuts and have a delicious nutty flavour and creamy texture. They need lengthy cooking and are much used in Mediterranean and Middle Eastern cooking. In India, they are known as gram and are ground into flour to make fritters and flat breads. Gram flour, also called besan, can be found in health food shops and Asian grocery stores.

Flageolet beans

These young haricot (navy) beans are removed from the pod before they are fully ripe, hence their fresh delicate flavour. A pretty, mint-green colour, they are the most expensive bean to buy and are best treated simply. Cook them until they are tender, then season and drizzle with a little olive oil and lemon juice.

Haricot (navy) beans

Most commonly used for canned baked beans, these versatile, ivory-coloured beans are small and oval in shape. Called navy or Boston beans in the USA, they suit slow-cooked dishes, such as casseroles and bakes.

Pinto beans

A smaller, paler version of the borlotti bean, the savoury-tasting pinto has an attractive speckled skin – it is aptly called the painted bean. One of the many relatives of the kidney bean, pinto beans feature extensively in Mexican cooking, most familiarly in refried beans,

Above: Quick and convenient, choose canned beans that do not have any added sugar or salt. Store in a cool, dry place and use within a year of purchase for best flavour and texture. Drain and rinse under cold running water before use.

when they are cooked until tender and fried with garlic, chilli and tomatoes. The beans are then mashed, resulting in a wonderful, spicy, rough purée that is usually served with warm tortillas. Soured cream and garlic-flavoured guacamole are good accompaniments.

Red kidney beans

Glossy, mahogany-red kidney beans retain their colour and shape when cooked. They have a soft, "mealy" texture and are much used in South American cooking. An essential ingredient in spicy chillies, they can also be used to make refried beans (although this dish is traditionally made from pinto beans). Cooked kidney beans can be used to make a variety of salads, but they are especially good combined with red onion and chopped flat leaf parsley and mint, then tossed in an olive oil dressing.

Mung beans

Instantly recognizable in their sprouted form as beansprouts, mung or moong beans are small, olive-coloured beans native to India. They are soft and sweet when cooked, and are used in the spicy curry, moong dahl. Soaking is not essential, but if they are soaked overnight this will reduce the usual 40 minutes cooking time by about half.

HERBS AND SPICES

In many vegetarian dishes, some ingredients are added to dishes to give essential extra flavour or to enhance those already present. Flavours provided by herbs and spices are naturally low in fat, and they contribute a lot of taste and colour, without extra fat, making them ideal for creating a wide range of delicious and nutritious low-fat vegetarian dishes.

Basil

One of the most popular herbs, basil has a wonderful intense aroma, sweet flavour and bright green colour. The sweet, tender leaves have a natural affinity with tomatoes, aubergines (eggplants), (bell) peppers, courgettes (zucchini) and cheese. Basil is perhaps best known as the basis of the Italian sauce pesto, but a handful of torn leaves will also enliven a green salad. Tear the leaves rather than chop them, as they bruise easily, and add basil to dishes towards the end of the cooking time.

Bay leaves

Picked from the hardy bay shrub or tree, bay leaves are widely used to flavour slow-cooked recipes such as low-fat stocks, soups and vegetable stews. They are invariably included in a bouquet garni. They are also threaded on to mixed vegetable kebab skewers or thrown on the barbecue to invigorate the smoky flavour.

Below: Bay leaves have a distinctively strong, aromatic, spicy flavour.

Chillies

These are the small fiery relatives of the sweet (bell) pepper family and are commonly used in vegetarian cooking. Chillies, both fresh and dried, may be used in spicy vegetable stews, as well as in stir-fries, curries and other hot dishes.

Chives

A member of the onion family, chives have a milder flavour and are best used as a garnish, snipped over egg or potato dishes, or added to salads or low-fat flans.

Coriander (cilantro)

Fresh coriander leaves impart a distinctive flavour to low-fat soups, vegetable stews, sauces and spicy dishes when added towards the end of cooking. Coriander is also used in salads and yogurt dishes.

Cumin seeds

These dark, spindly seeds play a major role in Indian, Mexican, Thai and Vietnamese cuisines. Cumin is a crucial ingredient of chilli powder. Cumin has a strong, spicy, sweet aroma with a slightly bitter, pungent taste. Cumin seeds are crushed or used whole.

Below: Chillies add intense heat and a crunchy texture to all dishes.

Above: Mixed herbs of lemon balm, marjoram, mint and oregano.

Dill

The mild, yet distinctive, aniseed flavour of the herb dill goes well with potatoes, courgettes (zucchini) and cucumber. It makes a good addition to sauces and can be added to a wide variety of egg dishes. It can also be used as a flavouring for low-fat dressings and marinades and is a good partner for mustard. Add to dishes just prior to serving as its mild flavour diminishes with cooking.

Below: Oregano is a wild form of marjoram and has a distinct aroma.

Above: Nutmeg makes a good addition to many sweet and savoury dishes.

Lemon balm

This herb makes a refreshing tea and is good in any sweet or savoury dish that uses lemon juice.

Marjoram

Closely related to oregano, marjoram has a slightly sweeter flavour. It goes well in Mediterranean-style vegetable dishes, such as ratatouille, or in vegetable casseroles and tomato sauces, but should be added at the last minute as its flavour diminishes when heated. It also goes well in marinades.

Mint

Chopped mint accompanies other herbs to enhance stuffed vegetables in countries such as Greece and in countries in the Middle East. Finely chopped mint adds a cooling tang to low-fat yogurt dishes as well as teas and iced drinks.

Nutmeg

The sweet, warm aroma of nutmeg makes a good addition to many sweet and savoury dishes, particularly those containing spinach, cheese and eggs. For the best flavour, buy whole nutmegs and grate them freshly as required.

Oregano

This herb is a wild form of marjoram, and has a slightly stronger flavour. It is a very popular herb, widely used in vegetarian cooking and is a classic addition to pizza-based recipes.

Parsley

Both flat leaf parsley and the tightly curled variety are widely used in vegetarian cooking. Parsley is commonly used to add flavour and colour, and it also makes an attractive garnish.

Pepper

This is one of the most versatile of all spices. There are several types of peppercorns, all of which are picked from the pepper vine. Black peppercorns have the strongest flavour, which is rich, earthy and pungent. Green peppercorns are the fresh unripe berries that are bottled while soft.

Rosemary

Wonderfully aromatic, rosemary is traditionally used in meat dishes, but it can also add a smoky flavour to hearty bean and vegetable dishes.

Sage

The leaves of this herb, which may be silver-grey or purple, have a potent aroma and only a small amount is needed. Sage is commonly added to meat dishes but used discreetly, it is delicious with beans, cheese, lentils and in stuffings.

Thyme

There are many types of thyme, from lemon thyme to plain garden thyme, ranging in colour from yellow to grey-green. A few sprigs will add a warm earthy flavour to vegetable soups, marinades and other vegetarian dishes. This robustly flavoured aromatic herb is good in tomato-based recipes, and with roasted vegetables, lentils and beans. It is also essential in a bouquet garni.

Above: Thyme

Tarragon

With its distinctive grey-green leaves, tarragon is a popular herb in French cooking. Tarragon has an affinity with all egg- and cheese-based dishes. The short slender-leafed French variety has a warm, aniseed flavour. Tarragon also makes a zesty addition to salads and vinaigrettes.

BUYING AND STORING FRESH HERBS

Fresh herbs are widely available, sold loose, in packets or growing in pots. Herbs in packets do not keep for as long and should be stored in the refrigerator. Place stems of fresh herbs in a half-filled jar of water and cover with a plastic bag. Sealed with an elastic band, the herbs should keep in the refrigerator for a week. Growing herbs should be kept on a sunny windowsill. If watered regularly, and not cut too often, they will keep for months.

Above: Rosemary (left) and sage (right).

Nuts and Dried Fruit

When it comes to nuts, eat sparingly, as they have high levels of mono-unsaturated and polyunsaturated fats, but they are also low in saturated fats and have no cholesterol. They contain plant protein, which makes them a good meat-substitute. Nuts are also a great source of vitamins E, B6, niacin, folic acid and minerals. Here are just a few of the many types available.

Almonds

Widely used in the Middle East, almonds are an important ingredient in sweet pastries as well as savoury dishes. Almonds are sold fresh in their green velvety shells in many Mediterranean markets. Due to their high-fat content, almonds should be used sparingly in low-fat cooking.

Chestnuts

Raw chestnuts are not recommended as they are not only unpleasant to eat but also contain tannic acid, which inhibits the absorption of iron. Most chestnuts originate from France and Spain and they are excellent after roasting – it complements their soft, floury texture. Unlike other nuts, they contain very little fat. Out of season, chestnuts can be bought dried, canned or puréed. Add whole chestnuts to winter stews, soups, stuffings or pies. The sweetened purée is delicious in desserts.

Coconuts

This versatile nut grows all over the tropics. The white dense meat, or flesh, is made into desiccated (dry, unsweetened shredded)

coconut, blocks of creamed coconut and a thick and creamy milk. A popular curry ingredient, coconut lends a sweet, creamy flavour to desserts, curries, soups and casseroles. Use coconut in moderation, as it is particularly high in fat.

Peanuts

Not strictly a nut but a member of the pulse family, peanuts bury themselves just below the earth after flowering – hence their

Left: Blanched, whole and shelled almonds; shelled cashews (in bowl); and shelled and whole Brazil nuts.

DRIED FRUIT AND VINE FRUIT

A useful source of energy, dried fruit is higher in calories than fresh fruit, and packed with vitamins and minerals. The drying process boosts the levels of vitamin C, beta carotene, potassium and iron. Apricots and prunes are the most popular types, but many other types such as dried apple rings, cherries and peaches are also available (*below left*).

Currants, sultanas and raisins are the most popular dried fruits. Traditionally, these vine fruits are used for fruit cakes and breads, but currants and raisins are also good in savoury vegetarian dishes. In Indian and North African cookery they are frequently used for their sweetness. Figs and dates are also popular – chopped or puréed (*below right*) – as an ingredient in low-fat cakes and tea breads.

It takes about 1.75–2.25kg/4–5lb fresh grapes to produce 450g/1lb sultanas, raisins or currants, while 1.5kg/3lb fresh figs and dates produces just 450g/1lb dried fruit. Although high in natural sugars, dried fruit is a concentrated source of nutrients, including iron, potassium, calcium, phosphorus, vitamin C, beta carotene and some B vitamins.

alternative name, groundnuts. They are widely used in South-east Asia, notably for satay sauce, and in African cuisines, where they are used as an ingredient in stews.

Use sparingly – like olive oil, peanut oil is a monounsaturated fat and helps lower LDL (bad) cholesterol.

Walnuts

When picked young, walnuts are referred to as "wet" and have fresh, milky-white kernels, which can be eaten raw, but are often pickled. Dried walnuts have a delicious bitter-sweet flavour and can be bought shelled, chopped or ground. They can be used to make excellent cakes and biscuits, but are also good added to savoury dishes such as stir-fries and salads – a low-fat Waldorf salad combines kernels with sliced celery and apples in a low-fat mayonnaise dressing.

OILS AND VINEGARS

Oils have positive health benefits – olive oil for example is heart-protective, because it is rich in monounsaturated fats – but use such oils sparingly because they can increase the fat content of your diet. Vinegars make excellent low-fat additions to sauces and salad dressings.

OILS

There is a wide variety of cooking oils and they are produced from a number of different sources: from cereals such as corn; from fruits such as olives; from nuts such as walnuts, almonds and hazelnuts; and from seeds such as rapeseed, safflower and sunflower.

Olive oil

This is one of the most popular oils, but should be used in moderation in low-fat cooking because of its high-fat content. Unlike other oils, which are extracted from the seeds or dried fruits of plants, olive oil is pressed from the pulp of ripe olives, which gives it an inimitable richness and flavour. Besides being high in monounsaturated fat and low in saturated fat, making it a healthy alternative to many other fats, olive oil is valued for its fine, nutty flavour. Different countries and regions produce distinctively different oils. The richest and best oil comes from the first cold pressing of the olives, with no further processing, producing a rich green 'extra virgin' oil. Virgin olive oil is pressed in the same way, but is usually from a second pressing. Extra virgin olive oil is ideal used 'raw' in salad dressings, uncooked sauces and for drizzling lightly over vegetables. Virgin olive oil is used for cooking and baking.

Extra virgin olive oil

This premium olive oil has a superior flavour. It comes from the first cold pressing of the olives and has a low acidity – less than 1 per cent. Extra virgin olive oil is not recommended for frying, as heat impairs its flavour, but it is good in salad dressings, especially when combined with lighter oils. It is delicious as a sauce on its own, stirred into pasta with chopped garlic and black pepper, or drizzled over steamed vegetables.

Corn oil

One of the most economical and widely used vegetable oils, corn oil has a deep golden colour and a fairly strong flavour. It is suitable for cooking and frying, but should not be used for salad dressings. Corn is rich in omega-6 (linoleic) fatty acids, which are believed to reduce harmful cholesterol in the body.

Safflower oil

This is a light, all-purpose oil, which comes from the seeds of the safflower. It can be used in place of sunflower and groundnut oils, but is a little thicker with a slightly stronger flavour. It is best used with other more strongly flavoured ingredients, and is ideal for cooking spicy foods. Safflower oil contains more polyunsaturated fat than any other type of oil and it is low in saturated fat.

Sunflower oil

Perhaps the best all-purpose oil, sunflower oil is very light and almost tasteless. It is very versatile, and can be used for cooking, or to make salad dressings, when it can be combined with a stronger flavoured oil such as olive oil or walnut oil. Sunflower oil is extracted from the seeds of the sunflower. It is very high in polyunsaturated fat and low in saturated fat.

Soya oil

This neutral flavoured, all-purpose oil, which is extracted from soya beans, is probably the most widely used oil in the world. It is useful for frying because it has a high smoking point, and remains stable at high temperatures. It is also widely used in margarines. It is rich in polyunsaturated and monounsaturated fats and low in saturates.

VINEGARS

One of our oldest condiments, vinegar is made by acetic fermentation, a process that occurs when a liquid containing less than 18 per cent alcohol is exposed to the air. Most countries produce their own type of vinegar, usually based on their most popular alcoholic drink – wine in France and Italy; sherry in Spain; rice wine in Asia; and beer and cider in Great Britain. Commonly used as a preservative in pickles and chutneys, it is also an ingredient in marinades and salad dressings. A spoonful or two of a good-quality vinegar can really add flavour to cooked dishes and sauces.

Balsamic vinegar

This is a rich, dark, mellow vinegar, which has become hugely popular. Traditionally made in Modena in northern Italy, balsamic vinegar is made from grape juice (predominantly from Trebbiano grapes), which is fermented in vast wooden barrels for a minimum of four to five years and up to 40 or more years, resulting in an intensely rich vinegar with a concentrated flavour. Balsamic vinegar is delicious in dressings or sprinkled over roasted vegetables.

Raspberry vinegar

Any soft fruit can be used to enhance the flavour of white wine vinegar but raspberries are the most popular. Raspberry vinegar can be made by macerating fresh raspberries in good-quality wine vinegar for 2–3 weeks. Once the mixture is strained, the vinegar is delicious as part of a salad dressing, or in sauces. It can be mixed with sparkling mineral water to make a refreshing drink.

Above: Make salad dressings with vinegars or predominantly unsaturated oils.

FAT AND CALORIE CONTENTS OF FOOD

The figures show the weight of fat (g) and the energy content per 100g (3½oz) of each foods used in low-fat cooking.

	Fat (g)	Energy		Fat (g)	Energy
VEGETABLES			Dried mixed fruit	0.4	268kcal/1114kJ
Asparagus	0	15kcals/63kJ	Figs	0	43kcal/185kJ
Aubergines (eggplants)	0.4	15kcal/63kJ	Grapefruit	0.1	30kcal/126kJ
Beetroot (beets), cooked	0.1	36kcal/151kJ	Grapes	0	63kcal/265kJ
Bell peppers	0.4	32kcal/128kJ	Lemons, with peel	0.2	9kcal/38kJ
Broad (fava) beans	0.8	48kcal/204kJ	Melon	0	32kcal/135kJ
Broccoli	0.9	33kcal/138kJ	Olives (green)	11	112kcal/422kJ
Cabbage	0.4	26kcal/109kJ	Oranges	0.1	37kcal/158kJ
Carrots	0.3	35kcal/146kJ	Peaches/nectarines	0.1	33kcal/142kJ
Cauliflower	0.9	34kcal/146kJ	Pears	0.1	40kcal/169kJ
Celery, raw	0.2	33kcal/142kJ	Pomegranate	0.2	51kcal/218kJ
Courgettes (zucchini)	0.4	18kcal/74kJ	Almonds	55.8	612kcal/2534kJ
Cucumber	0.1	10kcal/40kJ	Brazil nuts	68.2	682kcal/2813kJ
Fennel	0	14kcal/56kJ	Hazelnuts	63.5	650kcal/2685kJ
Globe artichoke	0	9kcal/35kJ	Peanut butter, smooth	53.7	623kcal/2581kJ
Green beans	0	22kcal/92kJ	Pine nuts	68.6	688kcal/2840kJ
Jerusalem artichoke	0	41kcal/207kJ	Pistachio nuts	58.3	632kcal/2650kJ
Mushrooms	0.5	13kcal/55kJ	Walnuts	68.5	688kcal/2840kJ
Okra	0	26kcal/110kJ			
Onions	0.2	36kcal/151kJ	**BEANS, RICE, GRAINS AND PASTA**		
Peas	1.5	83kcal/344kJ	Black-eyed beans (peas), cooked	1.8	116kcal/494kJ
Potatoes	0.2	75kcal/318kJ	Brown rice, raw	2.8	357kcal/1518kJ
Chips (French fries), home-made	6.7	189kcal/796kJ	Bulgur (cracked wheat)	2.5	319kcal/1340kJ
Chips, retail	12.4	239kcal/1001kJ	Butter beans, canned	0.5	77kcal/327kJ
Oven-chips, frozen, baked	4.2	162kcal/687kJ	Chickpeas, canned	2.9	115kcal/487kJ
Potato crisps (potato chips)	34.2	530kcal/1924kJ	Couscous (cooked)	0	112kcal/470kJ
Spinach (fresh, cooked)	0	21kcal/84kJ	Hummus	12.6	187kcal/781kJ
Tomatoes	0.3	17kcal/73kJ	Pasta, white, raw	1.8	342kcal/1456kJ
			Pasta, wholemeal (whole-wheat), uncooked	2.5	324kcal/1379kJ
FRUITS AND NUTS			Polenta	1.6	330kcal/1383kJ
Apples, eating	0.1	47kcal/199kJ	Red kidney beans, canned	0.6	100kcal/424kJ
Avocados	19.5	190kcal/784kJ	Red lentils, cooked	0.4	100kcal/424kJ
Bananas	0.3	95kcal/403kJ	White rice, raw	3.6	383kcal/1630kJ
Dates	0	226/kcal/970kJ			

Below: Vegetables are very low in fat. Eat them raw for a filling snack; steam them to retain maximum nutrition value.

Below: Vegetables contain plenty of dietary fibre and are valuable sources of vitamins, especially A, C and E.

BAKING AND SPREADS

	Fat (g)	Energy
Bread, brown	2.0	218kcal/927kJ
Bread, white	1.9	235kcal/1002kJ
Bread, wholemeal (whole-wheat)	2.5	215kcal/914kJ
Chocolate, milk	30.7	520kcal/2157kJ
Chocolate, plain (semisweet)	28.0	510kcal/2116kJ
Croissant	20.3	360kcal/1505kJ
Digestive biscuit (plain)	20.9	471kcal/1978kJ
Reduced-fat digestive biscuits	16.4	467kcal/1965kJ
Doughnut, jam	14.5	336kcal/1414kJ
Fatless sponge cake	6.1	294kcal/1245kJ
Flapjack	26.6	484kcal/2028kJ
Flour, plain (all-purpose) white	1.3	341kcal/1450kJ
Flour, self-raising (self-rising)	1.2	330kcal/1407kJ
Flour, wholemeal (whole-wheat)	2.2	310kcal/1318kJ
Fruit jam	0.26	268kcal/1114kJ
Honey	0	288kcal/1229kJ
Madeira cake	16.9	393kcal/1652kJ
Shortbread	26.1	498kcal/2087kJ
Sugar, white	0.3	94kcal/1680kJ

FATS, OILS AND EGGS

	Fat (g)	Energy
Butter	81.7	737kcal/3031kJ
Margarine	81.6	739kcal/3039kJ
Low-fat spread	40.5	390kcal/1605kJ
Very low-fat spread	25.0	273kcal/1128kJ
Cooking oil	99.9	899kcal/3696kJ
Corn oil	99.9	899kcal/3696kJ
Olive oil	99.9	899kcal/3696kJ
Safflower oil	99.9	899kcal/3696kJ
Eggs	10.8	147kcal/612kJ
Egg yolk	30.5	399kcal/1402kJ
Egg white	Trace	36kcal/153kJ
French dressing	49.4	462kcal/1902kJ
Fat-free dressing	1.2	67kcal/282kJ
Mayonnaise	75.6	691kcal/2843kJ
Mayonnaise, reduced calorie	28.1	288kcal/1188kJ

Below: Exotic fruits, with a few notable exceptions like avocado, have a very low fat content.

CREAM, MILK AND CHEESE

	Fat (g)	Energy
Cream, double (heavy)	48.0	449kcal/1849kJ
Reduced-fat double (heavy) cream	24.0	243kcal/1002kJ
Cream, single (light)	19.1	198kcal/817kJ
Cream, whipping	39.3	373kcal/1539kJ
Crème fraîche	40.0	379kcal/156kJ
Reduced-fat crème fraîche	15.0	165kcal/683kJ
Milk, skimmed	0.1	33kcal/130kJ
Milk, semi-skimmed (low-fat)	1.7	49kcal/204kJ
Milk, full cream (whole)	3.9	66kcal/275kJ
Brie	26.9	319kcal/1323kJ
Cheddar cheese	34.4	412kcal/1708kJ
Cheddar-type, reduced fat	15.0	261kcal/1091kJ
Cottage cheese	3.9	98kcal/413kJ
Cream cheese	47.4	439kcal/1807kJ
Curd cheese (medium fat)	11.7	173kcal/723kJ
Edam cheese	25.4	333kcal/1382kJ
Feta cheese	20.2	250kcal/1037kJ
Fromage frais, plain	7.1	113kcal/469kJ
Fromage frais, very low-fat	0.2	58kcal/247kJ
Mozzarella cheese	21.0	289kcal/1204kJ
Parmesan cheese	32.7	452kcal/1880kJ
Ricotta cheese	10	150kcal/625kJ
Skimmed-milk soft cheese	trace	74kcal/313kJ
Low-fat yogurt, natural (plain)	0.8	56kcal/236kJ
Greek (US strained plain) yogurt	9.1	115kcal/477kJ
Reduced-fat Greek yogurt	5.0	80kcal/335k

Below: Pasta, rice and beans play a key role in maintaining a healthy, low-fat, vegetarian diet.

SOUPS

*Vegetarian soups are ideal served as a light first
course, but many also provide a tasty, low-fat
vegetarian lunch, supper or more substantial meal
served with fresh crusty bread. In this chapter, there
is a tempting selection of recipes for chilled soups
to keep you cool in summer, as well as many hot
and hearty low-fat soups to warm you on
those chilly winter days.*

CHILLED TOMATO AND SWEET PEPPER SOUP ★

A LOW-FAT SOUP RECIPE INSPIRED BY THE CLASSICALLY COOL SPANISH GAZPACHO, WHERE RAW INGREDIENTS ARE COMBINED TO MAKE A REFRESHING CHILLED SOUP. IN THIS MODERN VARIATION THE PEPPERS, ONION, TOMATOES AND OTHER INGREDIENTS ARE COOKED FIRST AND THEN CHILLED.

SERVES FOUR

INGREDIENTS
   2 red (bell) peppers, halved
   10ml/2 tsp olive oil
   1 onion, finely chopped
   2 garlic cloves, crushed
   675g/1½lb ripe well-flavoured
     tomatoes
   150ml/¼ pint/⅔ cup red wine
   600ml/1 pint/2½ cups vegetable stock
   salt and ground black pepper
   chopped fresh chives, to garnish
For the croûtons
   2 slices day-old white bread,
     crusts removed
   10ml/2 tsp olive oil

COOK'S TIP
Any juice that accumulates in the pan after grilling (broiling) the peppers, or in the bowl, should be stirred into the soup. It will add a delectable flavour.

1 Cut each pepper half into quarters and seed. Place skin-side up on a grill (broiling) rack and grill (broil) until the skins have charred. Transfer to a bowl and cover with a plate.

2 Heat the oil in a large non-stick pan. Add the onion and garlic, and cook until soft. Meanwhile, remove the skin from the peppers and roughly chop them. Cut the tomatoes into chunks.

3 Add the peppers and tomatoes to the pan, then cover and cook gently for 10 minutes. Add the wine and cook for a further 5 minutes, then add the stock and salt and pepper, and simmer for 20 minutes.

4 Meanwhile, make the croûtons. Cut the bread into cubes. Heat the oil in a small non-stick frying pan, add the bread and fry until golden brown and crisp. Drain on kitchen paper, cool, then store in an airtight box.

5 Process the soup in a blender or food processor until smooth. Pour into a clean glass or ceramic bowl and leave to cool thoroughly before chilling for at least 3 hours. When the soup is cold, season to taste with salt and pepper.

6 Serve in bowls, topped with croûtons and garnished with chopped chives.

Energy 103Kcal/433kJ; Protein 2.4g; Carbohydrate 12.2g, of which sugars 11.5g; Fat 2.5g, of which saturates 0.5g; Cholesterol 0mg; Calcium 26mg; Fibre 3.3g; Sodium 148mg.

GAZPACHO ★

THIS CLASSIC CHILLED SOUP IS DEEPLY ROOTED IN ANDALUSIA. THE SOOTHING BLEND OF TOMATOES, SWEET PEPPERS AND GARLIC IS SHARPENED WITH SHERRY VINEGAR. SERVE IT WITH TRADITIONAL SMALL DISHES OF GARNISHES, IF YOU LIKE, BUT REMEMBER THESE WILL ADD EXTRA FAT AND CALORIES TO THE RECIPE.

SERVES FOUR

INGREDIENTS
 1.3–1.6kg/3–3½lb ripe tomatoes
 1 green (bell) pepper, seeded and
  roughly chopped
 2 garlic cloves, finely chopped
 2 slices stale bread, crusts removed
 20ml/4 tsp extra virgin olive oil
 60ml/4 tbsp sherry vinegar
 175ml/6fl oz/¾ cup tomato juice
 300ml/½ pint/1¼ cups iced water
 salt and ground black pepper
 ice cubes, to serve (optional)
For the garnishes
 10ml/2 tsp olive oil
 2–3 slices stale bread, diced
 1 small cucumber, peeled
  and finely diced
 1 small onion, finely chopped
 1 red (bell) and 1 green (bell)
  pepper, seeded and finely diced
 2 hard-boiled eggs, chopped
  (optional)

COOK'S TIP
In Spain, ripe tomatoes are used for salads and very ripe ones for sauces and soups. No further flavouring ingredients are needed. If you cannot find really ripe tomatoes, add a pinch of sugar to sweeten the soup slightly.

1 Skin the tomatoes, then quarter them and remove the cores and seeds, saving the juices. Put the pepper in a food processor and process for a few seconds. Add the tomatoes, reserved juices, garlic, bread, oil and vinegar and process. Add the tomato juice and process to combine.

2 Season the soup, then pour into a large bowl, cover with clear film (plastic wrap) and chill for at least 12 hours.

3 Prepare the garnishes. Heat the olive oil in a non-stick frying pan and lightly fry the bread cubes for 4–5 minutes until golden brown and crisp. Drain well on kitchen paper, then arrange in a small dish. Place each of the remaining garnishes in separate small dishes.

4 Just before serving, dilute the soup with the ice-cold water. The consistency should be thick but not too stodgy. If you like, stir a few ice cubes into the soup, then spoon into serving bowls and serve with the garnishes.

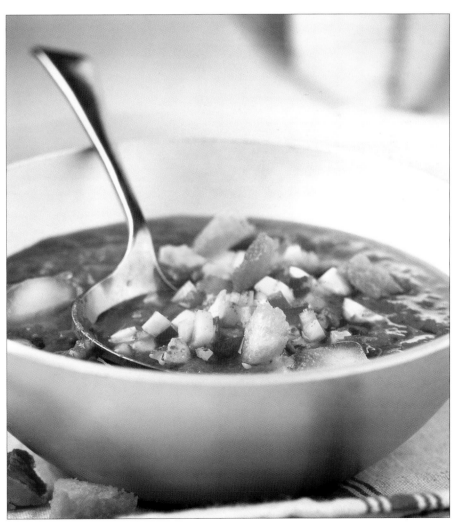

Energy 134Kcal/569kJ; Protein 4.2g; Carbohydrate 20.9g, of which sugars 14.4g; Fat 4.4g, of which saturates 0.8g; Cholesterol 0mg; Calcium 46mg; Fibre 4.4g; Sodium 202mg.

SPICED MANGO SOUP WITH YOGURT ★

THE RECIPE FOR DELICIOUS, LIGHT MANGO SOUP COMES FROM CHUTNEY MARY, THE FAMOUS ANGLO-INDIAN RESTAURANT IN LONDON. IT IS BEST WHEN SERVED LIGHTLY CHILLED.

SERVES FOUR

INGREDIENTS
2 ripe mangoes
15ml/1 tbsp gram flour
120ml/4fl oz/½ cup low-fat natural
  (plain) yogurt
900ml/1½ pints/3¾ cups cold water
2.5ml/½ tsp grated fresh root ginger
2 red chillies, seeded and
  finely chopped
10ml/2 tsp olive oil
2.5ml/½ tsp mustard seeds
2.5ml/½ tsp cumin seeds
8 curry leaves
salt and ground black pepper
fresh mint leaves, shredded,
  to garnish
low-fat natural (plain) yogurt, to serve

1 Peel the mangoes, remove the stones and cut the flesh into chunks. Purée the mango flesh in a blender or food processor until smooth. Pour the mango purée into a saucepan and gently stir in the gram flour, yogurt, water, ginger and chillies.

2 Bring slowly to the boil, stirring occasionally. Simmer for 4–5 minutes until thickened slightly, then remove the pan from the heat and set aside.

3 Heat the oil in a non-stick frying pan. Add the mustard seeds and cook for a few seconds until they begin to pop, then add the cumin seeds.

4 Add the curry leaves and cook gently for 5 minutes. Stir the spice mixture into the soup, return the soup to the heat and cook for 10 minutes.

5 Press the soup through a sieve (strainer), if you like, then season to taste with salt and pepper. Leave the soup to cool completely, then chill for at least 1 hour.

6 Ladle the soup into bowls, and top each with a dollop of yogurt. Garnish with shredded mint leaves and serve.

COOK'S TIP
Gram flour, also known as besan flour, is often used in Indian cooking and is made from ground chickpeas (*chana dhal*).

Energy 83Kcal/354kJ; Protein 3g; Carbohydrate 14.4g, of which sugars 12.7g; Fat 2g, of which saturates 0.5g; Cholesterol 0mg; Calcium 72mg; Fibre 2g; Sodium 28mg.

ROASTED TOMATO AND PASTA SOUP ★

WHEN THE ONLY TOMATOES YOU CAN BUY ARE NOT PARTICULARLY FLAVOURSOME, MAKE THIS TASTY LOW-FAT SOUP. THE OVEN-ROASTING GIVES THE TOMATOES A BIT OF ADDED PIQUANCY.

SERVES FOUR

INGREDIENTS
- 450g/1lb ripe Italian plum tomatoes, halved lengthways
- 1 large red (bell) pepper, quartered lengthways and deseeded
- 1 large red onion, quartered lengthways
- 2 garlic cloves, unpeeled
- 10ml/2 tsp olive oil
- 1.2 litres/2 pints/5 cups vegetable stock or water
- a good pinch of sugar
- 90g/3½oz/scant 1 cup dried small pasta shapes, such as tubetti or small macaroni
- salt and ground black pepper
- fresh basil leaves, to garnish

1 Preheat the oven to 190°C/375°F/ Gas 5. Spread out the tomatoes, red pepper, onion and garlic in a roasting pan and drizzle with the olive oil. Roast in the oven for 30–40 minutes, or until the vegetables are soft and charred, stirring and turning them halfway through the cooking time.

2 Tip the vegetables into a blender or food processor, add about 250ml/8fl oz/ 1 cup of the stock or water and process until puréed. Scrape the vegetable mixture into a sieve (strainer) placed over a large pan and press the purée through the sieve into the pan. Discard the contents of the sieve.

3 Add the remaining stock or water to the pan, then add the sugar, salt and pepper to taste. Bring to the boil, stirring.

4 Add the pasta to the pan, return to the boil, then simmer, stirring frequently for 7–8 minutes, or according to the packet instructions, until the pasta is tender or *al dente*. Adjust the seasoning to taste. Serve hot in soup bowls, garnished with fresh basil leaves.

COOK'S TIP
The soup can be frozen without the pasta. Thaw the soup and bring it gently to the boil before adding the pasta, then continue to cook as directed above.

Energy 142Kcal/599kJ; Protein 4.5g; Carbohydrate 26.9g, of which sugars 9.7g; Fat 2.5g, of which saturates 0.4g; Cholesterol 0mg; Calcium 30mg; Fibre 3.2g; Sodium 14mg.

SHIITAKE MUSHROOM AND RED ONION LAKSA ★

"NOODLES" OF THINLY SLICED RED ONIONS ENHANCE THE TRADITIONAL FLOUR NOODLES IN THIS TASTY, LOW-FAT SOUP, WHICH IS BASED ON THE CLASSIC SOUP, PENANG LAKSA.

SERVES SIX

INGREDIENTS

150g/5oz/2½ cups dried shiitake mushrooms
1.2 litres/2 pints/5 cups boiling vegetable stock
30ml/2 tbsp tamarind paste
250ml/8fl oz/1 cup hot water
6 large dried red chillies, stems removed and seeded
2 lemon grass stalks, thinly sliced
5ml/1 tsp ground turmeric
15ml/1 tbsp grated fresh galangal
1 onion, chopped
5ml/1 tsp dried shrimp paste
15ml/1 tbsp sunflower oil
10ml/2 tsp palm sugar
175g/6oz rice vermicelli
1 red onion, very thinly sliced
1 small cucumber, seeded and cut into strips
a handful of fresh mint leaves, to garnish

1 Place the mushrooms in a bowl and pour in enough boiling stock to cover them, then leave to soak for 30 minutes. Put the tamarind paste into a bowl and pour in the hot water. Mash the paste against the side of the bowl with a fork to extract as much flavour as possible, then strain and reserve the liquid, discarding the pulp.

2 Soak the chillies in enough hot water to cover for 5 minutes, then drain, reserving the liquid and soaked chillies separately.

3 Process the lemon grass, turmeric, galangal, onion, soaked chillies and shrimp paste in a blender or food processor, adding a little soaking water from the chillies to form a paste.

4 Heat the oil in a large, heavy, non-stick pan and cook the paste over a low heat for 4–5 minutes until fragrant.

5 Add the tamarind liquid and bring to the boil, then simmer for 5 minutes. Remove the pan from the heat.

6 Drain the mushrooms and reserve the stock. Discard the stems, then halve or quarter the mushrooms, if large. Add the mushrooms to the pan with their soaking liquid, the remaining stock and the palm sugar. Bring to the boil, then reduce the heat and simmer for 25–30 minutes, or until the mushrooms are tender.

7 Put the rice vermicelli into a large bowl and cover with boiling water, then leave to soak for 4 minutes or according to the packet instructions. Drain well, then divide among six bowls.

8 Top with onion and cucumber, then ladle in the boiling shiitake soup. Add a small bunch of mint leaves to each bowl and serve immediately.

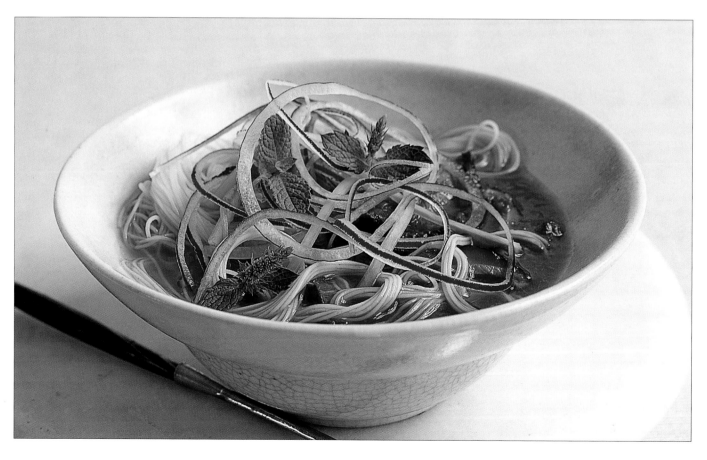

Energy 146Kcal/611kJ; Protein 4.4g; Carbohydrate 27.1g, of which sugars 3.7g; Fat 2.3g, of which saturates 0.3g; Cholesterol 4mg; Calcium 27mg; Fibre 1g; Sodium 54mg.

WILD MUSHROOM SOUP ★

DRIED PORCINI MUSHROOMS — THE KING OF MUSHROOMS IN ITALIAN COOKING — ARE PRICY BUT HAVE AN INTENSE FLAVOUR SO ONLY A SMALL QUANTITY IS NEEDED FOR THIS DELICIOUS LIGHT SOUP.

SERVES FOUR

INGREDIENTS

25g/1oz/½ cup dried porcini
  mushrooms
10ml/2 tsp olive oil
2 leeks, thinly sliced
2 shallots, roughly chopped
1 garlic clove, roughly chopped
225g/8oz/3 cups fresh wild
  mushrooms
about 1.2 litres/2 pints/5 cups
  vegetable stock
2.5ml/½ tsp dried thyme
30ml/2 tbsp single (light) cream
salt and ground black pepper
fresh thyme sprigs, to garnish

1 Put the dried porcini mushrooms in a bowl, add 250ml/8fl oz/1 cup warm water and leave to soak for 20–30 minutes. Lift the mushrooms out of the liquid and squeeze over the bowl to remove as much of the soaking liquid as possible. Strain all the liquid and reserve to use later. Finely chop the porcini and set aside.

2 Heat the olive oil in a large, non-stick pan. Add the leeks, shallots and garlic and cook gently for about 5 minutes, stirring the mixture frequently, until softened but not coloured.

COOK'S TIP
Store dried herbs, such as dried thyme, in airtight glass containers, and keep them in a cool, dark place.

3 Chop or slice the fresh mushrooms and add to the pan. Stir over a medium heat for a few minutes until they begin to soften. Pour in the stock and bring to the boil. Add the chopped porcini, reserved soaking liquid, dried thyme and salt and pepper to taste. Reduce the heat, half-cover the pan and simmer gently for 30 minutes, stirring occasionally.

4 Pour about three-quarters of the soup into a blender or food processor and process until smooth. Return to the soup left in the pan, stir in the cream and heat through gently, stirring. Check the consistency and add more hot stock if the soup is too thick. Adjust the seasoning to taste. Serve hot in soup bowls, garnished with fresh thyme sprigs.

Energy 62Kcal/257kJ; Protein 3.1g; Carbohydrate 4.2g, of which sugars 3.1g; Fat 3.8g, of which saturates 1.3g; Cholesterol 4mg; Calcium 36mg; Fibre 2.9g; Sodium 8mg.

SUMMER VEGETABLE SOUP ★

THIS BRIGHTLY COLOURED, FRESH-TASTING, LIGHT TOMATO SOUP MAKES THE MOST OF SUMMER VEGETABLES IN SEASON. ADD LOTS OF RED AND YELLOW PEPPERS TO MAKE A SWEETER VERSION.

SERVES FOUR

INGREDIENTS

450g/1lb ripe plum tomatoes
225g/8oz ripe yellow tomatoes
10ml/2 tsp olive oil
1 large onion, finely chopped
15ml/1 tbsp sun-dried tomato
  purée (paste)
225g/8oz green courgettes (zucchini),
  trimmed and roughly chopped
225g/8oz yellow courgettes (summer
  squash), trimmed and roughly
  chopped
3 waxy new potatoes, diced
2 garlic cloves, crushed
about 1.2 litres/2 pints/5 cups
  vegetable stock or water
60ml/4 tbsp shredded fresh basil
25g/1oz/⅓ cup grated
  fresh Parmesan cheese
salt and ground black pepper

1 Plunge all the tomatoes in boiling water for 30 seconds, refresh in cold water, then skin and chop finely. Heat the oil in a large non-stick pan, add the onion and cook gently for 5 minutes, until softened, stirring constantly. Stir in the sun-dried tomato purée, chopped tomatoes, courgettes, potatoes and garlic. Mix well and cook gently for 10 minutes, shaking the pan often.

2 Pour in the stock or water. Bring to the boil, reduce the heat, half-cover the pan and simmer gently for 15 minutes or until the vegetables are just tender. Add more stock or water, if necessary.

3 Remove the pan from the heat and stir in the basil and half the cheese. Add seasoning to taste. Serve hot, sprinkled with the remaining cheese.

Energy 146Kcal/615kJ; Protein 7.1g; Carbohydrate 19.9g, of which sugars 8.7g; Fat 4.7g, of which saturates 1.9g; Cholesterol 6mg; Calcium 121mg; Fibre 3.6g; Sodium 102mg.

HERB SOUP WITH CHARGRILLED RADICCHIO ★

THE SWEETNESS OF SHALLOTS AND LEEKS IN THIS TASTY, LOW-FAT SOUP IS BALANCED BEAUTIFULLY BY THE SLIGHTLY ACIDIC SORREL WITH ITS HINT OF LEMON, AND A BOUQUET OF SUMMER HERBS.

SERVES SIX

INGREDIENTS
30ml/2 tbsp dry white wine
2 shallots, finely chopped
1 garlic clove, crushed
2 leeks, sliced
1 large potato, about 225g/8oz,
  roughly chopped
2 courgettes (zucchini), chopped
600ml/1 pint/2½ cups water
115g/4oz sorrel, torn
a large handful of fresh chervil
a large handful of fresh
  flat leaf parsley
a large handful of fresh mint
1 round (butterhead) lettuce,
  separated into leaves
600ml/1 pint/2½ cups
  vegetable stock
1 small head of radicchio
5ml/1 tsp groundnut (peanut) oil
salt and ground black pepper

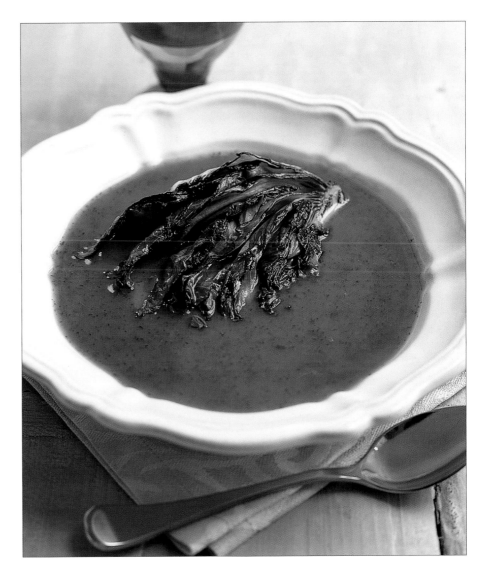

1 Put the wine, shallots and garlic into a heavy pan and bring to the boil. Cook for 2–3 minutes, until softened. Add the leeks, potato and courgettes with enough of the water to come about halfway up the vegetables.

2 Lay a wetted piece of greaseproof paper over the vegetables and put a lid on the pan, then cook gently for 10–15 minutes, or until softened. Remove and discard the paper and add the fresh herbs and lettuce. Cook for 1–2 minutes, or until wilted.

3 Pour in the remaining water and vegetable stock and bring to the boil, then reduce the heat and simmer for 10–12 minutes. Cool the soup slightly, then process it in a blender or food processor until smooth. Return the soup to the rinsed-out pan. Season well to taste with salt and pepper.

4 Cut the radicchio into thin wedges that hold together, then brush the cut sides with the oil. Heat a ridged griddle or frying pan until very hot and add the radicchio wedges.

5 Cook the radicchio wedges for 1 minute on each side, or until slightly charred. Reheat the soup over a low heat, stirring, then ladle it into warmed shallow bowls. Serve a wedge of charred radicchio on top of each portion.

COOK'S TIP
Radicchio is a ruby-leaved Italian chicory that is now grown in Britain as well as imported. Radicchio has a firm texture, a bitter but pleasant flavour, and adds an attractive colour to many dishes. It is often used raw, but may also be lightly cooked, as with this recipe.

Energy 75Kcal/314kJ; Protein 3.8g; Carbohydrate 11g, of which sugars 4.7g; Fat 1.6g, of which saturates 0.3g; Cholesterol 0mg; Calcium 85mg; Fibre 3.2g; Sodium 35mg.

CLASSIC PEA AND BASIL SOUP ★

THE PUNGENT FLAVOUR OF BASIL LIFTS THIS APPETIZING LOW-FAT ITALIAN SOUP OF PETITS POIS, WHILE THE ONION AND GARLIC GIVE DEPTH. SERVE IT WITH GOOD CRUSTY BREAD TO ENJOY IT AT ITS BEST.

2 Add the petits pois and stock to the pan and bring to the boil. Reduce the heat, add the basil and seasoning, then simmer for 10 minutes.

3 Spoon the soup into a blender or food processor (you may have to do this in batches) and process until the soup is smooth.

4 Return the soup to the rinsed out pan and reheat gently until piping hot, stirring. Ladle into warm bowls, sprinkle with shaved Parmesan and garnish with basil.

SERVES SIX

INGREDIENTS
 75ml/5 tbsp olive oil
 2 large onions, chopped
 1 celery stick, chopped
 1 carrot, chopped
 1 garlic clove, finely chopped
 400g/14oz/3½ cups frozen
  petits pois (baby peas)
 900ml/1½ pints/3¾ cups
  vegetable stock
 25g/1oz/1 cup fresh basil leaves,
  roughly torn, plus extra to garnish
 salt and ground black pepper
 shaved fresh Parmesan cheese,
  to serve

1 Heat the oil in a large, non-stick pan and add the onions, celery, carrot and garlic. Cover the pan and cook over a low heat for 45 minutes, or until the vegetables are soft, stirring occasionally to prevent the vegetables sticking.

COOK'S TIP
Remove the pan from the heat and allow the mixture to cool slightly before processing it in a blender or food processor.

VARIATIONS
You can also use mint or a mixture of parsley, mint and chives in place of the basil, if you like. Use frozen peas in place of petits pois (baby peas).

Energy 106Kcal/439kJ; Protein 5.6g; Carbohydrate 13.6g, of which sugars 6g; Fat 3.7g, of which saturates 0.6g; Cholesterol 0mg; Calcium 40mg; Fibre 4.5g; Sodium 9mg.

BROAD BEAN AND MANGETOUT MINESTRONE ★

THE CLASSIC, WINTRY ITALIAN MINESTRONE SOUP TAKES ON A SUMMER-FRESH IMAGE IN THIS LIGHT AND TASTY RECIPE. ANY SMALL PASTA SHAPES CAN BE USED INSTEAD OF THE SPAGHETTINI IF YOU PREFER.

SERVES SIX

INGREDIENTS

    15ml/1 tbsp olive oil
    2 onions, finely chopped
    2 garlic cloves, finely chopped
    2 carrots, very finely chopped
    1 celery stick, very finely chopped
    1.27 litres/2¼ pints/5⅔ cups
      boiling water
    450g/1lb shelled fresh broad
      (fava) beans
    225g/8oz mangetouts (snow peas),
      cut into thin strips
    3 tomatoes, skinned and chopped
    5ml/1 tsp tomato purée (paste)
    50g/2oz spaghettini, broken into
      4cm/1½in lengths
    225g/8oz baby spinach
    30ml/2 tbsp chopped fresh parsley
    handful of fresh basil leaves
    salt and ground black pepper
    basil sprigs, to garnish
    grated fresh Parmesan cheese,
      to serve

1 Heat the oil in a non-stick pan and add the onions and garlic. Cook for 4–5 minutes, until softened. Add the carrots and celery, and cook for 2–3 minutes. Add the boiling water and bring to the boil, then reduce the heat and simmer for 15 minutes, or until the vegetables are tender.

2 Cook the broad beans in pan of salted boiling water for 4–5 minutes. Remove with a slotted spoon, refresh under cold water and set aside.

3 Bring the pan of water back to the boil, add the mangetouts and cook for 1 minute, or until just tender. Drain, refresh under cold water, then set aside.

4 Add the tomatoes and tomato purée to the soup. Cook for 1 minute. Purée two or three large ladlefuls of the soup and a quarter of the broad beans in a blender or food processor until smooth. Set aside.

5 Add the spaghettini to the remaining soup in the pan and cook for 6–8 minutes, until tender. Stir in the purée and spinach and cook for 2–3 minutes. Add the rest of the broad beans, the mangetouts and parsley, and season well.

6 Heat gently until hot, then stir in the basil leaves. Ladle the soup into deep cups or bowls and garnish with sprigs of basil. Serve a little grated Parmesan with each portion of soup.

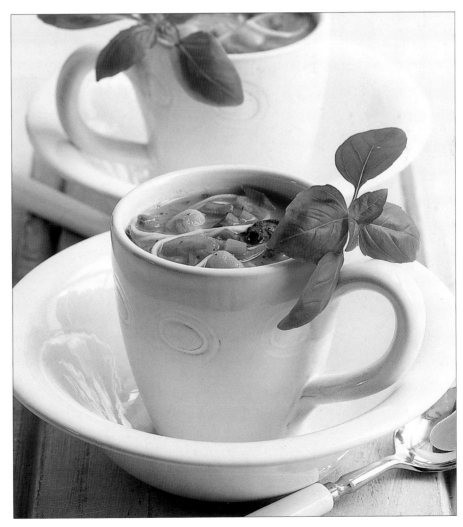

167Kcal/705kJ; Protein 10.7g; Carbohydrate 25.5g, of which sugars 9.8g; Fat 3.2g, of which saturates 0.5g; Cholesterol 0mg; Calcium 156mg; Fibre 8.8g; Sodium 76mg.

ITALIAN PASTA AND CHICKPEA SOUP ★

A SIMPLE, NOURISHING SOUP, IDEAL FOR AN APPEALING, LOW-FAT STARTER. YOU CAN USE OTHER PASTA SHAPES, BUT CONCHIGLIE ARE IDEAL BECAUSE THEY SCOOP UP THE CHICKPEAS AND BEANS.

SERVES SIX

INGREDIENTS
 1 onion
 2 carrots
 2 celery sticks
 15ml/1 tbsp olive oil
 400g/14oz can chickpeas, rinsed
  and drained
 200g/7oz can cannellini beans,
  rinsed and drained
 150ml/¼ pint/⅔ cup passata
  (bottled strained tomatoes)
 120ml/4fl oz/½ cup water
 1.5 litres/2½ pints/6¼ cups
  vegetable stock
 1 fresh or dried rosemary sprig
 200g/7oz/scant 2 cups dried
  conchiglie
 salt and ground black pepper
 fresh rosemary leaves, to garnish
 15ml/1 tbsp grated fresh Parmesan
  cheese, to serve

VARIATION
Use red kidney beans in place of
cannellini beans.

1 Chop the onion, carrots and celery sticks finely, either in a food processor or by hand.

2 Heat the olive oil in a large, non-stick pan, add the chopped vegetables and cook over a low heat, for 5–7 minutes, stirring frequently.

3 Add the chickpeas and cannellini beans, stir well to mix, then cook for 5 minutes.

4 Stir in the passata and water. Cook for 2–3 minutes, stirring.

5 Add 475ml/16fl oz/2 cups of the stock, the rosemary sprig and salt and pepper to taste. Bring to the boil, then reduce the heat, cover and simmer gently for 1 hour, stirring occasionally.

6 Pour in the remaining stock, add the pasta and bring to the boil, stirring. Reduce the heat and simmer for 7–8 minutes, or according to the packet instructions, until the pasta is tender or *al dente*, stirring frequently. Adjust the seasoning. Remove and discard the rosemary sprig, then serve the hot soup in soup bowls, topped with a few rosemary leaves and a little grated Parmesan.

COOK'S TIP
Choose beans or chickpeas canned in water, rather than in brine, if you like. Otherwise, rinse canned beans or chickpeas thoroughly under cold running water and drain well before use.

Energy 271Kcal/1151kJ; Protein 13.9g; Carbohydrate 50.3g, of which sugars 6.4g; Fat 3g, of which saturates 0.4g; Cholesterol 0mg; Calcium 98mg; Fibre 8.6g; Sodium 476mg.

BROWN LENTIL AND PASTA SOUP ★

THIS RUSTIC VEGETARIAN SOUP MAKES A WARMING WINTER MEAL. IT GOES WELL WITH GRANARY OR CRUSTY ITALIAN BREAD TO CREATE A HEALTHY, LOW-FAT SUPPER DISH.

SERVES SIX

INGREDIENTS
175g/6oz/¾ cup brown lentils
3 garlic cloves
1 litre/1¾ pints/4 cups water
15ml/1 tbsp olive oil
1 onion, finely chopped
2 celery sticks, finely chopped
30ml/2 tbsp sun-dried tomato
  purée (paste)
1.75 litres/3 pints/7½ cups
  vegetable stock
a few fresh marjoram leaves
a few fresh basil leaves
leaves from 1 fresh thyme sprig
50g/2oz/½ cup dried small pasta
  shapes, such as tubetti
salt and ground black pepper
tiny fresh herb leaves, to garnish

COOK'S TIP
Use green lentils instead of brown if you like, but don't use the orange or red ones as they will go mushy.

1 Put the lentils in a large pan. Smash 1 garlic clove (there's no need to peel it first) and add it to the lentils. Pour in the water and bring to the boil. Reduce the heat to a gentle simmer and cook, for about 20 minutes, or until the lentils are just tender, stirring occasionally. Tip the lentils into a sieve (strainer), remove the garlic and set it aside. Rinse the lentils under the cold tap, then leave them to drain.

2 Heat the oil in a large, non-stick pan. Add the onion and celery and cook over a low heat for 5–7 minutes, or until softened, stirring frequently.

3 Crush the remaining garlic, then peel and mash the reserved garlic. Add to the vegetables with the tomato purée and the lentils. Stir, then add the stock, the fresh herbs and salt and pepper to taste. Bring to the boil, then reduce the heat and simmer for 30 minutes, stirring occasionally.

4 Add the pasta to the pan and bring back to the boil, stirring. Simmer for 7–8 minutes, or according to the packet instructions, until the pasta is tender or *al dente*, stirring frequently. Adjust the seasoning to taste. Serve hot, sprinkled with the herb leaves.

Energy 140Kcal/592kJ; Protein 7g; Carbohydrate 24.4g, of which sugars 0.8g; Fat 2.3g, of which saturates 0.3g; Cholesterol 0mg; Calcium 20mg; Fibre 1.6g; Sodium 17mg.

CARROT <u>AND</u> ORANGE SOUP ★

THIS TRADITIONAL, BRIGHT AND SUMMERY LOW-FAT SOUP IS ALWAYS POPULAR FOR ITS WONDERFULLY CREAMY CONSISTENCY AND VIBRANTLY FRESH CITRUS FLAVOUR. USE A GOOD, HOME-MADE, LOW-FAT VEGETABLE STOCK IF YOU CAN FOR THE BEST RESULTS.

SERVES SIX

INGREDIENTS
  25g/1oz/2 tbsp butter
  3 leeks, thinly sliced
  450g/1lb carrots, sliced
  1.2 litres/2 pints/5 cups
    vegetable stock
  grated rind and juice of 2 oranges
  2.5ml/½ tsp freshly grated nutmeg
  150ml/¼ pint/⅔ cup reduced-fat
    Greek (US strained plain) yogurt
  salt and ground black pepper
  fresh sprigs of coriander (cilantro),
    to garnish

1 Melt the butter in a large, non-stick pan. Add the leeks and carrots and stir well, lightly coating the vegetables with the butter. Cover and cook for about 10 minutes, until the vegetables are beginning to soften but not colour.

2 Pour in the stock and the orange rind and juice. Add the nutmeg and season to taste with salt and pepper. Bring to the boil then reduce the heat, cover and simmer for about 40 minutes, or until the vegetables are tender.

3 Leave to cool slightly, then process the soup in a blender or food processor until smooth.

4 Return the soup to the rinsed-out pan and add 30ml/2 tbsp of the yogurt, then adjust the seasoning to taste, if necessary. Reheat gently, stirring.

5 Ladle the soup into warm individual bowls and put a swirl of yogurt in the centre of each. Sprinkle the fresh sprigs of coriander over each bowl to garnish, and serve immediately.

Energy 93Kcal/389kJ; Protein 3.4g; Carbohydrate 10.7g, of which sugars 9.7g; Fat 4.4g, of which saturates 2.5g; Cholesterol 9mg; Calcium 91mg; Fibre 4g; Sodium 67mg.

BORSCHT ★

BEETROOT IS THE MAIN INGREDIENT OF BORSCHT, AND ITS FLAVOUR AND COLOUR DOMINATE THIS WELL-KNOWN LOW-FAT RUSSIAN OR POLISH SOUP. FOR THIS VEGETARIAN VERSION, THE USUAL BEEF STOCK HAS BEEN REPLACED WITH VEGETABLE STOCK.

SERVES SIX

INGREDIENTS
900g/2lb uncooked beetroot, peeled
2 carrots, peeled
2 celery sticks
25g/1oz/2 tbsp butter
2 onions, sliced
2 garlic cloves, crushed
4 tomatoes, skinned, seeded
  and chopped
1 bay leaf
1 large fresh parsley sprig
2 cloves
4 whole black peppercorns
1.2 litres/2 pints/5 cups
  well-flavoured vegetable stock
150ml/¼ pint/⅔ cup beetroot *kvas*
  (see Cook's Tip) or the liquid from
  pickled beetroot
salt and ground black pepper
sour cream, garnished with chopped
  fresh chives or sprigs of fresh dill,
  to serve

1 Cut the beetroot, carrots and celery into fairly thick strips. Set aside. Melt the butter in a large, non-stick pan and cook the onions over a low heat for 5 minutes, stirring occasionally.

2 Add the beetroot, carrots and celery and cook for a further 5 minutes, stirring occasionally.

VARIATION
Use 6–8 shallots in place of onions.

3 Add the garlic and chopped tomatoes to the pan and cook for a further 2 minutes, stirring.

COOK'S TIP
Beetroot *kvas*, fermented beetroot juice, adds an intense colour and a slight tartness. If unavailable, peel and grate 1 beetroot, add 150ml/¼ pint/⅔ cup stock and 10ml/2 tsp lemon juice. Bring to the boil, then remove the pan from the heat, cover and leave for 30 minutes. Strain before using.

4 Place the bay leaf, parsley, cloves and peppercorns in a piece of muslin (cheesecloth) and tie with string.

5 Add the muslin bag to the pan with the stock. Bring to the boil, then reduce the heat, cover and simmer for 1¼ hours, or until the vegetables are very tender. Discard the muslin bag. Stir in the beetroot *kvas* and season to taste with salt and pepper. Bring back to the boil. Ladle the soup into bowls and serve with sour cream, garnished with chives or dill.

Energy 127Kcal/535kJ; Protein 4g; Carbohydrate 20.2g, of which sugars 17.7g; Fat 4g, of which saturates 2.3g; Cholesterol 9mg; Calcium 60mg; Fibre 5g; Sodium 143mg.

CORN AND SWEET POTATO SOUP ★

THE COMBINATION OF CORN AND SWEET POTATO GIVES THIS LIGHT VEGETARIAN SOUP A REAL DEPTH OF FLAVOUR, AS WELL AS MAKING IT LOOK VERY COLOURFUL.

SERVES SIX

INGREDIENTS
    15ml/1 tbsp olive oil
    1 onion, finely chopped
    2 garlic cloves, crushed
    1 small red chilli, seeded and
        finely chopped
    1.75 litres/3 pints/7½ cups
        vegetable stock
    10ml/2 tsp ground cumin
    1 medium sweet potato, diced
    ½ red (bell) pepper, seeded and
        finely chopped
    450g/1lb corn kernels
    salt and ground black pepper
    lime wedges, to serve

COOK'S TIP
Use frozen or canned (drained weight) corn kernels for this recipe.

1 Heat the oil in a non-stick pan, add the onion and cook for 5 minutes, until softened, stirring occasionally. Add the garlic and chilli and cook for a further 2 minutes.

2 Add 300ml/½ pint/1¼ cups of the stock to the pan, then bring to the boil, reduce the heat and simmer for 10 minutes.

3 In a small bowl, mix the cumin with a little stock to form a paste, then stir this into the soup. Add the sweet potato, stir, then simmer for 10 minutes. Add salt and pepper to taste.

4 Add the red pepper, corn and remaining stock. Simmer for 10 minutes. Process half of the soup in a blender until smooth, then stir the purée into the chunky soup. Reheat gently. Serve with lime wedges.

Energy 127Kcal/535kJ; Protein 4g; Carbohydrate 20.2g, of which sugars 17.7g; Fat 4g, of which saturates 2.3g; Cholesterol 9mg; Calcium 60mg; Fibre 5g; Sodium 143mg.

GENOESE MINESTRONE ★

THE VARIATIONS ON THIS SOUP ARE ENDLESS. THIS LIGHT, PASTA-FREE VEGETARIAN VERSION IS PACKED WITH HEAPS OF VEGETABLES TO MAKE A SUBSTANTIAL, HEARTY LUNCH — IDEAL SERVED WITH CRUSTY BREAD.

SERVES SIX

INGREDIENTS
    1.75 litres/3 pints/7½ cups
        vegetable stock
    1 large onion, chopped
    3 celery sticks, chopped
    2 carrots, finely diced
    2 large floury potatoes, finely diced
    ½ head of cabbage, very finely diced
    225g/8oz runner (green) beans,
        sliced diagonally
    2 x 400g/14oz cans cannellini beans,
        rinsed and drained
    30ml/2 tbsp ready-made pesto sauce
    salt and ground black pepper
    crusty bread, to serve
    grated fresh Parmesan cheese,
        to serve

1 Pour the stock into a large pan. Add the onion, celery and carrots. Simmer for 10 minutes.

2 Add the potatoes, cabbage, and beans and simmer for 10–12 minutes, or until the potatoes are tender.

3 Stir in the cannellini beans and pesto, then return the mixture to the boil. Season to taste with salt and pepper and serve hot with crusty bread and a sprinkling of grated fresh Parmesan cheese.

Energy 233Kcal/983kJ; Protein 12.1g; Carbohydrate 40.1g, of which sugars 10.7g; Fat 3.7g, of which saturates 0.6g; Cholesterol 1mg; Calcium 151mg; Fibre 10.9g; Sodium 556mg.

CHICKPEA, LEMON AND PARSLEY SOUP ★

LEMON ENHANCES THE FLAVOUR OF FRESH PARSLEY IN THIS TASTY NORTH AFRICAN INSPIRED LOW-FAT SOUP, WHICH MAKES A SUBSTANTIAL VEGETARIAN LUNCH SERVED WITH CRUSTY BREAD.

2 Place the onion and parsley in a blender or food processor and process until finely chopped.

3 Heat the mixed oils in a large, non-stick frying pan and gently cook the onion mixture over a low heat for about 4 minutes, or until slightly softened.

4 Add the chickpeas, cook gently for about 2 minutes, then add the stock. Season well. Bring the soup to the boil, then reduce the heat, cover and simmer for 20 minutes, or until the chickpeas are very tender.

5 Leave the soup to cool a little and then part-purée it in a blender or food processor, or mash the chickpeas fairly coarsely with a fork, so that the soup is thick, but still quite chunky.

SERVES SIX

INGREDIENTS

   225g/8oz/1¼ cups chickpeas,
     soaked overnight
   1 small onion, coarsely chopped
   1 bunch fresh parsley (about
     40g/1½oz/¾ cup)
   15ml/1 tbsp olive oil and sunflower
     oil, mixed
   1.2 litres/2 pints/5 cups
     vegetable stock
   juice of ½ lemon
   salt and ground black pepper
   lemon wedges and thinly pared
     and shredded lemon rind,
     to garnish
   crusty bread, to serve

1 Drain the chickpeas and rinse well under cold running water. Cook them in a pan of rapidly boiling water for 10 minutes, then simmer for 1–1½ hours, or until tender. Drain, then, using your fingertips, gently peel away the skins.

6 Return the soup to the rinsed-out pan, stir in the lemon juice, then adjust the seasoning to taste. Heat it through gently, then serve, garnished with lemon wedges and shredded lemon rind, and accompanied by crusty bread.

Energy 140Kcal/591kJ; Protein 8.1g; Carbohydrate 19.4g, of which sugars 1.5g; Fat 3.9g, of which saturates 0.5g; Cholesterol 0mg; Calcium 63mg; Fibre 4.2g; Sodium 15mg.

CURRIED CAULIFLOWER SOUP ★

THIS SPICY, CREAMY LOW-FAT SOUP IS PERFECT FOR LUNCH ON A COLD WINTER'S DAY SERVED WITH FLATBREAD SUCH A PITTA AND GARNISHED WITH FRESH CORIANDER.

SERVES FOUR

INGREDIENTS
750ml/1¼ pints/3 cups
  semi-skimmed (low-fat) milk
1 large cauliflower
15ml/1 tbsp garam masala
salt and ground black pepper

1 Pour the milk into a large pan and place over a medium heat. Cut the cauliflower into florets and add to the milk with the garam masala. Season to taste with salt and pepper.

2 Bring the milk to the boil, then reduce the heat, half-cover the pan and simmer for about 20 minutes, or until the cauliflower is tender, stirring occasionally.

3 Remove the pan from the heat and allow the mixture to cool for a few minutes, then transfer to a blender or food processor and process until smooth (you may have to do this in two batches).

4 Return the purée to the rinsed-out pan and reheat gently, stirring. Adjust the seasoning to taste, and serve immediately.

Energy 151Kcal/636kJ; Protein 12.9g; Carbohydrate 14.7g, of which sugars 13.2g; Fat 5g, of which saturates 2.4g; Cholesterol 11mg; Calcium 276mg; Fibre 3.7g; Sodium 107mg.

EGG FLOWER SOUP ★

THIS SIMPLE, HEALTHY SOUP IS FLAVOURED WITH FRESH ROOT GINGER AND CHINESE FIVE-SPICE POWDER. IT IS QUICK AND DELICIOUS AND CAN EASILY BE MADE AT THE LAST MINUTE.

SERVES FOUR

INGREDIENTS
    1.2 litres/2 pints/5 cups fresh
      vegetable stock
    10ml/2 tsp grated fresh root ginger
    10ml/2 tsp light soy sauce
    5ml/1 tsp sesame oil
    5ml/1 tsp Chinese five-spice powder
    15–30ml/1–2 tbsp cornflour
      (cornstarch)
    2 eggs
    salt and ground black pepper
    1 spring onion (scallion), very thinly
      sliced diagonally and 15ml/1 tbsp
      roughly chopped fresh coriander
      (cilantro) or fresh flat leaf parsley,
      to garnish

COOK'S TIP
This soup is a good way of using up leftover egg yolks or whites, which have been stored in the freezer.

1 Put the vegetable stock into a large pan with the ginger, soy sauce, sesame oil and five-spice powder. Bring to the boil and allow to simmer gently for about 10 minutes.

2 Blend the cornflour in a measuring jug (cup) with 60–75ml/4–5 tbsp water and stir into the stock. Cook until slightly thickened, stirring constantly. Season to taste with salt and pepper.

3 In a jug, beat the eggs together with 30ml/2 tbsp cold water, until the mixture becomes frothy.

4 Bring the soup just back to the boil and drizzle in the egg mixture, stirring vigorously with chopsticks. Choose a jug with a fine spout to form a very thin drizzle. Serve the soup immediately, sprinkled with the sliced spring onion and chopped coriander or parsley.

Energy 118Kcal/497kJ; Protein 3.2g; Carbohydrate 19.8g, of which sugars 10.9g; Fat 3.5g, of which saturates 0.6g; Cholesterol 0mg; Calcium 84mg; Fibre 6g; Sodium 66mg.

MISO BROTH WITH TOFU ★

THIS VEGETARIAN BROTH IS HIGHLY NUTRITIOUS AND MAKES A GOOD APPETIZER OR LIGHT LUNCH.
A STAPLE IN JAPAN, MISO IS A RICH, SALTY CONDIMENT; TOFU IS A SOFT CHEESE-LIKE FOOD.

SERVES FOUR

INGREDIENTS

- 1 bunch of spring onions (scallions) or 5 baby leeks
- 15g/½oz fresh coriander (cilantro)
- 3 thin slices fresh root ginger
- 2 star anise
- 1 small dried red chilli
- 1.2 litres/2 pints/5 cups vegetable stock
- 225g/8oz pak choi (bok choy) or other Asian greens, thickly sliced
- 200g/7oz firm tofu, cut into 2.5cm/1in cubes
- 60ml/4 tbsp red miso
- 30–45ml/2–3 tbsp Japanese soy sauce
- 1 fresh red chilli, seeded and shredded (optional)

1 Cut the coarse green tops off the spring onions or baby leeks and slice the rest of the spring onions or leeks finely on the diagonal.

2 Place the coarse green tops in a large pan with the stalks from the coriander, the fresh root ginger, star anise, dried chilli and vegetable stock.

3 Heat the mixture over a low heat until boiling, then reduce the heat and simmer for about 10 minutes. Strain the broth, return it to the pan and reheat until simmering. Add the green portion of the sliced spring onions or leeks to the soup with the pak choi or Asian greens and tofu. Cook for 2 minutes.

4 In a small bowl, combine the miso with a little soup, then stir the mixture into the pan. Add soy sauce to taste.

5 Coarsely chop the coriander leaves and stir most of them into the soup with the white part of the spring onions or leeks. Cook for 1 minute, then ladle the soup into warmed bowls. Sprinkle with the remaining chopped coriander and the shredded fresh red chilli, if using, and serve immediately.

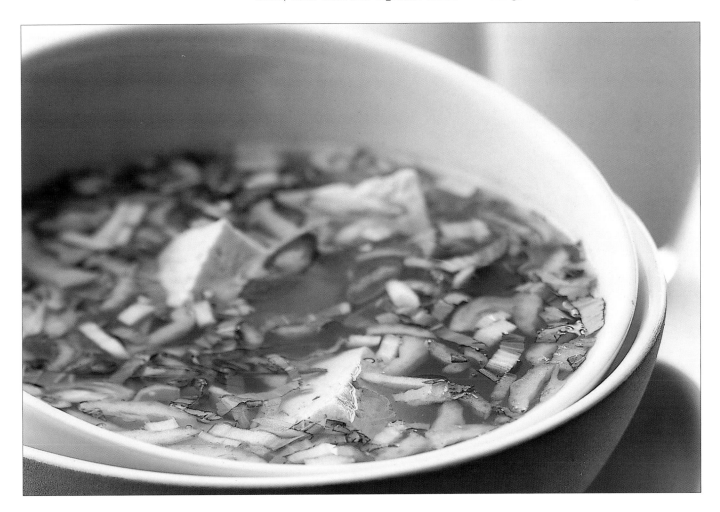

Energy 25Kcal/103kJ; Protein 2.4g; Carbohydrate 2.6g, of which sugars 2.4g; Fat 0.6g, of which saturates 0.1g; Cholesterol 0mg; Calcium 107mg; Fibre 1.6g; Sodium 882mg.

APPETIZERS

There are many low-fat options when it comes to appetizers — all of which can be prepared and eaten at any time of day. From tempting cold dishes such as Garlicky Green Salad with Raspberry Vinaigrette or Artichoke and Cumin Dip, to popular warm delights such as Peperonata or Vegetable Samosas, these dishes provide satisfying dishes while staying below the low-fat threshold.

GARLICKY GREEN SALAD WITH RASPBERRY VINAIGRETTE ★

ADDING A SPLASH OF RASPBERRY VINEGAR TO THE DRESSING ENLIVENS A SIMPLE GREEN SALAD, TRANSFORMING IT INTO THIS SOPHISTICATED LOW-FAT SIDE DISH.

SERVES SIX

INGREDIENTS
30ml/2 tbsp olive oil
2 garlic cloves, thinly sliced
6 handfuls green salad leaves
15ml/1 tbsp raspberry vinegar
salt and ground black pepper

1 Heat the oil in a small, non-stick pan and add the garlic. Cook gently for 1–2 minutes, or until just golden, being careful not to burn the garlic. Remove the garlic with a slotted spoon and drain on kitchen paper. Pour the oil into a small bowl.

2 Arrange the salad leaves in a serving bowl. Whisk the raspberry vinegar into the reserved oil and season to taste with salt and pepper.

3 Pour the garlic dressing over the salad leaves and toss to combine. Sprinkle over the fried garlic slices and serve immediately.

Energy 45Kcal/185kJ; Protein 0.7g; Carbohydrate 1.4g, of which sugars 1.4g; Fat 4.1g, of which saturates 0.6g; Cholesterol 0mg; Calcium 23mg; Fibre 0.8g; Sodium 3mg.

WILD ROCKET AND COS LETTUCE SALAD WITH HERBS ★

THIS AROMATIC SALAD FOLLOWS A GREEK RECIPE COMBINING A LEMONY FLAVOUR WITH THE STRONG SWEET TASTE OF COS LETTUCE. WILD ROCKET IS ADDED TO GIVE A SHARP NEW EDGE.

SERVES FOUR

INGREDIENTS
  a large handful of rocket
    (arugula) leaves
  2 cos or romaine lettuce hearts
  3 or 4 fresh flat leaf parsley sprigs,
    coarsely chopped
  30–45ml/2–3 tbsp finely
    chopped fresh dill
  90ml/6 tbsp low-fat French dressing
  salt and ground black pepper

COOK'S TIP
It is important to balance the bitterness
of the rocket and the sweetness of the
cos or romaine lettuce, and the best way
to find this out is by taste.

1 If the rocket leaves are young and
tender they can be left whole, but older
ones should be trimmed of thick stalks
and then sliced coarsely. Discard any
tough stalks.

2 Slice the cos or romaine lettuce
hearts into thin ribbons and place these
in a bowl, then add the rocket and
chopped parsley and dill.

3 Taste the dressing and adjust the
seasoning to taste. Just before serving,
pour the dressing over the salad and
toss lightly to coat everything with the
dressing. Serve the salad with
crusty bread.

Energy 26Kcal/110kJ; Protein 1g; Carbohydrate 4.4g, of which sugars 4.2g; Fat 0.6g, of which saturates 0.1g; Cholesterol 0mg; Calcium 35mg; Fibre 1.2g; Sodium 341mg.

CARROT AND ORANGE SALAD ★

THIS IS A WONDERFUL, FRESH-TASTING LOW-FAT SALAD WITH SUCH A FABULOUS COMBINATION OF CITRUS FRUIT AND VEGETABLES THAT IT IS DIFFICULT TO KNOW WHETHER IT IS A SALAD OR A DESSERT. IT MAKES A REFRESHING, LOW-FAT ACCOMPANIMENT TO VEGETARIAN MAIN DISHES.

2 Cut a thin slice of peel and pith from each end of the oranges. Place cut side down on a plate, then cut off the peel and pith in strips. Holding the oranges over a bowl, cut out each segment leaving the membrane behind. Squeeze the juice from the membrane.

3 Combine the oil, lemon juice and orange juice in a small bowl. Season with salt and pepper, and sugar, if you like.

SERVES FOUR

INGREDIENTS
  450g/1lb carrots
  2 large Navelina oranges, such as
    Washington or Bahia
  15ml/1 tbsp extra virgin
    olive oil
  30ml/2 tbsp freshly squeezed
    lemon juice
  pinch of granulated sugar (optional)
  30ml/2 tbsp chopped pistachio nuts
    or toasted pine nuts (optional)
  salt and ground black pepper

1 Peel the carrots and coarsely grate them into a large bowl.

4 Toss the oranges with the carrots and pour the dressing over. Sprinkle over the nuts, if using. Serve.

Energy 92Kcal/385kJ; Protein 1.5g; Carbohydrate 15.3g, of which sugars 14.7g; Fat 3.2g, of which saturates 0.5g; Cholesterol 0mg; Calcium 64mg; Fibre 4g; Sodium 32mg.

WATERMELON <u>AND</u> FETA SALAD <u>WITH</u> OLIVES ★

THE COMBINATION OF SWEET WATERMELON WITH SALTY FETA CHEESE MAKES FOR A ZESTY COMBINATION SALAD — ESPECIALLY WITH THE EXTRA INGREDIENTS OF BLACK OLIVES, LIGHTLY TOASTED PUMPKIN SEEDS AND SUNFLOWER SEEDS FOR ADDED PIQUANCY.

SERVES SIX

INGREDIENTS
  6 slices watermelon, chilled
  115g/4oz feta cheese, cut into
    bitesize pieces
  15–30ml/1–2 tbsp mixed seeds,
    such as pumpkin seeds and
    sunflower seeds, lightly toasted
  10 whole black olives

COOK'S TIP
The best choice of olives for this recipe
is plump black ones, such as *kalamata*,
dry-cured black olives or other shiny,
brined varieties.

1 Cut the rind off the watermelon and
remove as many seeds as possible.
The sweetest and juiciest part is right
in the core, and you may want to cut off
any whiter flesh just under the skin.

2 Cut the flesh into triangular chunks.
Mix the watermelon, feta cheese, mixed
seeds and olives in a bowl. Cover and
chill the salad in the refrigerator for 30
minutes before serving.

Energy 136Kcal/572kJ; Protein 4.9g; Carbohydrate 15g, of which sugars 14.6g; Fat 6.7g, of which saturates 3.4g; Cholesterol 15mg; Calcium 98mg; Fibre 0.5g; Sodium 429mg.

PEPERONATA ★

THIS RICHLY FLAVOURED LOW-FAT DIP COMBINES SPICY TOMATO WITH SWEET RED PEPPER. BEST COMPLEMENTED WITH CRISP ITALIAN-STYLE BREADSTICKS, IT IS DELICIOUS SERVED HOT, COLD OR AT ROOM TEMPERATURE AND CAN BE STORED IN THE REFRIGERATOR FOR SEVERAL DAYS.

SERVES SIX

INGREDIENTS
  30ml/2 tbsp garlic-infused olive oil
  2 large red (bell) peppers, halved,
    seeded and sliced
  a pinch of dried chilli flakes
  400g/14oz can pomodorino tomatoes
  salt and ground black pepper

COOK'S TIP
Long, slow cooking helps to bring out the sweetness of the peppers and tomatoes, so don't be tempted to cheat on the cooking time by cooking over a higher heat.

1 Heat the oil in a large, non-stick pan over a low heat and add the sliced peppers. Cook very gently for 3–4 minutes, stirring occasionally.

2 Add the chilli flakes to the pan and cook for 1 minute, then stir in the tomatoes. Season with salt and pepper. Cook gently for 50 minutes to 1 hour, stirring occasionally.

Energy 66Kcal/274kJ; Protein 1.1g; Carbohydrate 6.3g, of which sugars 6.1g; Fat 4.1g, of which saturates 0.7g; Cholesterol 0mg; Calcium 10mg; Fibre 1.7g; Sodium 9mg.

ARTICHOKE AND CUMIN DIP ★

THIS LOW-FAT VEGETARIAN DIP IS SO EASY TO MAKE AND IS REALLY TASTY. SERVE WITH OLIVES, LOW-FAT HUMMUS AND WEDGES OF PITTA BREAD AS A SUMMERY SNACK SELECTION. GRILLED ARTICHOKES BOTTLED IN OIL HAVE A FABULOUS FLAVOUR AND CAN BE USED INSTEAD OF CANNED ARTICHOKES BUT REMEMBER TO DRAIN THEM WELL BEFORE USE. YOU CAN ALSO VARY THE FLAVOURINGS — TRY ADDING CHILLI POWDER IN PLACE OF THE CUMIN AND ADD A HANDFUL OF FRESH BASIL LEAVES TO THE ARTICHOKES BEFORE PROCESSING.

SERVES SIX

INGREDIENTS
  2 x 400g/14oz cans artichoke hearts,
    drained
  2 garlic cloves, peeled
  2.5ml/½ tsp ground cumin
  30ml/2 tbsp olive oil
  salt and ground black pepper

COOK'S TIP
Canned artichoke hearts tend to be preserved in brine; rinse and drain them before serving to reduce their high sodium content.

1 Put the artichoke hearts in a food processor with the garlic and ground cumin, and a generous drizzle of olive oil. Process to a smooth purée and season to taste with plenty of salt and ground black pepper.

2 Spoon the purée into a serving bowl and serve with an extra drizzle of olive oil swirled on the top and slices of warm pitta bread for dipping.

Energy 42Kcal/172kJ; Protein 0.6g; Carbohydrate 1.2g, of which sugars 0.9g; Fat 3.9g, of which saturates 0.5g; Cholesterol 0mg; Calcium 41mg; Fibre 1.2g; Sodium 60mg.

BABY SPINACH WITH TOASTED SESAME SEEDS ★

BASED ON A JAPANESE SPECIALITY — O-HITASHI — SEASONAL GREEN VEGETABLES ARE SIMPLY BLANCHED AND COOLED AND FORMED INTO LITTLE TOWERS. WITH A LITTLE HELP FROM SOY SAUCE AND SESAME SEEDS, THEY WRAP UP A SUPERB ORIENTAL FLAVOUR.

SERVES FOUR

INGREDIENTS
450g/1lb fresh young or baby
  spinach leaves
30ml/2 tbsp shoyu or soy sauce
30ml/2 tbsp water
15ml/1 tbsp sesame seeds
salt

VARIATION
Japanese spinach, the long-leaf type with the stalks and pink root intact, is best, but you can use ordinary young spinach leaves, or any soft and deep-green salad leaves – such as watercress, rocket (arugula) or lamb's lettuce.

1 Blanch the spinach leaves in a pan of lightly salted, boiling water for 15 seconds. For Japanese-type spinach, hold the leafy part and slip the stems into the pan. After 15 seconds, drop in the leaves and cook for 20 seconds.

2 Drain immediately and place the spinach under cold running water. Squeeze out all the excess water by hand. Now what looked like a large amount of spinach has become a ball, roughly the size of an orange. Mix the shoyu or soy sauce and water in a small bowl, then pour it on to the spinach. Mix well and leave to cool.

3 Meanwhile, put the sesame seeds in a dry frying pan and stir or toss over a low heat until they start to pop. Remove the pan from the heat and leave to cool.

4 Drain the spinach and squeeze out the excess sauce with your hands. Form the spinach into a log shape about 4cm/1½in in diameter on a chopping board. Squeeze again to make it firm. With a sharp knife, cut it across into four cylinders.

5 Place the spinach cylinders on a large plate or individual serving dishes. Sprinkle with the toasted sesame seeds and a little salt and serve.

Energy 54Kcal/222kJ; Protein 4.1g; Carbohydrate 2.5g, of which sugars 2.3g; Fat 3.1g, of which saturates 0.4g; Cholesterol 0mg; Calcium 218mg; Fibre 2.7g; Sodium 692mg.

VEGETABLE SAMOSAS ★

A SELECTION OF HIGHLY SPICED VEGETABLES IN A LIGHT, CRISPY PASTRY CASING MAKES THESE SAMOSAS A TASTY VEGETARIAN SNACK AT ANY TIME OF THE DAY. SERVE THESE DELICIOUS PASTRIES FRESHLY BAKED AND HOT FROM THE OVEN.

MAKES TWENTY-EIGHT

INGREDIENTS

14 sheets filo pastry, thawed and
   wrapped in a damp dish towel
45ml/3 tbsp sunflower oil
For the filling
3 large potatoes, boiled and
   coarsely mashed
75g/3oz/¾ cup frozen peas, thawed
50g/2oz/⅓ cup canned corn
   kernels, drained
5ml/1 tsp ground coriander
5ml/1 tsp ground cumin
5ml/1 tsp dry mango powder
   (amchur)
1 small onion, finely chopped
2 fresh green chillies, seeded and
   finely chopped
30ml/2 tbsp chopped fresh coriander
   (cilantro) leaves
30ml/2 tbsp chopped fresh
   mint leaves
juice of 1 lemon
salt

1 Preheat the oven to 200°C/400°F/ Gas 6. Cut each sheet of filo pastry in half lengthways and fold each piece in half lengthways to give 28 thin strips. Lightly brush with oil.

2 Toss all the filling ingredients together in a large mixing bowl until they are well blended. Adjust the seasoning with salt and lemon juice, if necessary.

3 Using one strip of the pastry at a time, place about 15ml/1 tbsp of the filling mixture at one end of the strip and diagonally fold the pastry up to form a triangle shape. Brush the samosas with oil, place on a baking sheet and bake in the oven for 10–15 minutes, or until cooked and golden brown. Serve.

COOK'S TIP
Work with one or two sheets of filo pastry at a time and keep the rest covered with a damp dish towel to prevent it drying out.

Energy 56Kcal/235kJ; Protein 1.3g; Carbohydrate 10g, of which sugars 0.8g; Fat 1.4g, of which saturates 0.2g; Cholesterol 0mg; Calcium 16mg; Fibre 0.7g; Sodium 8mg.

STUFFED VINE LEAVES ★

THIS POPULAR LOW-FAT GREEK DISH, DOLMADES, KEEPS MOIST WHEN COOKED SLOWLY IN A CLAY POT.
FRESH VINE LEAVES GIVE THE BEST FLAVOUR, BUT PRESERVED OR CANNED ONES WILL ALSO WORK WELL.

SERVES FOUR

INGREDIENTS
    12 fresh vine leaves
    10ml/2 tsp olive oil
    1 small onion, chopped
    15g/½oz pine nuts
    1 garlic clove, crushed
    115g/4oz/1 cup cooked long
       grain rice
    2 tomatoes, skinned, seeded and
       finely chopped
    15ml/1 tbsp chopped fresh mint
    1 lemon, sliced
    150ml/¼ pint/⅔ cup dry white wine
    200ml/7fl oz/scant 1 cup
       vegetable stock
    salt and ground black pepper
    lemon wedges and fresh mint sprigs,
       to garnish

COOK'S TIPS
• You can use preserved vine leaves; do
not rinse, but blanch them before use.
• A lidded clay pot, or "brick", is a useful
piece of equipment for sealing in the
juices of food while it cooks. It must be
thoroughly soaked in water before use.
• This delicious dish can be served as a
starter or as part of a meze table.

2 Heat the oil in a non-stick frying pan,
add the onion and cook for 5–6 minutes
until softened, stirring frequently. Add
the pine nuts and garlic and cook
until the onions and pine nuts are
golden, stirring constantly.

3 Stir the onion mixture into the rice,
then add and stir in the tomatoes and
chopped mint. Season to taste with salt
and pepper.

4 Place a spoonful of the rice mixture at
the stalk end of each vine leaf. Fold the
sides over the filling and roll up tightly.

5 Place the stuffed vine leaves close
together, seam-side down, in the clay
pot. Place the lemon slices on top and
in between the stuffed vine leaves. Pour
over the white wine and sufficient stock
just to cover the stuffed vine leaves and
lemon slices.

6 Cover the dish with the lid and place
in an unheated oven. Set the oven to
200°C/400°F/Gas 6 and cook for 30
minutes. Reduce the oven temperature
to 160°C/325°F/Gas 3 and cook for a
further 30 minutes.

7 Serve hot or cold, and drizzle with a
little fruity extra virgin olive oil, if you
like. Garnish with lemon wedges and a
few sprigs of fresh mint.

1 Soak the clay pot in cold water for
20 minutes, then drain. Blanch the
vine leaves in a pan of boiling water for
about 2 minutes, or until they darken
and soften. Rinse the leaves under cold
running water and leave to drain.

Energy 131Kcal/549kJ; Protein 2.6g; Carbohydrate 14.5g, of which sugars 5.2g; Fat 4.7g, of which saturates 0.5g; Cholesterol 0mg; Calcium 41mg; Fibre 1.9g; Sodium 10mg.

CHINESE-STYLE BRAISED TOFU WITH MUSHROOMS ★

FOUR DIFFERENT KINDS OF MUSHROOMS COMBINE SUCCULENTLY WITH TOFU IN THIS ROBUST LOW-FAT RECIPE. CHINESE FLAVOURINGS ENHANCE ALL THE INGREDIENTS TO MAKE THIS AN INTERESTING VEGETARIAN VARIATION TO TRY OUT.

SERVES SIX

INGREDIENTS

    350g/12oz firm tofu
    2.5ml/½ tsp sesame oil
    10ml/2 tsp light soy sauce
    15ml/1 tbsp vegetable oil
    2 garlic cloves, finely chopped
    2.5ml/½ tsp grated fresh root ginger
    115g/4oz/scant 2 cups fresh shiitake
      mushrooms, stalks removed
    175g/6oz/scant 2 cups fresh oyster
      mushrooms
    115g/4oz/scant 2 cups drained,
      canned straw mushrooms
    115g/4oz/scant 2 cups button (white)
      mushrooms, halved
    15ml/1 tbsp Chinese rice wine or
      dry sherry
    15ml/1 tbsp dark soy sauce
    90ml/6 tbsp vegetable stock
    5ml/1 tsp cornflour (cornstarch)
    15ml/1 tbsp cold water
    salt and ground white pepper
    2 shredded spring onions (scallions),
      to garnish

1 Put the tofu in a dish or bowl and sprinkle with the sesame oil, light soy sauce and a large pinch of pepper. Leave to marinate for 10 minutes, then drain and cut into 2.5 x 1cm/1 x ½in pieces using a sharp knife.

2 Heat the vegetable oil in a large non-stick frying pan or wok. When the oil is very hot, add the garlic and ginger and stir-fry for a few seconds. Add all the mushrooms and stir-fry for a further 2 minutes.

3 Stir in the Chinese rice wine or dry sherry, dark soy sauce and stock. Season to taste with salt, if necessary, and white pepper. Reduce the heat and simmer gently for 4 minutes.

4 Place the cornflour in a bowl with the water. Mix to make a smooth paste. Stir the cornflour mixture into the pan or wok and cook until thickened, stirring constantly to prevent lumps forming.

VARIATIONS

Use galangal instead of root ginger. Stir-fry 1–2 seeded and chopped fresh red chillies with the garlic and garnish with chopped coriander (cilantro).

5 Carefully add the pieces of tofu, toss gently to coat thoroughly in the sauce and simmer for 2 minutes.

6 Sprinkle the shredded spring onions over the top of the mixture to garnish, transfer to a warm serving dish or individual plates, and serve immediately.

COOK'S TIPS

• If fresh shiitake mushrooms are not available, use dried Chinese mushrooms. Soak them in hot water for about 20–30 minutes, then drain. Use the soaking liquid instead of vegetable stock for a more intense flavour.

• Straw mushrooms, so called because they are grown on beds of straw, are rarely available fresh in the West. However, they are widely available canned. Their main contribution to this dish – and to Chinese cooking in general – is their slippery texture rather than their flavour which is quite bland.

Energy 85Kcal/356kJ; Protein 6.4g; Carbohydrate 3.3g, of which sugars 0.6g; Fat 5g, of which saturates 0.6g; Cholesterol 0mg; Calcium 304mg; Fibre 1g; Sodium 186mg.

LIGHT MEALS

Vegetarian meals offer plenty of scope for the cook's imagination. The selection of recipes in this chapter combines an extensive variety of fresh vegetables, fruit, beans, grains, seeds and tofu, perfect for lunchtimes and lighter dinner options. Tempting dishes include Spanish Omelette, Potato and Onion Cakes with Beetroot, Stuffed Aubergines and Lemony Couscous Salad.

COURGETTE AND FLAGEOLET BEAN SALAD ★

SERVE THIS MARINATED VEGETABLE DISH AS A DELICIOUS ACCOMPANIMENT TO A LIGHT VEGETARIAN MAIN MEAL OR AS A SUMMER LUNCH IN ITS OWN RIGHT.

SERVES SIX

INGREDIENTS

  3 courgettes (zucchini), halved
    lengthways and sliced
  400g/14oz can flageolet or cannellini
    beans, rinsed and drained
  30ml/2 tbsp garlic-infused olive oil
  finely grated rind and juice of
    1 unwaxed lemon
  salt and ground black pepper

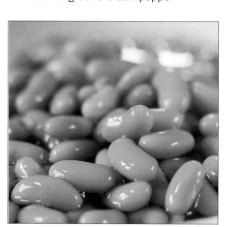

1 Cook the courgettes in a pan of salted boiling water for 2–3 minutes, or until just tender. Drain well and refresh under cold running water.

2 Transfer the drained courgettes to a bowl with the beans, then stir in the oil and lemon rind and juice. Season to taste with salt and pepper. Chill the salad in the refrigerator for 30 minutes before serving.

VARIATION
To add extra flavour to the salad, add 30ml/2 tbsp chopped fresh herbs before chilling. Basil and mint both have fresh, distinctive flavours that will work very well in this salad.

COOK'S TIP
When buying courgettes (zucchini), choose firm vegetables with unbroken skin and a good green colour. Avoid courgettes with soft or brown patches. Wrap loosely and store in the refrigerator.

Energy 106Kcal/445kJ; Protein 5.5g; Carbohydrate 11.9g, of which sugars 3.5g; Fat 4.4g, of which saturates 0.7g; Cholesterol 0mg; Calcium 62mg; Fibre 4.4g; Sodium 228mg.

ARTICHOKE SALAD <u>WITH</u> SALSA AGRODOLCE ★

AGRODOLCE IS AN ITALIAN SWEET-AND-SOUR SAUCE WHICH MAKES AN IDEAL ACCOMPANIMENT FOR THIS TASTY, LOW-FAT ARTICHOKE AND BEAN SALAD.

SERVES FOUR TO SIX

INGREDIENTS
   6 small globe artichokes
   juice of 1 lemon
   15ml/1 tbsp olive oil
   2 onions, roughly chopped
   175g/6oz/1 cup fresh or frozen broad
      (fava) beans (shelled weight)
   175g/6oz/1½ cups fresh or frozen
      peas (shelled weight)
   salt and ground black pepper
   fresh mint leaves, to garnish
For the salsa agrodolce
   120ml/4fl oz/½ cup white
      wine vinegar
   15ml/1 tbsp caster (superfine) sugar
   a handful of fresh mint leaves,
      roughly torn

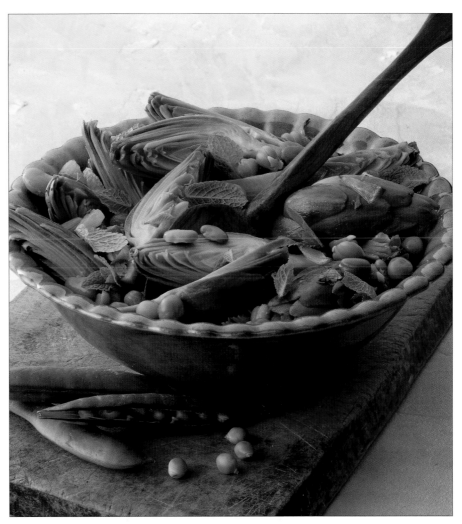

1 Peel and discard the outer leaves from the artichokes and cut into quarters. Place the artichokes in a bowl of water with the lemon juice. Set aside.

2 Heat the oil in a large, non-stick pan and add the onions. Cook until the onions are golden, stirring occasionally. Add the broad beans and stir, then drain the artichokes and add to the pan. Pour in about 300ml/½ pint/ 1¼ cups of water and bring to the boil, then reduce the heat and cook, covered, for 10–15 minutes.

3 Add the peas, season to taste with salt and pepper and cook for a further 5 minutes until the vegetables are tender, stirring occasionally. Strain through a sieve (strainer), discard the liquid, then place all the vegetables in a bowl, leave to cool, cover and chill.

4 To make the salsa agrodolce, mix the vinegar, sugar and torn mint leaves in a small pan. Heat gently for 2–3 minutes, until the sugar has dissolved, then simmer for 5 minutes, stirring occasionally. Remove the pan from the heat and leave to cool. To serve, drizzle the salsa over the vegetables and garnish with mint leaves.

VARIATION
Use 6–8 shallots in place of onions.

COOK'S TIP
Leave the root end intact when chopping or slicing an onion. This will prevent the release of the strong juices and fumes that can cause eyes to water.

Energy 98Kcal/411kJ; Protein 5.4g; Carbohydrate 14g, of which sugars 7.2g; Fat 2.7g, of which saturates 0.4g; Cholesterol 0mg; Calcium 71mg; Fibre 4.9g; Sodium 54mg.

ORANGE AND RED ONION SALAD WITH CUMIN ★

IN THIS SPANISH-DERIVED DISH, JUICY ORANGES PERFECTLY PARTNER THINLY SLICED RED ONIONS AND BLACK OLIVES. CUMIN SEEDS AND MINT ARE ADDED TO COMPLETE THIS MOUTHWATERING SALAD.

SERVES SIX

INGREDIENTS
 6 oranges
 2 red onions
 15ml/1 tbsp cumin seeds
 5ml/1 tsp coarsely ground
  black pepper
 15ml/1 tbsp chopped fresh mint
 40ml/8 tsp olive oil
 salt
 fresh mint sprigs and whole black
  olives, to garnish

COOK'S TIP
It is important to let the salad stand before serving. This allows the flavours to develop and the pungent taste of the onion to soften slightly.

1 Using a sharp knife, slice the oranges thinly, working over a bowl to catch any juice. Then, holding each orange slice in turn over the bowl, cut round the middle fleshy section with scissors to remove the peel and pith. Reserve the juice. Slice the red onions thinly and separate the rings.

2 Arrange the orange and onion slices in layers in a shallow dish, sprinkling each layer with cumin seeds, pepper, mint, olive oil and salt. Pour in the reserved orange juice. Leave to marinate in a cool place for about 2 hours. Just before serving, scatter with the mint sprigs and black olives.

Energy 110Kcal/460kJ; Protein 2.3g; Carbohydrate 16.7g, of which sugars 15.6g; Fat 4.3g, of which saturates 0.6g; Cholesterol 0mg; Calcium 83mg; Fibre 3.3g; Sodium 9mg.

SPANISH MIXED SALAD WITH OLIVES AND CAPERS ★

THIS COLOURFUL LOW-FAT VEGETARIAN SALAD ORIGINATES FROM SPAIN WHERE, TYPICALLY, THE BOWL OF SALAD IS PUT IN THE CENTRE OF THE TABLE FOR EVERYONE TO HELP THEMSELVES WITH A FORK.

SERVES FOUR

INGREDIENTS
 4 large tomatoes
 ½ cucumber
 1 bunch spring onions (scallions)
 1 bunch watercress or rocket
  (arugula), washed
 8 pimiento-stuffed olives
 30ml/2 tbsp drained pickled capers
For the dressing
 1 garlic clove, finely chopped
 105ml/7 tbsp low-fat French dressing
 5ml/1 tsp paprika
 2.5ml/½ tsp ground cumin
 salt and ground black pepper

COOK'S TIP
Scallions, or "green onions" are immature onions and and have a mild flavour for soups and stews. They can be eaten raw.

1 To skin the tomatoes, place them in a heatproof bowl, pour over boiling water to cover and leave to stand for 1 minute. Lift out the tomatoes with a slotted spoon and plunge them into a bowl of cold water. Leave for 1 minute, then drain. Slip off the skins and chop the flesh finely. Put in a salad bowl.

2 Peel the cucumber, finely dice and add it to the tomatoes. Trim and chop half the spring onions, then add them to the bowl.

3 Toss the vegetables together, then break the watercress or rocket into small sprigs. Add the olives and capers to the tomato mixture.

4 Make the dressing. Crush the garlic to a paste with a little salt, using the flat of a knife. Put in a bowl and mix in the French dressing and spices. Whisk together to mix well, then season to taste. Dress the salad, and serve garnished with the remaining spring onions.

Energy 42Kcal/177kJ; Protein 1.4g; Carbohydrate 6.7g, of which sugars 6.3g; Fat 1.3g, of which saturates 0.3g; Cholesterol 0mg; Calcium 22mg; Fibre 1.7g; Sodium 573mg.

HERB POLENTA WITH GRILLED TOMATOES ★

GOLDEN POLENTA FLAVOURED WITH FRESH SUMMER HERBS AND SERVED WITH SWEET GRILLED TOMATOES CREATES THIS TASTY LOW-FAT ITALIAN DISH, IDEAL FOR LUNCH OR SUPPER.

SERVES SIX

INGREDIENTS
  750ml/1¼ pints/3 cups vegetable
    stock or water
  5ml/1 tsp salt
  175g/6oz/1½ cups polenta
  15g/½oz/1 tbsp butter
  75ml/5 tbsp chopped mixed fresh
    parsley, chives and basil, plus extra
    to garnish
  10ml/2 tsp olive oil
  4 large plum or beefsteak
    tomatoes, halved
  salt and ground black pepper

1 Prepare the polenta in advance: place the stock or water in a pan with the salt, and bring to the boil.

2 Reduce the heat and gradually add the polenta, stirring constantly to ensure that it doesn't form any lumps.

3 Stir constantly over a medium heat for 5 minutes, until the polenta begins to thicken and comes away from the sides of the pan.

4 Remove the pan from the heat and stir in the butter, chopped herbs and pepper.

5 Transfer the polenta mixture to a wide, lightly greased dish or baking tin (pan) and spread it out evenly. Leave until it is completely cool and has set.

6 Turn the polenta out on to a chopping board and cut it into squares or stamp out rounds with a large biscuit cutter. Lightly brush the squares or rounds with oil.

7 Lightly brush the tomatoes with oil and sprinkle with salt and pepper.

8 Cook the tomatoes and polenta over a medium hot barbecue or under a preheated grill (broiler) for 5 minutes, turning once. Serve hot, garnished with herbs.

VARIATION
Any mixture of fresh herbs can be used, or try using just basil or chives alone, for a really distinctive flavour.

Energy 146Kcal/611kJ; Protein 3.2g; Carbohydrate 23.4g, of which sugars 2.1g; Fat 4.2g, of which saturates 1.5g; Cholesterol 5mg; Calcium 6mg; Fibre 1.3g; Sodium 349mg.

SUMMER VEGETABLES WITH YOGURT PESTO ★

CHARGRILLED VEGETABLES CREATE A DELICIOUS LIGHT MEAL ON THEIR OWN, OR ARE EQUALLY GOOD SERVED AS A MEDITERRANEAN-STYLE ACCOMPANIMENT TO VEGETARIAN MAIN MEALS.

SERVES FOUR

INGREDIENTS
2 small aubergines (eggplants)
2 large courgettes (zucchini)
1 red (bell) pepper
1 yellow (bell) pepper
1 fennel bulb
1 red onion
10ml/2 tsp olive oil
salt and ground black pepper
For the yogurt pesto
150ml/¼ pint/⅔ cup fat-free Greek (US strained plain) yogurt
15ml/1 tbsp pesto

1 Cut the aubergines into 1cm/½in slices. Sprinkle with salt and leave to drain for about 30 minutes. Rinse well in cold running water and pat dry.

2 Cut the courgettes in half lengthways. Cut the peppers in half, removing the seeds but leaving the stalks intact. Set aside.

3 Slice the fennel bulb and the red onion into thick wedges. Set aside.

COOK'S TIP
Baby vegetables make excellent candidates for grilling (broiling) whole, so look out for baby aubergines (eggplants) and (bell) peppers, in particular. There's no need to salt the aubergines if they're small.

4 Stir the yogurt and pesto lightly together in a serving bowl, to make a marbled sauce. Set aside.

5 Arrange the vegetables over a hot barbecue, or under a hot grill (broiler), lightly brush with the olive oil and sprinkle with plenty of salt and pepper.

6 Cook the vegetables until golden brown and tender, turning occasionally. The aubergines and peppers will take about 6–8 minutes to cook, and the courgettes, onion and fennel will take about 4–5 minutes. Serve the vegetables immediately, with the yogurt pesto.

Energy 107Kcal/448kJ; Protein 5.7g; Carbohydrate 13g, of which sugars 12.1g; Fat 4g, of which saturates 1g; Cholesterol 2mg; Calcium 133mg; Fibre 4.5g; Sodium 56mg.

SPANISH OMELETTE ★★

SPANISH TORTILLA, OR OMELETTE, CONSISTS SIMPLY OF POTATOES, ONIONS AND EGGS. THIS VARIATION FROM NORTHERN SPAIN HAS OTHER VEGETABLES INCLUDING WHITE BEANS, AND MAKES A HEARTY LOW-FAT VEGETARIAN MAIN COURSE OR, BECAUSE IT IS GOOD SERVED COLD, AN EXCELLENT PICNIC FOOD.

SERVES EIGHT

INGREDIENTS
15ml/1 tbsp olive oil
1 Spanish (Bermuda) onion, chopped
1 small red (bell) pepper, seeded
  and diced
2 celery sticks, chopped
225g/8oz potatoes, diced and cooked
400g/14oz can cannellini beans,
  rinsed and drained
8 eggs
salt and ground black pepper
sprigs of fresh oregano, to garnish
green salad and olives, to serve

1 Heat the oil in a 30cm/12in non-stick frying pan or paella pan. Add the onion, red pepper and celery and cook for 3–5 minutes until the vegetables are soft, but not coloured.

2 Add the potatoes and beans and cook for several minutes to heat through.

3 In a small bowl, beat the eggs with a fork, then season well and pour over the ingredients in the pan.

4 Stir the egg mixture with a wooden spatula until it begins to thicken, then allow it to cook over a low heat for about 8 minutes. The omelette should be firm, but still moist in the middle. Cool slightly then invert on to a serving plate.

5 Cut the omelette into wedges. Serve warm or cool with a green salad and olives. Garnish with fresh oregano sprigs.

COOK'S TIP
In Spain, this omelette is often served as a tapas dish or appetizer. It is delicious served cold, cut into bitesize pieces and accompanied by a low-fat chilli sauce for dipping. Other sliced seasonal vegetables, baby artichoke hearts and chickpeas can also be used in this recipe.

Energy 223Kcal/937kJ; Protein 15.2g; Carbohydrate 25.1g, of which sugars 5.4g; Fat 7.7g, of which saturates 1.9g; Cholesterol 190mg; Calcium 82mg; Fibre 6.8g; Sodium 86mg.

POTATO AND ONION CAKES WITH BEETROOT ★★

THESE IRRESISTIBLE LOW-FAT PANCAKES ARE BASED ON LATKE (JEWISH CRISPY, SAVOURY POTATO CAKES TRADITIONALLY EATEN AT HANUKKAH). THEY ARE ESPECIALLY DELICIOUS SERVED WITH A SWEET-SHARP BEETROOT RELISH AND SOUR CREAM, AND ARE A TREAT ANYTIME.

SERVES FOUR

INGREDIENTS

500g/1¼lb potatoes (such as King Edward, Estima or Desirée)
1 small Bramley cooking apple, peeled, cored and coarsely grated
1 small onion, finely chopped
50g/2oz/½ cup plain (all-purpose) flour
2 large (US extra large) eggs, beaten
30ml/2 tbsp chopped fresh chives
30ml/2 tbsp vegetable oil
salt and ground black pepper
fresh dill sprigs and fresh chives or chive flowers, to garnish
250ml/8fl oz/1 cup sour cream or reduced-fat crème fraîche, to serve (optional)

For the beetroot relish
250g/9oz beetroot (beets), cooked and peeled
1 large dessert apple, cored and finely chopped
15ml/1 tbsp finely chopped red onion
15–30ml/1–2 tbsp tarragon vinegar
15ml/1 tbsp chopped fresh dill
15ml/1 tbsp light olive oil
a pinch of caster (superfine) sugar (optional)

1 To make the relish, finely dice the beetroot, then mix it with the apple and onion in a bowl. Add 15ml/1 tbsp of the vinegar, the dill and oil. Season, adding a little more vinegar and a pinch of caster sugar to taste. Set aside.

2 Coarsely grate the potatoes, then rinse, drain and dry them on a clean dish towel.

3 Mix the potatoes, cooking apple and onion in a bowl. Stir in the flour, eggs and chives. Season and mix again.

4 Heat the oil in a non-stick frying pan and cook spoonfuls of the potato mixture. Flatten them to make pancakes 7.5–10cm/3–4in across and cook for 3–4 minutes on each side, until browned. Drain on kitchen paper and keep warm until the mixture is used up.

VARIATION
Use sweet potatoes in place of standard potatoes.

5 Serve a stack of pancakes – there should be about 16–20 in total – with spoonfuls of sour cream or crème fraîche if you like, and the beetroot relish. Garnish with dill sprigs and chives or chive flowers and grind black pepper on top just before serving.

VARIATION
To make a leek and potato cake, melt 15g/½oz/1 tbsp butter in a non-stick pan, add 400g/14oz thinly sliced leeks and cook until tender. Season well. Coarsely grate 500g/1¼lb peeled potatoes, then season. Melt another 25g/1oz/2 tbsp butter in a non-stick frying pan and add a layer of half the potatoes. Cover with the leeks, then add the remaining potatoes, pressing down with a spatula to form a cake. Cook over a low heat for 20–25 minutes until the potatoes are browned, then turn over and cook for 15–20 minutes, until the potatoes are browned.

Energy 265Kcal/1116kJ; Protein 7.8g; Carbohydrate 38.8g, of which sugars 10g; Fat 9.9g, of which saturates 1.7g; Cholesterol 95mg; Calcium 57mg; Fibre 3.6g; Sodium 92mg.

LEMONY COUSCOUS SALAD ★

*THIS IS A POPULAR SALAD OF OLIVES, ALMONDS AND COURGETTES MIXED WITH FLUFFY COUSCOUS
AND TOSSED WITH A LIGHT, HERBY DRESSING. IT HAS A DELICATE FLAVOUR AND MAKES AN EXCELLENT
ACCOMPANIMENT TO CHARGRILLED MIXED VEGETABLE KEBABS.*

SERVES FOUR

INGREDIENTS
  275g/10oz/1⅔ cups couscous
  550ml/18fl oz/2½ cups boiling
    vegetable stock
  2 small courgettes (zucchini)
  16–20 whole black olives
  25g/1oz/¼ cup flaked (sliced)
    almonds, toasted
  75ml/5 tbsp low-fat French or tomato
    dressing (*see recipes on page 14*)
  15ml/1 tbsp chopped fresh
    coriander (cilantro)
  15ml/1 tbsp chopped fresh parsley
  a good pinch of ground cumin
  a good pinch of cayenne pepper

1 Place the couscous in a bowl and pour over the boiling stock. Stir with a fork, then set aside for 10 minutes to allow the stock to be absorbed. Fluff up with a fork.

2 Trim the courgettes at both ends then cut into pieces about 2.5cm/1in long. Slice into thin julienne strips. Halve the black olives, discarding the stones (pits).

3 Carefully mix the courgettes, olives and almonds into the couscous.

4 Whisk together the French or tomato dressing, coriander, parsley, cumin and cayenne in a small bowl. Stir into the salad, tossing gently to mix through. Transfer to a large serving dish and serve immediately.

Energy 211Kcal/879kJ; Protein 6g; Carbohydrate 38.4g, of which sugars 2.8g; Fat 4.5g, of which saturates 0.4g; Cholesterol 0mg; Calcium 42mg; Fibre 1.1g; Sodium 451mg.

TOFU AND WILD RICE SALAD ★

THE FLAVOURS IN THIS LIGHT, VEGETARIAN SALAD ARE INFLUENCED BY THE CUISINES OF NORTH AFRICA AND THE EASTERN SEABOARDS OF THE MEDITERRANEAN. IT GOES PARTICULARLY WELL WITH CHARGRILLED VEGETABLES SUCH AS RED ONIONS, TOMATOES, COURGETTES AND PEPPERS.

SERVES SIX

INGREDIENTS
 175g/6oz/scant 1 cup basmati rice
 50g/2oz/generous ¼ cup wild rice
 250g/9oz firm tofu, drained and
  cubed
 25g/1oz preserved lemon, finely
  chopped (see Cook's Tip)
 20g/¾oz fresh parsley, chopped
For the dressing
 1 garlic clove, crushed
 10ml/2 tsp clear honey
 10ml/2 tsp of the preserved lemon
  juice
 15ml/1 tbsp balsamic vinegar
 15ml/1 tbsp olive oil
 1 small fresh red chilli, seeded and
  finely chopped
 5ml/1 tsp harissa paste (optional)
 salt and ground black pepper

1 Cook the basmati rice and the wild rice in separate pans until tender. The basmati rice will take about 10–15 minutes to cook, while the wild rice will take about 45–50 minutes. Drain both lots of rice, rinse under cold water and drain again, then place in a large bowl together.

2 Meanwhile, whisk together all the dressing ingredients in a small bowl. Add the tofu, stir to coat and leave to marinate while the rice cooks.

VARIATIONS
Keep an eye open for rose harissa paste, which is available from the special range in some large supermarkets or from delicatessens or food halls. It is exceptionally delicious in this recipe and still fiery hot.

3 Gently fold the tofu, dressing, preserved lemon and parsley into the rice, adjust the seasoning to taste and serve.

COOK'S TIP
Preserved lemons, packed in salt, are available from Middle Eastern delicatessens or from large food halls and some supermarkets.

Energy 183Kcal/766kJ; Protein 5.8g; Carbohydrate 31.5g, of which sugars 1.4g; Fat 3.6g, of which saturates 0.5g; Cholesterol 0mg; Calcium 199mg; Fibre 0g; Sodium 2mg.

STUFFED AUBERGINES ★

THIS DISH FROM THE LIGURIAN REGION OF ITALY IS SPIKED WITH PAPRIKA AND ALLSPICE, A LEGACY FROM THE DAYS WHEN SPICES FROM THE EAST CAME INTO NORTHERN ITALY VIA THE PORT OF GENOA.

SERVES SIX

INGREDIENTS

2 aubergines (eggplants), about
    225g/8oz each, stalks removed
275g/10oz potatoes, diced
15ml/1 tbsp olive oil
1 small onion, finely chopped
1 garlic clove, finely chopped
a good pinch of ground allspice
    and paprika
30ml/2 tbsp skimmed milk
25g/1oz grated fresh Parmesan
    cheese
15ml/1 tbsp fresh white breadcrumbs
salt and ground black pepper
fresh mint sprigs, to garnish
salad leaves, to serve

1 Bring a large pan of lightly salted water to the boil. Add the whole aubergines and cook for 5 minutes, turning frequently. Remove with a slotted spoon and set aside. Add the diced potatoes to the pan and boil for about 15 minutes or until cooked.

2 Meanwhile, cut the aubergines in half lengthways and gently scoop out the flesh with a small sharp knife and a spoon, leaving 5mm/¼in of the shell intact. Select an ovenproof baking dish that will hold the aubergine shells snugly in a single layer. Brush it lightly with oil. Put the shells in the baking dish and chop the aubergine flesh roughly. Set aside.

3 Heat the remaining oil in a non-stick frying pan, add the onion and cook gently until softened, stirring frequently. Add the chopped aubergine flesh and the garlic. Cook for 6–8 minutes, stirring frequently. Tip the mixture into a bowl and set aside. Preheat the oven to 190°C/375°F/Gas 5.

4 Drain and mash the potatoes. Add to the aubergine mixture with the ground spices and milk, mixing well. Set aside 15ml/1 tbsp of the Parmesan cheese and add the rest to the aubergine mixture, stirring in salt and pepper to taste.

5 Spoon the mixture into the aubergine shells. Mix the breadcrumbs with the reserved Parmesan cheese and sprinkle the mixture evenly over the aubergines. Bake in the oven for 30–40 minutes or until the topping is crisp. Garnish with mint sprigs and serve with salad leaves.

COOK'S TIPS
• To make fine fresh breadcrumbs quickly, drop pieces or small slices of fresh bread through the feeder tube onto the moving blade of a food processor.
• If you only need a small amount of breadcrumbs, such as with this recipe, use a coffee grinder to grind small pieces of fresh bread.
• Freshly made breadcrumbs will keep in a polythene freezer bag in the freezer for up to 6 months.

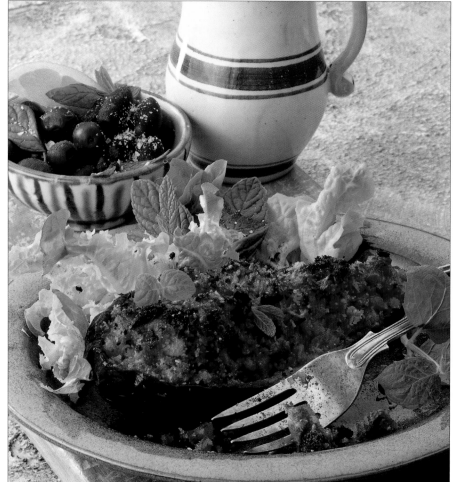

Energy 94Kcal/396kJ; Protein 3.8g; Carbohydrate 12.2g, of which sugars 3.1g; Fat 3.8g, of which saturates 1.3g; Cholesterol 4mg; Calcium 73mg; Fibre 2.3g; Sodium 74mg.

ITALIAN STUFFED PEPPERS ★

THESE FLAVOURFUL ITALIAN STUFFED PEPPERS ARE EASY TO MAKE FOR A LIGHT AND HEALTHY LUNCH OR SUPPER, AND ARE IDEAL SERVED WITH A MIXED LEAF SALAD.

SERVES FOUR

INGREDIENTS
  10ml/2 tsp olive oil
  1 red onion, sliced
  1 courgette (zucchini), diced
  115g/4oz/1½ cups mushrooms, sliced
  1 garlic clove, crushed
  400g/14oz can chopped tomatoes
  15ml/1 tbsp tomato purée (paste)
  25g/1oz pine nuts (optional)
  30ml/2 tbsp torn fresh basil leaves
  4 large (bell) peppers
  25g/1oz/⅓ cup finely grated fresh
    Parmesan or Fontina cheese
    (optional)
  salt and ground black pepper
  fresh basil leaves, to garnish

1 Preheat the oven to 180°C/350°F/ Gas 4. Heat the oil in a non-stick pan, add the onion, courgette, mushrooms and garlic and cook gently for 3 minutes, stirring occasionally.

COOK'S TIP
Tear fresh basil leaves with your fingers, instead of chopping them with a knife, to avoid losing the flavour and colour too quickly from this delicate leaved herb.

2 Stir in the tomatoes and tomato purée, then bring to the boil and simmer, uncovered, for 10–15 minutes until thickened slightly, stirring occasionally. Remove the pan from the heat and stir in the basil, seasoning and pine nuts, if using. Set aside.

3 Cut the peppers in half lengthways and deseed them. Blanch the pepper halves in a pan of boiling water for about 3 minutes. Drain.

4 Place the peppers cut side up in a shallow ovenproof dish and fill with the vegetable mixture.

5 Cover the dish with foil and bake in the oven for 20 minutes. Uncover, sprinkle each pepper half with a little grated cheese, if using, and bake, uncovered, for a further 5–10 minutes. Garnish with fresh basil leaves and serve immediately.

Energy 108Kcal/450kJ; Protein 4.2g; Carbohydrate 17g, of which sugars 16.1g; Fat 2.9g, of which saturates 0.6g; Cholesterol 0mg; Calcium 40mg; Fibre 4.9g; Sodium 28mg.

LEMONY OKRA AND TOMATO TAGINE ★

IN THIS SPICY VEGETABLE DISH, THE HEAT OF THE CHILLI IS OFFSET BY THE REFRESHING FLAVOUR OF LEMON JUICE. BASED ON A MOROCCAN RECIPE, THIS IS IDEAL SERVED WITH A MIXED LEAF SIDE SALAD.

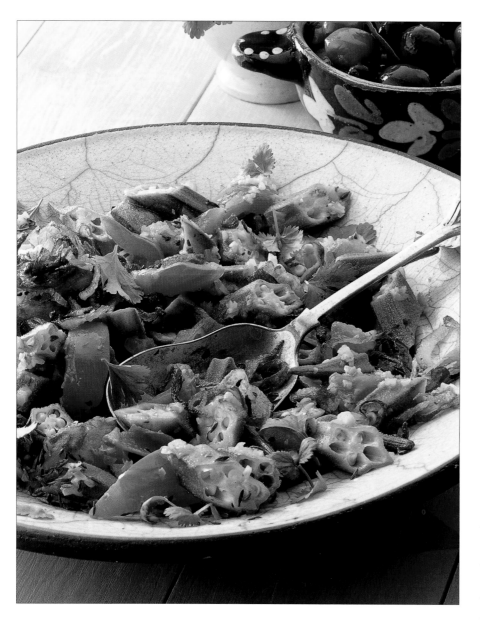

4 Heat the sunflower oil in a large, non-stick pan. Thinly slice the second onion and cook it gently in the oil for about 5–6 minutes, or until soft and golden brown. Transfer the cooked onion slices to a plate with a slotted spoon.

5 Reduce the heat and pour the onion and coriander mixture into the pan. Cook for 1–2 minutes, stirring frequently. Add the okra pieces, chopped tomatoes, lemon juice and about 120ml/4fl oz/½ cup water. Stir well to mix, cover tightly, and simmer gently over a low heat for about 15 minutes, or until the okra is tender.

6 Transfer to a large warmed serving dish, sprinkle with the fried onion rings, garnish with fresh coriander and serve immediately.

VARIATIONS
Use vine-ripened or plum tomatoes for this recipe. Use 2 small red onions or 4–6 shallots in place of standard onions.

SERVES FOUR

INGREDIENTS
350g/12oz okra
5–6 tomatoes
2 small onions
2 garlic cloves, crushed
1 fresh green chilli, seeded
5ml/1 tsp paprika
a small handful of fresh coriander (cilantro), plus extra to garnish
15ml/1 tbsp sunflower oil
juice of 1 lemon

1 Trim the okra and then cut them into 1cm/½in lengths. Set aside.

2 Cut the tomatoes in half and scoop out the seeds with a teaspoon. Chop the flesh coarsely and set aside.

3 Coarsely chop one of the onions, then place it in a blender or food processor with the garlic, green chilli, paprika, coriander and 60ml/4 tbsp water. Process to a smooth paste.

Energy 79Kcal/329kJ; Protein 3.7g; Carbohydrate 7.3g, of which sugars 6.4g; Fat 4.1g, of which saturates 0.7g; Cholesterol 0mg; Calcium 176mg; Fibre 5.3g; Sodium 21mg.

SPICED TURNIPS <u>WITH</u> SPINACH <u>AND</u> TOMATOES ★

SWEET BABY TURNIPS, TENDER SPINACH AND RIPE TOMATOES MAKE TEMPTING PARTNERS IN THIS SIMPLE BUT VERY TASTY LIGHT, EASTERN MEDITERRANEAN VEGETABLE STEW.

SERVES SIX

INGREDIENTS

450g/1lb plum tomatoes
25ml/5 tsp olive oil
2 onions, sliced
450g/1lb baby turnips, peeled
5ml/1 tsp paprika
2.5ml/½ tsp granulated sugar
60ml/4 tbsp chopped fresh
  coriander (cilantro)
450g/1lb fresh young spinach
salt and ground black pepper

VARIATION

Try this with celery hearts instead of baby turnips. It is also good with fennel or drained canned artichoke hearts.

1 Plunge the tomatoes into a bowl of boiling water for 30 seconds or so, then refresh in a bowl of cold water. Drain, peel away the tomato skins and chop the flesh roughly.

2 Heat the olive oil in a large, non-stick frying pan or sauté pan, add the onions and cook gently for about 5 minutes until golden. Ensure that they do not blacken.

3 Add the baby turnips, tomatoes and paprika to the pan with 60ml/4 tbsp water and cook until the tomatoes are pulpy. Cover the pan with a lid and continue cooking until the baby turnips have softened.

4 Stir in the sugar and coriander, then add the spinach and a little salt and pepper. Cook the mixture for a further 2–3 minutes or until the spinach has wilted. The dish can be served warm or cold.

Energy 77Kcal/320kJ; Protein 3.4g; Carbohydrate 8.3g, of which sugars 7.8g; Fat 3.6g, of which saturates 0.5g; Cholesterol 0mg; Calcium 172mg; Fibre 4.3g; Sodium 123mg.

TOFU AND GREEN BEAN RED CURRY ★

*THIS IS ONE OF THOSE VERSATILE RECIPES THAT SHOULD BE IN EVERY COOK'S REPERTOIRE. THIS
VERSION USES GREEN BEANS, BUT OTHER TYPES OF VEGETABLE WORK EQUALLY WELL.*

SERVES FOUR

INGREDIENTS
  600ml/1 pint/2½ cups canned
    coconut milk
  15ml/1 tbsp Thai red curry paste
  10ml/2 tsp palm sugar or honey
  225g/8oz/3¼ cups button
    (white) mushrooms
  115g/4oz/scant 1 cup green
    beans, trimmed
  175g/6oz firm tofu, rinsed, drained
    and cut into 2cm/¾in cubes
  4 kaffir lime leaves, torn
  2 fresh red chillies, seeded
    and sliced
  fresh coriander (cilantro) leaves,
    to garnish

1 Pour about one-third of the coconut milk into a wok or pan. Cook until it starts to separate and an oily sheen appears on the surface.

2 Add the red curry paste and palm sugar or honey to the coconut milk. Mix thoroughly, then add the mushrooms. Stir and cook for 1 minute.

3 Stir in the remaining coconut milk. Bring back to the boil, then add the green beans and tofu cubes. Simmer gently for 4–5 minutes more.

4 Stir in the kaffir lime leaves and sliced red chillies. Spoon the curry into a serving dish, garnish with the coriander leaves and serve immediately.

Energy 89kcal/375kJ; Protein 5.7g; Carbohydrate 11.3g, of which sugars 10.7g; Fat 2.7g, of which saturates 0.6g; Cholesterol 0mg; Calcium 282mg; Fibre 1.2g; Sodium 437mg

CHINESE OMELETTE VEGETABLE PARCELS ★★

STIR-FRIED FRESH VEGETABLES COOKED IN CHINESE SAVOURY BLACK BEAN SAUCE MAKE A REALLY
INTERESTING OMELETTE FILLING, FOR AN UNUSUAL MAIN MEAL.

SERVES FOUR

INGREDIENTS
130g/4½oz broccoli, cut into
small florets
15ml/1 tbsp groundnut (peanut) oil
1cm/½in piece of fresh root ginger,
finely grated
1 large garlic clove, crushed
2 fresh red chillies, seeded and
thinly sliced
4 spring onions (scallions),
sliced diagonally
175g/6oz/3 cups pak choi (bok
choy), shredded
50g/2oz/2 cups fresh coriander
(cilantro) leaves, plus extra to
garnish
115g/4oz/½ cup beansprouts
45ml/3 tbsp black bean sauce
4 eggs
salt and ground black pepper

1 Blanch the broccoli in a pan of salted boiling water for 2 minutes, drain well, then refresh under cold running water. Set aside.

2 Meanwhile, heat 5ml/1 tsp oil in a non-stick frying pan or wok. Add the ginger, garlic and half the chilli and stir-fry for 1 minute. Add the spring onions, broccoli and pak choi and stir-fry for 2 minutes, tossing the vegetables to prevent them sticking.

3 Chop three-quarters of the coriander and add it to the frying pan or wok. Add the beansprouts and stir-fry for 1 minute, then add the black bean sauce and heat through for a further minute. Remove the pan from the heat and keep warm.

4 Beat the eggs lightly and season well with salt and pepper. Heat a little of the remaining groundnut oil in a small, non-stick frying pan and add a quarter of the beaten egg. Swirl the egg until it covers the base of the pan, then sprinkle over a quarter of the reserved coriander leaves. Cook until set, then carefully turn out on to a plate and keep warm in the oven while you make three more omelettes, adding a little more oil when necessary.

5 Spoon the vegetable stir-fry on to the omelettes and roll up. Cut in half crossways and serve garnished with coriander leaves and the remaining sliced chilli.

VARIATIONS
Use cauliflower florets or green beans (cut into 5cm/2in lengths), in place of broccoli. Use sesame oil in place of groundnut (peanut) oil.

COOK'S TIP
Black bean sauce is available in jars or cans from most large supermarkets.

Energy 148Kcal/614kJ; Protein 10.4g; Carbohydrate 6.2g, of which sugars 5.4g; Fat 9.3g, of which saturates 2.2g; Cholesterol 190mg; Calcium 152mg; Fibre 3g; Sodium 323mg.

WILD RICE WITH GRILLED VEGETABLES ★

THE MIXTURE OF WILD RICE AND LONG GRAIN RICE WORKS VERY WELL IN THIS DISH, COMBINED WITH
THE GRILLED PEPPERS, MUSHROOMS, COURGETTES AND AUBERGINE, TO MAKE A COMFORTING LIGHT MEAL.

2 Make the dressing. Whisk the French dressing, garlic and seasoning together in a bowl or shake in a screw-top jar until thoroughly blended. Set aside while you grill (broil) the vegetables.

SERVES FOUR

INGREDIENTS

225g/8oz/generous 1 cup mixed wild and long grain rice
1 large aubergine (eggplant), thickly sliced
1 red, 1 yellow and 1 green (bell) pepper, seeded and cut into quarters
2 red onions, sliced
225g/8oz/3 cups brown cap (cremini) or shiitake mushrooms
2 small courgettes (zucchini), cut in half lengthways
10ml/2 tsp olive oil
30ml/2 tbsp chopped fresh thyme, plus extra to garnish
For the dressing
120ml/4fl oz/½ cup low-fat French dressing (*see recipe on page 14*)
2 garlic cloves, crushed
salt and ground black pepper

1 Put all the rice in a pan of salted cold water. Bring to the boil, then reduce the heat, cover and cook gently for 30–40 minutes (or according to the instructions on the packet) until tender.

3 Preheat the grill (broiler) to high. Arrange all the vegetables on a grill (broiler) rack. Lightly brush the vegetables with olive oil and grill for about 5 minutes.

4 Turn the vegetables over, lightly brush them with a little more olive oil and grill for a further 5–8 minutes, or until tender and charred in places.

5 Drain the rice, transfer it to a bowl and toss in half the dressing. Spoon the rice on to individual plates and arrange the grilled vegetables on top. Pour over the remaining dressing, scatter over the chopped thyme and serve.

VARIATION
Use standard onions in place of red onions.

Energy 296Kcal/1237kJ; Protein 7.8g; Carbohydrate 59.3g, of which sugars 13.5g; Fat 3g, of which saturates 0.5g; Cholesterol 0mg; Calcium 39mg; Fibre 4.7g; Sodium 460mg.

LENTILS <u>WITH</u> MUSHROOMS <u>AND</u> ANIS ★

IN THIS SPANISH RECIPE, LENTEJAS CON CHAMPIÑONES, *LENTILS ARE FLAVOURED WITH ANOTHER PRODUCT OF CASTILLE, ANIS SPIRIT, PLUS A LARGE QUANTITY OF PARSLEY. SERVE THIS DELICATE LOW-FAT DISH ON ITS OWN, OR WITH FRESH CRUSTY BREAD.*

SERVES FOUR

INGREDIENTS
15ml/1 tbsp olive oil
1 large onion, sliced
2 garlic cloves, finely chopped
250g/9oz/generous 3 cups brown cap (cremini) mushrooms, sliced
150g/5oz/generous ½ cup brown or green lentils, soaked overnight and drained
4 tomatoes, each cut into eighths
1 bay leaf
25g/1oz/½ cup chopped fresh parsley
30ml/2 tbsp anis spirit or anisette
salt, paprika and black pepper

COOK'S TIP
If you forget to soak the lentils, add at least 30 minutes to the cooking time.

1 Heat the oil in a flameproof casserole. Add the onion and cook gently, with the garlic, until softened but not browned.

2 Add the mushrooms and stir to combine with the onion and garlic. Continue cooking for a couple of minutes, stirring gently.

3 Add the lentils, tomatoes and bay leaf with 175ml/6fl oz/¾ cup water. Simmer gently, covered, for 30–40 minutes until the lentils are soft, and the liquid has almost disappeared.

4 Stir in the parsley and anis. Season with salt, paprika and black pepper.

Energy 216Kcal/910kJ; Protein 12.4g; Carbohydrate 29.3g, of which sugars 9.6g; Fat 4.5g, of which saturates 0.7g; Cholesterol 0mg; Calcium 72mg; Fibre 6.9g; Sodium 26mg.

CHINESE LEAVES AND BLACK RICE STIR-FRY ★

THE SLIGHTLY NUTTY, CHEWY BLACK GLUTINOUS RICE CONTRASTS BEAUTIFULLY WITH THE CHINESE LEAVES, TO CREATE THIS FLAVOURFUL LIGHT VEGETARIAN DISH.

SERVES FOUR

INGREDIENTS

225g/8oz/generous 1 cup black
  glutinous rice or brown rice
900ml/1½ pints/3¾ cups
  vegetable stock
10ml/2 tsp vegetable oil
225g/8oz Chinese leaves (Chinese
  cabbage), cut into 1cm/½in strips
4 spring onions (scallions),
  thinly sliced
salt and ground white pepper
2.5ml/½ tsp sesame oil

1 Rinse the rice until the water runs clear, then drain and transfer to a pan. Add the stock and bring to the boil. Reduce the heat, cover the pan and cook gently for 30 minutes. Remove the pan from the heat and leave to stand for 15 minutes without lifting the lid.

2 Heat the vegetable oil in a non-stick frying pan or wok. Stir-fry the Chinese leaves for 2 minutes, adding a little water to prevent them burning.

3 Drain the rice, stir it into the pan and cook for 4 minutes, using two spatulas or wooden spoons to toss it with the Chinese leaves over the heat.

4 Add the spring onions, with the salt and pepper and sesame oil. Cook for a further 1 minute. Serve immediately.

Energy 236Kcal/988kJ; Protein 5.7g; Carbohydrate 45.3g, of which sugars 3g; Fat 2.9g, of which saturates 0.3g; Cholesterol 0mg; Calcium 41mg; Fibre 1.3g; Sodium 6mg.

TOASTED NOODLES <u>WITH</u> VEGETABLES ★

SLIGHTLY CRISP NOODLE CAKES TOPPED WITH VEGETABLES CREATE THIS SUPERB LOW-FAT LUNCH OR SUPPER DISH. EACH NOODLE CAKE SERVES TWO PEOPLE.

SERVES FOUR

INGREDIENTS
175g/6oz/1½ cups dried egg vermicelli
10ml/2 tsp vegetable oil
2 garlic cloves, finely chopped
115g/4oz/1 cup baby corn cobs
115g/4oz/1½ cups fresh shiitake
  mushrooms, halved
3 celery sticks, sliced
1 carrot, sliced diagonally
115g/4oz/1 cup mangetouts (snow peas)
75g/3oz/¾ cup canned, sliced
  bamboo shoots, drained
15ml/1 tbsp cornflour (cornstarch)
15ml/1 tbsp cold water
15ml/1 tbsp dark soy sauce
5ml/1 tsp caster (superfine) sugar
300ml/½ pint/1¼ cups
  vegetable stock
salt and ground white pepper
spring onion (scallion) curls,
  to garnish

1 Bring a pan of water to the boil. Add the egg vermicelli and cook according to instructions on the packet until just tender. Drain, refresh under cold water, drain again, then dry thoroughly on kitchen paper. Set aside.

2 Heat 2.5ml/½ tsp oil in a non-stick frying pan or wok. When it starts to smoke, spread half the noodles over the base. Cook for 2–3 minutes until lightly toasted. Carefully turn the noodles over (they stick together like a cake), cook the other side, then slide on to a heated serving plate. Repeat with the remaining noodles to make two cakes. Keep hot.

3 Heat the remaining oil in the clean pan, then cook the garlic for a few seconds. Halve the corn cobs lengthways, add to the pan with the mushrooms, then stir-fry for 3 minutes, adding a little water, if needed, to prevent the mixture burning. Add the celery, carrot, mangetouts and bamboo shoots. Stir-fry for 2 minutes or until the vegetables are tender-crisp.

4 In a small bowl, mix the cornflour to a paste with the water. Add the mixture to the pan with the soy sauce, sugar and stock. Cook until the sauce thickens, stirring. Season to taste with salt and pepper. Divide the vegetable mixture between the noodle cakes, garnish with the spring onion curls and serve immediately.

Energy 230Kcal/964kJ; Protein 7.9g; Carbohydrate 44.6g, of which sugars 5.4g; Fat 2.4g, of which saturates 0.3g; Cholesterol 0mg; Calcium 52mg; Fibre 2.8g; Sodium 623mg.

Main Courses

Take advantage of the wide variety of grains, beans lentils, and vegetables to make some delicious, wholesome and satisfying meals, such as Mixed Bean and Aubergine Tagine with Mint Yogurt, Fresh Herb Risotto, or Hot Vegetable Couscous with Harissa. All the recipes in this section will make a fabulous main course, as they are all filling, packed full of nutrients and full of flavour.

MIXED VEGETABLES MONK-STYLE ★

*CHINESE MONKS EAT NEITHER MEAT NOR FISH, SO "MONK-STYLE" DISHES ARE IDEAL FOR
VEGETARIANS. THIS TASTY VEGETABLE MIXTURE CREATES A TANGY, LOW-FAT SIDE DISH.*

SERVES FOUR

INGREDIENTS
  50g/2oz dried beancurd or
    tofu sticks
  115g/4oz fresh lotus root, or
    50g/2oz dried
  10g/¼oz dried cloud ears (wood ears)
  8 dried Chinese mushrooms
  10ml/2 tsp vegetable oil
  75g/3oz/¾ cup drained, canned
    straw mushrooms
  115g/4oz/1 cup baby corn cobs,
    cut in half
  30ml/2 tbsp light soy sauce
  15ml/1 tbsp dry sherry
  10ml/2 tsp caster (superfine) sugar
  150ml/¼ pint/⅔ cup vegetable stock
  75g/3oz mangetouts (snow peas),
    trimmed and cut in half
  5ml/1 tsp cornflour (cornstarch)
  15ml/1 tbsp cold water
  salt

1 Put the beancurd or tofu sticks in a
bowl. Cover with hot water and leave to
soak for 1 hour. If using fresh lotus root,
peel and slice it; if using dried lotus
root, place it in a bowl of hot water and
leave to soak for 1 hour.

VARIATIONS
• Use sugar-snap peas in place of
mangetouts (snow peas).
• Use canned or frozen (defrosted) corn
kernels in place of baby corn cobs.
• If you can't easily find dried Chinese
mushrooms, substitute button or
chestnut mushrooms.

2 Prepare the dried wood ears and
Chinese mushrooms by soaking them in
separate bowls of hot water for 15
minutes. Drain the wood ears, trim off
and discard the hard base from each
and cut the rest into bitesize pieces.
Drain the soaked mushrooms, trim off
and discard the stems and chop the
caps roughly.

3 Drain the beancurd or tofu sticks.
Cut them into 5cm/2in long pieces,
discarding any hard pieces. If using
dried lotus root, drain it well.

4 Heat the oil in a non-stick wok or
frying pan. Add the wood ears, Chinese
mushrooms and lotus root and stir-fry
for about 30 seconds.

5 Add the pieces of beancurd or tofu
sticks, straw mushrooms, baby corn cobs,
soy sauce, sherry, sugar and stock.

6 Bring to the boil, then reduce the
heat, cover the wok or pan, lower the
heat and simmer for about 20 minutes.

7 Stir in the mangetouts, with salt to
taste, then cook, uncovered, for a
further 2 minutes.

8 In a small bowl, mix the cornflour
and water to a smooth paste. Add the
cornflour mixture to the wok or pan.
Cook until the sauce thickens, stirring.
Serve immediately.

COOK'S TIP
The flavour of this tasty vegetable mix
improves on keeping, so any leftovers
would taste even better the next day.

Energy 48Kcal/203kJ; Protein 3.3g; Carbohydrate 6.2g, of which sugars 4.6g; Fat 0.9g, of which saturates 0.1g; Cholesterol 0mg; Calcium 90mg; Fibre 1.4g; Sodium 882mg.

MIXED BEAN AND AUBERGINE TAGINE WITH MINT YOGURT ★★

IN THIS TRADITIONAL-STYLE, HEARTY BUT LOW-FAT MOROCCAN DISH, THE MIXED BEANS AND AUBERGINE PROVIDE BOTH TEXTURE AND FLAVOUR, WHICH ARE ENHANCED BY THE HERBS AND CHILLIES.

SERVES SIX

INGREDIENTS

115g/4oz/generous ½ cup dried red
  kidney beans, soaked overnight in
  cold water and drained
115g/4oz/generous ½ cup dried
  black-eyed beans (peas) or
  cannellini beans, soaked overnight
  in cold water and drained
600ml/1 pint/2½ cups water
2 bay leaves
2 celery sticks, each cut into
  4 batons
45ml/3 tbsp olive oil
1 aubergine (eggplant), about 350g/
  12oz, cut into small chunks
1 onion, thinly sliced
3 garlic cloves, crushed
1–2 fresh red chillies, seeded
  and chopped
30ml/2 tbsp tomato purée (paste)
5ml/1 tsp paprika
2 large tomatoes, roughly chopped
300ml/½ pint/1¼ cups
  vegetable stock
15ml/1 tbsp each chopped fresh mint,
  parsley and coriander (cilantro)
salt and ground black pepper
fresh herb sprigs, to garnish
For the mint yogurt
150ml/¼ pint/⅔ cup low-fat natural
  (plain) yogurt
30ml/2 tbsp chopped fresh mint
2 spring onions (scallions), chopped

COOK'S TIPS
When using dried beans, first rinse them
in a sieve (strainer) under cold running
water to wash off any loose, floury matter
before cooking, as this will minimise the
formation of scum during cooking. Then,
soak the beans in plenty of cold water,
overnight, then drain and use as
required. When you store dried beans in
a jar or container, always make a note
of the 'best-before' date. Older dried
beans will still be quite edible, but
fresh ones will need less cooking time.

1 Place the soaked and drained kidney
beans in a large pan of unsalted boiling
water. Bring back to the boil and boil
rapidly for 10 minutes, then drain.
Place the soaked and drained black-
eyed or cannellini beans in a separate
large pan of unsalted boiling water and
boil rapidly for 10 minutes, then drain.

2 Place the 600ml/1 pint/2½ cups of
water in a large tagine or casserole, and
add the bay leaves, celery and beans.
Cover and place in an unheated oven.
Set the oven temperature to 190°C/
375°F/Gas 5. Cook for 1–1½ hours or
until the beans are tender, then drain.
Discard the bay leaves and celery.

3 Heat 30ml/2 tbsp of the oil in a large,
non-stick frying pan or cast-iron tagine
base. Add the aubergine chunks and
cook for 4–5 minutes, until evenly
browned, stirring. Remove the
aubergines from the pan and set aside.

4 Add the remaining oil to the frying
pan or tagine base, then add the onion
and cook for about 4–5 minutes, until
softened, stirring. Add the garlic and
red chillies and cook for a further
5 minutes until the onion is golden,
stirring frequently.

5 Reset the oven temperature to
160°C/325°F/Gas 3. Add the tomato
purée and paprika to the onion mixture
and cook for 1–2 minutes. Add the
tomatoes, aubergine chunks, beans
and stock, then season to taste with
salt and pepper.

6 Cover the tagine base with the lid or,
if using a frying pan, transfer the
contents to a clay tagine or casserole.
Place in the oven and cook for 1 hour.

7 Meanwhile, mix together the yogurt,
mint and spring onions in a small
serving bowl. Just before serving, add
the chopped mint, parsley and
coriander to the tagine and lightly mix
through the vegetables. Garnish with
fresh herb sprigs and serve with the
mint yogurt.

Energy 210Kcal/885kJ; Protein 12.1g; Carbohydrate 26.8g, of which sugars 8.8g; Fat 6.9g, of which saturates 1.1g; Cholesterol 0mg; Calcium 145mg; Fibre 8.5g; Sodium 55mg.

CONCHIGLIE WITH ROASTED VEGETABLES ★★

NOTHING COULD BE SIMPLER — OR MORE DELICIOUS — THAN TOSSING FRESHLY COOKED PASTA WITH ROASTED VEGETABLES. THE COMBINATION IS SUPERB AND THIS DISH IS LOW IN FAT TOO!

SERVES SIX

INGREDIENTS
1 red (bell) pepper, seeded and cut into 1cm/½in squares
1 yellow or orange (bell) pepper, seeded and cut into 1cm/½in squares
1 small aubergine (eggplant), roughly diced
2 courgettes (zucchini), roughly diced
30ml/2 tbsp extra virgin olive oil
15ml/1 tbsp chopped fresh flat leaf parsley
5ml/1 tsp dried oregano or marjoram
250g/9oz baby Italian plum tomatoes, halved lengthways
2 garlic cloves, roughly chopped
350–400g/12–14oz/3–3½ cups dried conchiglie
salt and ground black pepper
4–6 fresh marjoram or oregano flowers, to garnish

1 Preheat the oven to 190°C/375°F/ Gas 5. Rinse the prepared peppers, aubergine and courgettes in a colander under cold running water, drain well, then put the vegetables in a large, non-stick roasting pan.

2 Drizzle the olive oil over the vegetables and sprinkle with the chopped fresh and dried herbs. Add salt and pepper to taste and toss to mix well. Roast in the oven for about 30 minutes, stirring two or three time during cooking.

3 Stir the halved tomatoes and chopped garlic into the vegetable mixture, then roast for a further 20 minutes, stirring once or twice. Meanwhile, cook the pasta according to the instructions on the packet.

4 Drain the pasta and transfer it to a warmed serving bowl. Add the roasted vegetables and any cooking juices and toss to mix well. Serve the hot pasta and vegetables in warmed bowls, sprinkling each portion with fresh herb flowers, to garnish.

Energy 277Kcal/1171kJ; Protein 9.5g; Carbohydrate 50.3g, of which sugars 8.7g; Fat 5.5g, of which saturates 0.8g; Cholesterol 0mg; Calcium 52mg; Fibre 4.6g; Sodium 11mg.

TOMATOES AND WILD MUSHROOMS ★

T... RD STAND-BY AS IT DOESN'T RELY ON ANYTHING FRESH, APART FROM
TH... PERFECT FOR A LOW-FAT END-OF-WEEK MEAL.

SERVE...

INGRED...
2 x 15...
wild ...
175ml/...
10ml/2 t...
2 shallots...
2 garlic cl...
a few sprigs...
chopped, p...
1 handful fres...
parsley, chop...
15g/½oz/1 tbsp...
400g/14oz can...
400g/14oz/3½ cu...
25g/1oz/⅓ cup gra...
Parmesan cheese...
salt and ground blac...

1 Put the dried mushroo...
pour the warm water over...
leave to soak for 15–20 mi...
into a fine sieve (strainer) s...
bowl and squeeze the mushr...
your fingers to release as muc...
as possible. Reserve the mushr...
and the strained liquid.

2 Heat the oil in a non-stick frying
pan and cook the shallots, garlic and
chopped herbs over a low heat for
about 5 minutes, stirring frequently.
Add the butter and soaked mushrooms,
and stir until the butter has melted.
Season well with salt and pepper.

3 Stir in the tomatoes and the reserved
liquid from the soaked mushrooms.
Bring to the boil, then reduce the heat,
cover and simmer for about 20 minutes,
stirring occasionally. Meanwhile, cook
the pasta according to the instructions
on the packet.

4 Taste the sauce and adjust the
seasoning. Drain the pasta, reserving
some of the cooking water, and tip the
pasta into a warmed large bowl. Add the
sauce and the grated Parmesan and toss
to mix. Add a little cooking water if you
prefer a runnier sauce. Serve immediately,
garnished with marjoram sprigs.

VARIATION
If you have a bottle of wine open, red or
white, add a splash when you add the
canned tomatoes.

COOK'S TIP
Serve with a little extra Parmesan
cheese, which can be handed around
separately, if you like, but remember
this will add to the calorie and fat
content of the dish.

Energy 281Kcal/1193kJ; Protein 10.4g; Carbohydrate 52.3g, of which sugars 4.9g; Fat 4.9g, of which saturates 1.9g; Cholesterol 7mg; Calcium 75mg; Fibre 2.8g; Sodium 62mg.

PENNE WITH GREEN VEGETABLE SAUCE ★★

*LIGHTLY COOKED FRESH GREEN VEGETABLES ARE TOSSED WITH HOT PASTA TO CREATE THIS
DELICATELY-FAVOURED LOW-FAT DISH, IDEAL FOR A DECEPTIVELY FILLING SUPPER.*

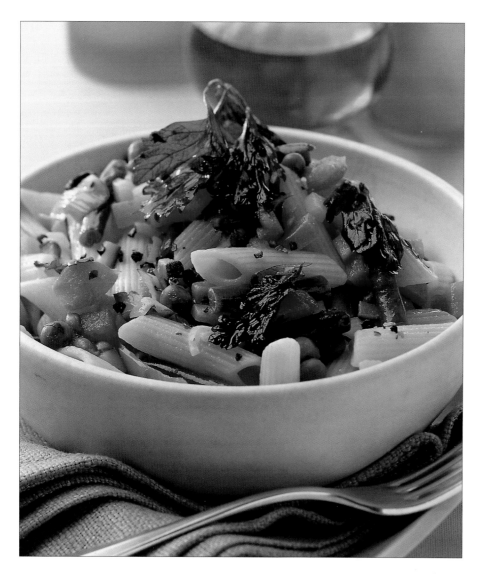

2 Heat the oil in a non-stick frying pan.
Add the carrots and leek. Sprinkle the
sugar over and cook for about 5
minutes, all the time stirring.

3 Stir in the courgette, green beans,
peas and plenty of salt and pepper.
Cover and cook over a low to medium
heat for 5–8 minutes, or until the
vegetables are tender, stirring
occasionally.

4 Meanwhile, cook the pasta in a large
pan of salted boiling water, according to
the packet instructions, until it is tender
or *al dente*. Drain the pasta well and
keep it hot until it is ready to serve.

5 Stir the chopped parsley and plum
tomatoes into the vegetable mixture and
adjust the seasoning to taste. Toss the
vegetable mixture with the cooked pasta
and serve immediately.

SERVES FOUR

INGREDIENTS
  2 carrots
  1 courgette (zucchini)
  75g/3oz green beans
  1 small leek
  2 ripe Italian plum tomatoes
  1 handful fresh flat leaf parsley
  15ml/1 tbsp extra virgin olive oil
  2.5ml/½ tsp granulated sugar
  115g/4oz/1 cup frozen peas
  350g/12oz/3 cups dried penne
  salt and ground black pepper

1 Dice the carrots and the courgette
finely. Trim the green beans, then cut
them into 2cm/¾in lengths. Slice the
leek thinly. Skin and dice the tomatoes.
Finely chop the parsley and set aside.

VARIATIONS
Use 1 standard or red onion in place of
leek. Use frozen baby broad (fava) beans
in place of peas.

Energy 400Kcal/1692kJ; Protein 15.3g; Carbohydrate 76.9g, of which sugars 11.7g; Fat 5.6g, of which saturates 0.9g; Cholesterol 0mg; Calcium 76mg; Fibre 7.2g; Sodium 21mg.

PASTA WITH TOMATO AND CHILLI SAUCE ★★

THIS DELICIOUS LOW-FAT PASTA DISH COMES FROM LAZIO, IN ITALY, WHERE IT IS DESCRIBED AS "ALL'ARRABBIATA" WHICH MEANS ANGRY — REFERRING TO THE HEAT THAT COMES FROM THE CHILLI.

SERVES FOUR

INGREDIENTS

500g/1¼lb sugocasa (see Cook's Tip)
2 garlic cloves, crushed
150ml/¼ pint/½ cup dry white wine
15ml/1 tbsp sun-dried tomato paste
1 fresh red chilli
300g/11oz/2¾ cups penne or tortiglioni
60ml/4 tbsp finely chopped fresh flat
   leaf parsley
salt and ground black pepper
grated fresh Pecorino cheese,
   to serve

COOK'S TIP

Sugocasa resembles passata (bottled strained tomatoes), but it is rougher.

3 Remove the chilli from the tomato sauce and add 30ml/2 tbsp of the parsley. Taste for seasoning. If you prefer a hotter taste, chop some or all of the chilli and return it to the sauce.

4 Drain the pasta and transfer it to a warmed large bowl. Pour the tomato sauce over the pasta and toss to mix. Serve at once, sprinkled with grated Pecorino and the remaining parsley.

1 Mix the sugocasa, garlic, wine, sun-dried tomato paste and whole chilli in a pan and bring to the boil. Cover and simmer gently, stirring occasionally.

2 Meanwhile, drop the pasta into a large pan of salted rapidly boiling water. Reduce the heat and simmer for 10–12 minutes or until *al dente*.

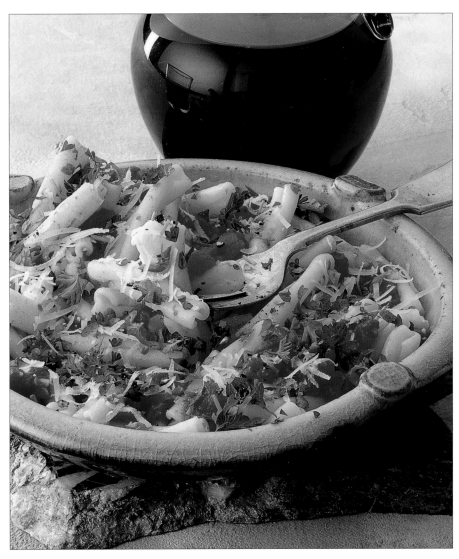

Energy 310Kcal/1316kJ; Protein 10.5g; Carbohydrate 60.6g, of which sugars 7.4g; Fat 1.9g, of which saturates 0.3g; Cholesterol 0mg; Calcium 57mg; Fibre 4.2g; Sodium 28mg.

TAGLIATELLE ON BROCCOLI AND SPINACH ★★

THIS IS A HEARTY, FRESHLY-PREPARED VEGETARIAN SUPPER DISH. IT IS NUTRITIOUS AND FILLING, AND NEEDS NO ACCOMPANIMENT. IF YOU LIKE, YOU CAN USE TAGLIATELLE FLECKED WITH HERBS.

SERVES FOUR

INGREDIENTS
2 heads of broccoli
450g/1lb fresh spinach,
  stalks removed
freshly grated nutmeg, to taste
450g/1lb fresh or dried
  egg tagliatelle
30ml/2 tbsp extra virgin olive oil
juice of ½ lemon, or to taste
salt and ground black pepper
grated fresh Parmesan cheese,
  to serve

COOK'S TIP
Always grate nutmeg freshly as the ground spice loses its flavour quickly.

1 Put the broccoli in the basket of a steamer, cover and steam over a pan of boiling water for 10 minutes. Add the spinach to the broccoli, cover and steam for 4–5 minutes or until both are tender. Towards the end of the cooking time, sprinkle the vegetables with freshly grated nutmeg and salt and pepper to taste. Transfer the vegetables to a colander.

2 Add salt to the water in the steamer and fill the steamer pan with boiling water, then add the pasta and cook according to the instructions on the packet. Meanwhile, chop the broccoli and spinach in the colander.

3 Drain the pasta. Heat the oil in the pasta pan, add the pasta and chopped vegetables and toss over a medium heat until evenly mixed. Sprinkle in the lemon juice and plenty of black pepper, then taste and add more lemon juice, salt and nutmeg, if you like. Serve immediately, sprinkled with grated fresh Parmesan cheese and black pepper.

VARIATIONS
• If you like, add a sprinkling of crushed dried chillies with the black pepper in Step 3.
• To add both texture and protein, garnish the finished dish with one or two handfuls of toasted pine nuts. They are often served with broccoli and spinach in Italy. Remember though, they will add extra calories and fat to the recipe.

Energy 504Kcal/2130kJ; Protein 22.2g; Carbohydrate 87.4g, of which sugars 7.3g; Fat 9.6g, of which saturates 1.4g; Cholesterol 0mg; Calcium 290mg; Fibre 8.9g; Sodium 171mg.

PASTA WITH ONION AND SHREDDED CABBAGE ★★

SLOWLY-COOKED ONIONS, CABBAGE, PARMESAN AND PINE NUTS COMBINE WITH BALSAMIC VINEGAR TO PRODUCE A LOVELY SPICY TANG TO THIS PASTA CLASSIC.

SERVES SIX

INGREDIENTS

   15g/½oz/1 tbsp butter
   15ml/1 tbsp extra virgin olive oil
   500g/1¼lb Spanish (Bermuda)
     onions, halved and thinly sliced
   5–10ml/1–2 tsp balsamic vinegar
   400–500g/14oz–1¼lb cavolo nero,
     spring greens (collards), kale or
     Brussels sprout tops, shredded
   400–500g/14–1¼lb/3½–5 cups
     dried pasta shapes (such as penne
     or fusilli)
   50g/2oz/⅔ cup grated fresh
     Parmesan cheese
   25g/1oz/¼ cup pine nuts, toasted,
     to serve
   salt and ground black pepper

VARIATION

To make a delicious pilaff, cook 250g/ 9oz/1¼ cups brown basmati rice and use in place of the pasta.

1 Heat the butter and olive oil together in a large, non-stick pan. Stir in the onions, cover and cook very gently for about 20 minutes, until very soft, stirring occasionally.

2 Uncover the pan and continue to cook gently until the onions have turned golden. Add the balsamic vinegar and season well, then cook for a further 1–2 minutes. Remove from the heat and set aside.

3 Blanch the cavolo nero, spring greens, kale or Brussels sprout tops in a pan of lightly salted boiling water for about 3 minutes. Drain well and add to the onions, then cook over a low heat for 3–4 minutes.

4 Cook the pasta in a separate pan of lightly salted boiling water for 8–12 minutes, or according to the packet instructions, until *al dente*. Drain the pasta, then add it to the pan of onions and greens and toss thoroughly to mix.

5 Season well with salt and pepper and stir in half the grated Parmesan cheese. Transfer the pasta to warmed plates. Scatter the pine nuts and more Parmesan on top and serve immediately.

Energy 349Kcal/1472kJ; Protein 13.2g; Carbohydrate 59.3g, of which sugars 10.2g; Fat 8.1g, of which saturates 3.4g; Cholesterol 14mg; Calcium 171mg; Fibre 4.5g; Sodium 115mg.

FRESH RAVIOLI WITH PUMPKIN ★★

THIS IS A VERY SIMPLE, LOW-FAT VERSION OF A CHRISTMAS EVE SPECIALITY FROM LOMBARDY. IN TRADITIONAL RECIPES THE PUMPKIN FILLING IS FLAVOURED WITH MOSTARDA DI FRUTTA (A KIND OF SWEET FRUIT PICKLE), CRUSHED AMARETTI AND SUGAR. HERE THE PUMPKIN IS SEASONED WITH FRESH PARMESAN AND NUTMEG. IT IS QUITE SWEET ENOUGH FOR MOST TASTES.

SERVES EIGHT

INGREDIENTS
　1 quantity Pasta with Eggs
　40g/1½oz/3 tbsp butter
　grated fresh Parmesan cheese,
　　to serve
For the filling
　450g/1lb piece of pumpkin
　10ml/2 tsp olive oil
　25g/1oz/⅓ cup grated fresh
　　Parmesan cheese
　freshly grated nutmeg, to taste
　salt and ground black pepper

1 Make the filling. Preheat the oven to 220°C/425°F/Gas 7. Cut the piece of pumpkin into chunks and remove the seeds and fibres. Put the chunks, skin side down, in a roasting pan and drizzle the oil over the pumpkin flesh. Roast in the oven for 30 minutes, turning the pieces over once or twice.

2 Leave the roasted pumpkin until it is cool enough to handle, then scrape the flesh out into a bowl and discard the pumpkin skin.

3 Mash the roasted pumpkin flesh with a fork, then add the grated Parmesan and freshly grated nutmeg and salt and pepper to taste. Stir well to mix, then set aside until cold.

4 Using a pasta machine, roll out one-quarter of the pasta into a 90cm–1m/36in–1yd strip. Cut the strip with a sharp knife into two 45–50cm/18–20in lengths (you can do this during rolling if the strip gets too long to manage).

5 Using a teaspoon, put 10–12 little mounds of the filling along one side of one of the pasta strips, spacing them evenly.

6 Brush a little water around each mound, then fold the plain side of the pasta strip over the mounds of filling. Starting from the folded edge, press down gently with your fingertips around each mound, pushing the air out at the unfolded edge. Sprinkle lightly with flour.

VARIATION
You can buy *mostarda di frutta* at Italian delicatessens, especially at Christmas time. If you would like to try some in the filling, add about 45ml/3 tbsp, together with a few crushed amaretti.

7 With a fluted pasta wheel, cut along each long side, then in between each mound to make small square shapes. Put the ravioli on floured dish towels, sprinkle lightly with flour and leave to dry, while repeating the process with the remaining pasta to get 80–96 ravioli altogether.

8 Drop the ravioli into a large pan of salted boiling water, bring back to the boil and boil for 4–5 minutes. Meanwhile, melt the butter in a small pan until it is sizzling.

9 Drain the ravioli and divide them equally among eight warmed dinner plates or large bowls. Drizzle the sizzling butter over the ravioli and serve immediately, sprinkled with grated Parmesan. Hand round a little more grated Parmesan separately, if you like.

Energy 236Kcal/998kJ; Protein 7.7g; Carbohydrate 38.3g, of which sugars 2.6g; Fat 6.9g, of which saturates 3.5g; Cholesterol 14mg; Calcium 67mg; Fibre 2g; Sodium 66mg.

SPAGHETTI WITH FRESH TOMATO SAUCE ★★

*THE HEAT FROM THE PASTA WILL RELEASE THE AROMATIC FLAVOURS OF SOFT PLUM OR SWEET
CHERRY TOMATOES — TOP QUALITY TOMATOES REALLY ADD TO THE TASTE OF THIS SAUCE.*

SERVES FOUR

INGREDIENTS
  675g/1½lb ripe Italian
    plum tomatoes or sweet
    cherry tomatoes
  30ml/2 tbsp extra virgin olive oil or
    sunflower oil
  1 onion, finely chopped
  350g/12oz fresh or dried spaghetti
  a small handful of fresh basil leaves
  salt and ground black pepper
  coarsely shaved fresh Parmesan
    cheese, to serve

COOK'S TIPS
• The Italian plum tomatoes called San
Marzano are the best variety to use.
When fully ripe, they have thin skins that
peel off easily.
• In Italy, cooks often make this sauce in
bulk in the summer months and freeze it
for later use. Let it cool, then freeze in
usable quantities in rigid containers.
Thaw, before reheating thoroughly.

1 With a sharp knife, cut a cross in the
base end of each tomato. Plunge the
tomatoes, a few at a time, into a bowl of
boiling water. Leave for 30 seconds or
so, then lift them out with a slotted
spoon and drop them into a bowl of
cold water. Drain well. The skin will
have begun to peel back from the
crosses. Remove it entirely.

2 Place the tomatoes on a chopping
board and cut into quarters, then
eighths, then chop as finely as possible.

3 Heat the oil in a large, non-stick pan,
add the onion and cook over a low heat
for about 5 minutes until softened and
lightly coloured, stirring frequently.

4 Add the tomatoes, season with salt
and pepper to taste, bring to a simmer,
then reduce the heat to low and
cover the pan with a lid. Cook for
30–40 minutes until the mixture is
thick, stirring occasionally.

5 Meanwhile, cook the pasta according
to the instructions on the packet. Shred
the basil leaves finely, or tear them into
small pieces.

6 Remove the sauce from the heat, stir
in the basil and adjust the seasoning to
taste. Drain the pasta in a colander.
Transfer the spaghetti to a warmed
bowl, pour the sauce over and toss the
mixture well. Serve immediately, with
shaved Parmesan handed around in a
separate bowl.

Energy 383Kcal/1623kJ; Protein 11.9g; Carbohydrate 71.3g, of which sugars 9g; Fat 7.6g, of which saturates 1.1g; Cholesterol 0mg; Calcium 38mg; Fibre 4.4g; Sodium 18mg.

FRESH HERB RISOTTO ★

HERE IS A LIGHT AND TASTY RISOTTO TO CELEBRATE THE ABUNDANCE OF SUMMER HERBS. AN
AROMATIC BLEND OF OREGANO, CHIVES, PARSLEY AND BASIL IS COMBINED WITH ARBORIO RICE.

SERVES SIX

INGREDIENTS
  90g/3½oz/½ cup wild rice
  15g/½oz/1 tbsp butter
  10ml/2 tsp olive oil
  1 small onion, finely chopped
  450g/1lb/2¼ cups arborio rice
  300ml/½ pint/1¼ cups dry white
    wine
  1.2 litres/2 pints/5 cups simmering
    vegetable stock
  45ml/3 tbsp chopped fresh oregano
  45ml/3 tbsp chopped fresh chives
  60ml/4 tbsp chopped fresh flat
    leaf parsley
  60ml/4 tbsp chopped fresh basil
  40g/1½oz/½ cup grated fresh
    Parmesan cheese
  salt and ground black pepper

1 Cook the wild rice in a pan of salted boiling water according to the instructions on the packet, then drain and set aside.

2 Heat the butter and oil in a large, heavy, non-stick pan. When the butter has melted, add the onion and cook for 3 minutes. Add the arborio rice and cook for 2 minutes, stirring to coat.

COOK'S TIPS
Risotto rice is essential to achieve the correct creamy texture in this dish. Other types of rice simply will not do. Fresh herbs are also a must, but you can use tarragon, chervil, marjoram or thyme instead of the ones listed here, if you prefer.

3 Pour in the white wine and bring to the boil. Reduce the heat and cook for 10 minutes, or until all the wine has been absorbed.

4 Add the hot vegetable stock, a little at a time, waiting for each quantity to be absorbed before adding more, and stirring constantly. After 20–25 minutes the rice should be tender and creamy. Season well with salt and pepper.

5 Add the chopped herbs and wild rice, then heat for 2 minutes, stirring frequently. Stir in two-thirds of the Parmesan, if using, and cook until melted. Serve sprinkled with the remaining Parmesan, if using.

Energy 378Kcal/1578kJ; Protein 9.6g; Carbohydrate 72.8g, of which sugars 0.7g; Fat 4.8g, of which saturates 2.1g; Cholesterol 9mg; Calcium 115mg; Fibre 0.5g; Sodium 83mg.

RISOTTO WITH BASIL AND RICOTTA ★★

THIS IS A WELL-FLAVOURED, LIGHT VEGETARIAN RISOTTO, WHICH BENEFITS FROM THE DISTINCTIVE PUNGENCY OF BASIL, MELLOWED WITH SMOOTH RICOTTA.

SERVES FOUR

INGREDIENTS
10ml/2 tsp olive oil
1 onion, finely chopped
275g/10oz/scant 1½ cups risotto rice
1 litre/1¾ pints/4 cups simmering
  vegetable stock
175g/6oz/¾ cup ricotta cheese
50g/2oz/generous 1 cup finely
  chopped fresh basil leaves, plus
  extra leaves to garnish
40g/1½oz/½ cup grated fresh
  Parmesan cheese
salt and ground black pepper

1 Heat the oil in a large, non-stick pan and cook the onion pieces over a gentle heat stirring frequently until they are soft.

2 Stir in the rice. Cook for a few minutes until the rice is coated with oil and is slightly translucent, stirring.

3 Pour in about a quarter of the stock. Cook until all the stock has been absorbed, stirring, then add another ladleful of stock. Continue in this manner, adding more stock when the previous ladleful has been absorbed, for about 20 minutes, or until the rice is just tender.

4 Spoon the ricotta cheese into a bowl and break it up a little with a fork. Stir into the risotto along with the basil and Parmesan. Adjust the seasoning to taste, then cover and allow to stand for 2–3 minutes before serving, garnished with basil leaves.

Energy 373Kcal/1557kJ; Protein 16.1g; Carbohydrate 57.9g, of which sugars 2.7g; Fat 8.8g, of which saturates 4.6g; Cholesterol 21mg; Calcium 213mg; Fibre 0.8g; Sodium 305mg.

ROSEMARY RISOTTO <u>WITH</u> BORLOTTI BEANS ★★

THIS IS A TASTY, LOW-FAT RISOTTO WITH A SUBTLE AND COMPLEX TASTE, FROM THE HEADY FLAVOURS OF ROSEMARY TO THE SAVOURY BEANS AND THE FRUITY-SWEET TASTES OF THE CHEESES.

SERVES FOUR

INGREDIENTS
- 400g/14oz can borlotti beans
- 10ml/2 tsp olive oil
- 1 onion, chopped
- 2 garlic cloves, crushed
- 275g/10oz/scant 1½ cups risotto rice
- 175ml/6fl oz/¾ cup dry white wine
- 900ml–1 litre/1½–1¾ pints/ 3¾–4 cups simmering vegetable stock
- 30ml/2 tbsp mascarpone
- 40g/1½oz/½ cup grated fresh Parmesan cheese, plus extra to serve (optional)
- 5ml/1 tsp chopped fresh rosemary
- salt and ground black pepper

1 Drain the canned borlotti beans, rinse them well under plenty of cold water and drain again.

2 Purée about two-thirds of the beans fairly coarsely in a blender or food processor. Set the remainder aside.

3 Heat the oil in a large, non-stick pan and gently cook the onion and garlic for 6–8 minutes, or until very soft. Add the rice and cook over a medium heat for a few minutes until the grains are thoroughly coated in oil and are slightly translucent, stirring constantly.

VARIATION
Fresh thyme or marjoram could be used for this risotto instead of rosemary, if you prefer. Experiment with different herbs to make your own speciality dish.

4 Pour in the wine. Cook over a medium heat for 2–3 minutes until the wine has been absorbed, stirring constantly. Gradually add the stock, a ladleful at a time, waiting for each quantity to be absorbed before adding more, and stirring constantly.

5 When the rice is about three-quarters cooked, stir in the bean purée. Continue to cook the risotto, adding any stock that remains, until it has reached a creamy consistency and the rice is tender but still has a bit of "bite".

6 Add the reserved beans, with the mascarpone, Parmesan and rosemary, then season to taste with salt and pepper. Stir thoroughly, then cover and leave to stand for about 5 minutes, so that the risotto absorbs the flavours fully and the rice finishes cooking. Serve with extra Parmesan, if you like.

Energy 419Kcal/1752kJ; Protein 15.1g; Carbohydrate 68.8g, of which sugars 3.9g; Fat 6.2g, of which saturates 2.7g; Cholesterol 12mg; Calcium 198mg; Fibre 4.5g; Sodium 412mg.

THREE-ALLIUM RISOTTO ★★

GARLIC AND CHIVES ARE ADDED TO SOFTENED, GOLDEN BROWN ONIONS TO CREATE THIS FLAVOURFUL RISOTTO. FRIED ONIONS BRING A DELICIOUS CHANGE OF TEXTURE TO THE COOKED DISH.

SERVES SIX

INGREDIENTS
25g/1oz/2 tbsp butter
30ml/2 tbsp olive oil
1 onion, finely chopped
4 garlic cloves, finely chopped
350g/12oz/1¾ cups risotto rice
150ml/¼ pint/⅔ cup dry white wine
a pinch of saffron threads
about 1.2 litres/2 pints/5 cups hot
  vegetable stock
1 large yellow onion, thinly sliced
15g/½oz fresh chives, chopped,
  plus extra to garnish
25g/1oz/⅓ cup grated fresh
  Parmesan cheese
salt and ground black pepper

1 Melt half the butter with 15ml/1 tbsp of the oil in a large, deep, non-stick frying pan or heavy pan. Add the onion with a pinch of salt and cook over a very low heat, for 10–15 minutes, until softened and just turning golden, stirring frequently.

2 Add the garlic and rice and cook, for 3–4 minutes, until the rice is coated and looks translucent, stirring constantly. Season to taste with a little salt and pepper.

3 Pour in the wine and stir in the saffron with a ladleful of hot stock. Cook slowly until the liquid is absorbed, stirring frequently.

4 Continue cooking for 18–20 minutes, adding 1–2 ladlefuls of stock at a time, until the rice is swollen and tender outside, but still *al dente* on the inside. Keep the heat low and stir frequently. The finished risotto should be moist, but not like soup.

5 Meanwhile, separate the slices of yellow onion into rings while the risotto is cooking. Heat the remaining oil in a non-stick frying pan. Cook the onion rings slowly at first until soft, then increase the heat and fry briskly until they are brown and crisp. Drain on kitchen paper.

6 Beat the chives, the remaining butter and half the Parmesan into the risotto until it looks creamy. Taste and adjust the seasoning, if necessary.

7 Serve the risotto in warm serving bowls, topped with the crisp onions and chives.

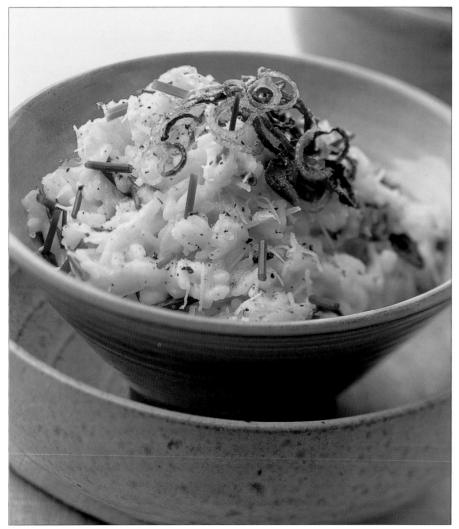

Energy 316Kcal/1316kJ; Protein 6.3g; Carbohydrate 48.3g, of which sugars 1.3g; Fat 8.8g, of which saturates 3.6g; Cholesterol 13mg; Calcium 69mg; Fibre 0.3g; Sodium 72mg.

HOT VEGETABLE COUSCOUS WITH HARISSA ★★

A NORTH AFRICAN FAVOURITE, THIS DELICIOUSLY SPICY DISH, MADE RICH WITH TOMATOES AND PRUNES, MAKES AN EXCELLENT AND UNUSUAL LOW-FAT MEAL FOR VEGETARIANS.

SERVES FOUR

INGREDIENTS
  15ml/1 tbsp extra virgin olive oil or
    sunflower oil
  1 onion, chopped
  2 garlic cloves, crushed
  5ml/1 tsp ground cumin
  5ml/1 tsp paprika
  400g/14oz can chopped tomatoes
  300ml/½ pint/1¼ cups
    vegetable stock
  1 cinnamon stick
  a generous pinch of saffron threads
  4 baby aubergines (eggplants),
    quartered
  8 baby courgettes (zucchini), trimmed
  8 baby carrots
  225g/8oz/1⅓ cups couscous, soaked
  400g/14oz can chickpeas, rinsed
    and drained
  175g/6oz/¾ cup pitted prunes
  45ml/3 tbsp chopped fresh parsley
  45ml/3 tbsp chopped fresh
    coriander (cilantro)
  10–15ml/2–3 tsp harissa
  salt

COOK'S TIPS
Harissa is a very hot chilli sauce from North Africa. It looks rather like puréed tomatoes but needs to be treated with a great deal more caution. Use it sparingly. When choosing a steamer, metal sieve (strainer) or colander for steaming the couscous, check that it fits neatly over the pan in which you intend to cook the vegetables.

1 Heat the oil in a large, non-stick pan. Add the onion and garlic and cook gently for 5 minutes. Add the cumin and paprika and cook for 1 minute, stirring.

2 Add the tomatoes, stock, cinnamon stick, saffron, aubergines, courgettes and carrots, with water to cover. Season with salt. Bring to the boil, then reduce the heat, cover and cook for 20 minutes until the vegetables are just tender.

3 Line a steamer with muslin (cheesecloth). Steam the couscous according to the instructions on the packet. Add the chickpeas and prunes to the vegetables and cook for 5 minutes.

4 Place the couscous on top of the vegetable pan, cover, and cook for 5 minutes until the couscous is hot.

5 Stir the parsley and coriander into the vegetables. Heap the couscous on to a warmed serving plate. Using a slotted spoon, arrange the vegetables over the couscous. Spoon over a little of the remaining liquid and combine.

6 Stir the harissa into the remaining reserved liquid and serve separately.

Energy 396Kcal/1667kJ; Protein 15.1g; Carbohydrate 73.2g, of which sugars 28.3g; Fat 6.6g, of which saturates 0.9g; Cholesterol 0mg; Calcium 138mg; Fibre 12.2g; Sodium 43mg.

PROVENÇAL RICE ★★

SWEET CHERRY TOMATOES, PURPLE AUBERGINES AND TENDER GREEN COURGETTES ARE A DELICIOUS
COMBINATION IN THIS FLAVOURFUL LOW-FAT DISH ORIGINATING FROM THE SOUTH OF FRANCE.

SERVES FOUR

INGREDIENTS

2 onions
30ml/2 tbsp extra virgin olive oil or
    sunflower oil
225g/8oz/generous 1 cup long grain
    brown rice
10ml/2 tsp mustard seeds
600ml/1 pint/2½ cups vegetable stock
1 large or 2 small red (bell) peppers,
    seeded and cut into chunks
1 small aubergine (eggplant), diced
2–3 courgettes (zucchini), sliced
about 12 cherry tomatoes
5–6 fresh basil leaves, torn into pieces
2 garlic cloves, finely chopped
60ml/4 tbsp white wine
60ml/4 tbsp passata (bottled strained
    tomatoes) or tomato juice
2 hard-boiled eggs, peeled and cut
    into wedges
8 stuffed green olives, sliced
15ml/1 tbsp capers
3 sun-dried tomatoes in oil, drained
    and sliced (optional)
salt and ground black pepper

1 Preheat the oven to 200°C/400°F/
Gas 6. Roughly chop 1 onion. Heat
10ml/2 tsp of the oil in a non-stick pan
and cook the chopped onion over a low
heat for 5–6 minutes until softened.

2 Add the rice and mustard seeds.
Cook for 2 minutes, stirring, then add
the stock and a little salt. Bring to the
boil, then reduce the heat, cover and
simmer for 35 minutes or until the rice
is tender and fairly dry.

3 Meanwhile, cut the remaining onion
into wedges. Put these in a roasting pan
with the peppers, aubergine, courgettes
and cherry tomatoes. Sprinkle over
the basil and garlic. Drizzle over the
remaining oil and sprinkle with salt
and pepper. Roast in the oven for
15–20 minutes or until the vegetables
begin to char, stirring halfway through
cooking. Remove from the oven, then
reduce the oven temperature to 180°C/
350°F/Gas 4.

4 Spoon the rice into an earthenware
casserole. Put the roasted vegetables on
top, together with any juices from the
roasting pan, then pour over the combined
wine and passata or tomato juice.

5 Arrange the egg wedges on top of
the vegetables, with the sliced olives,
capers and sun-dried tomatoes, if using.
Cover and cook for 15–20 minutes until
heated through. Serve immediately, in
warmed bowls.

Energy 359Kcal/1511kJ; Protein 9.5g; Carbohydrate 59.2g, of which sugars 12.1g; Fat 10g, of which saturates 1.8g; Cholesterol 48mg; Calcium 74mg; Fibre 5.7g; Sodium 114mg.

SPICED TOMATO RICE ★★

THIS RECIPE IS PROOF THAT YOU DON'T NEED ELABORATE INGREDIENTS OR COMPLICATED COOKING
METHODS TO CREATE A DELICIOUS LOW-FAT VEGETARIAN DISH.

SERVES FOUR

INGREDIENTS
  15ml/1 tbsp sunflower oil
  2.5ml/½ tsp onion seeds
  1 onion, sliced
  4 tomatoes, sliced
  1 orange or yellow (bell) pepper,
    seeded and sliced
  5ml/1 tsp grated fresh root ginger
  1 garlic clove
  5ml/1 tsp chilli powder
  1 potato, diced
  7.5ml/1½ tsp salt
  400g/14oz/2 cups basmati
    rice, soaked
  750ml/1¼ pints/3 cups water
  30–45ml/2–3 tbsp chopped
    fresh coriander (cilantro)

1 Heat the oil in a non-stick pan and cook the onion seeds for 30 seconds. Add the onion and cook for about 5 minutes.

2 Stir in the tomatoes, pepper, ginger, garlic, chilli powder, potato and salt. Stir-fry over a medium heat for about 5 minutes.

3 Drain the rice and add it to the pan, then stir for about 1 minute until the grains are well coated. Pour in the water and bring the rice to the boil, then reduce the heat, give the mixture a stir, cover the pan and cook the rice for 12–15 minutes.

4 Remove the pan from the heat, without lifting the lid, and leave the rice to stand for 5 minutes. Stir in the chopped coriander. Serve in warmed bowls, forking the rice over gently as you do so. If you like, sprinkle a little extra coriander on top of each portion.

Energy 463Kcal/1940kJ; Protein 10g; Carbohydrate 96.2g, of which sugars 7.6g; Fat 4.1g, of which saturates 0.5g; Cholesterol 0mg; Calcium 57mg; Fibre 3g; Sodium 21mg.

SIDE DISHES AND ACCOMPANIMENTS

Vegetarian side dishes provide a tasty anytime snack in themselves or can be served to accompany any of the main courses featured in this book. In this chapter, a collection of low-fat side dishes are presented, including aromatic dishes such as Green Beans with Tomatoes, Marinated Mushrooms and Thai-Spiced Rice, so you'll find the perfect accompaniment to complement your meal.

FENNEL GRATIN ★

SWEET AND AROMATIC FENNEL MAKES A HEALTHY AND TASTY LOW-FAT LIGHT SNACK OR VEGETABLE ACCOMPANIMENT. MUCH USED IN MEDITERRANEAN COOKING IT IS A VERY VERSATILE STAND-BY.

SERVES SIX

INGREDIENTS

   2 fennel bulbs, about 675g/
     1½lb total
   300ml/½ pint/1¼ cups semi-
     skimmed (low-fat) milk
   15g/½oz/1 tbsp butter
   15ml/1 tbsp plain (all-purpose) flour
   25g/1oz/scant ½ cup dry
     white breadcrumbs
   40g/1½oz Gruyère cheese, grated
   salt and ground black pepper

1 Preheat the oven to 240°C/475°F/ Gas 9. Discard the fennel stalks and root ends. Slice the fennel into quarters and place in a large pan. Pour over the milk, bring to boil; reduce the heat and simmer for 10–15 minutes, or until tender.

2 Grease a small ovenproof dish. Remove the fennel pieces with a slotted spoon, reserving the milk. Arrange the fennel pieces in the ovenproof dish.

3 Melt the butter in a small, non-stick pan and add the flour. Stir well, then gradually whisk in the reserved milk.

4 Cook the sauce until thickened, stirring. Pour the sauce over the fennel pieces, then sprinkle with the breadcrumbs and Gruyère. Season to taste with salt and pepper, then bake in the oven for about 20 minutes, or until browned. Serve.

VARIATIONS
• Instead of the Gruyère, fresh Parmesan, Pecorino, mature Cheddar or any other strong cheese would work perfectly in this recipe.
• Use dry wholemeal (wholewheat) breadcrumbs in place of white breadcrumbs.

Energy 101Kcal/423kJ; Protein 5.4g; Carbohydrate 9.6g, of which sugars 4.4g; Fat 4.9g, of which saturates 2.9g; Cholesterol 13mg; Calcium 156mg; Fibre 2.9g; Sodium 135mg.

ITALIAN SWEET AND SOUR ONIONS ★

ONIONS ARE NATURALLY SWEET, AND WHEN THEY ARE COOKED AT A HIGH TEMPERATURE THE SWEETNESS INTENSIFIES TO GIVE FANTASTIC LOW-FAT FLAVOURING TO MANY SAVOURY DISHES. SERVE THESE DELICIOUS ONIONS WITH A SELECTION OF COOKED FRESH VEGETABLES.

SERVES SIX

INGREDIENTS

   25g/1oz/2 tbsp butter
   75ml/5 tbsp granulated sugar
   120ml/4fl oz/½ cup white wine
     vinegar
   30ml/2 tbsp balsamic vinegar
   675g/1½lb small pickling (pearl)
     onions, peeled
   salt and ground black pepper

VARIATION
This recipe also looks and tastes delicious when made with either yellow or red onions, cut into slices. Cooking times vary, depending on the size of the pieces.

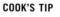

1 Melt the butter in a large pan over a gentle heat. Add the sugar and cook until it begins to dissolve. Stir constantly.

2 Add the vinegars to the pan with the onions and heat gently. Season to taste, then cover the pan and cook over a medium heat for 20–25 minutes, until the onions are soft when pierced with a knife, stirring occasionally. Serve hot.

COOK'S TIP
When buying onions, choose firm onions with a dry skin and no signs of blemishes or discolouration. Avoid onions that are showing signs of sproutung.

Energy 121Kcal/506kJ; Protein 1.4g; Carbohydrate 22g, of which sugars 19.4g; Fat 3.7g, of which saturates 2.2g; Cholesterol 9mg; Calcium 36mg; Fibre 1.6g; Sodium 29mg.

ROASTED PLUM TOMATOES <u>WITH</u> GARLIC ★

THESE ARE SO SIMPLE TO PREPARE YET TASTE ABSOLUTELY WONDERFUL. USE A LARGE, SHALLOW EARTHENWARE DISH THAT WILL ALLOW THE TOMATOES TO SEAR AND CHAR IN A HOT OVEN.

SERVES FOUR

INGREDIENTS
    8 plum tomatoes
    12 garlic cloves
    20ml/4 tsp extra virgin olive oil
    3 bay leaves
    salt and ground black pepper
    45ml/3 tbsp fresh oregano leaves,
      to garnish

COOK'S TIPS
• Use ripe plum tomatoes for this recipe
as they keep their shape and do not fall
apart when roasted at such a high
temperature. Leave the stalks on,
if possible.
• To give the tomatoes a bit of extra zing,
add a couple of dashes of hot pepper
sauce to the olive oil.

1 Preheat the oven to 230°C/450°F/
Gas 8. Select an ovenproof dish that
will hold all the tomatoes snugly in a
single layer.

2 Cut the plum tomatoes in half
lengthways. Place them in the dish, cut
sides uppermost, and push the whole,
unpeeled garlic cloves between them.

3 Brush the tomatoes with the oil,
add the bay leaves and sprinkle pepper
over the top. Roast in the oven for
about 45 minutes, or until the tomatoes
have softened and are sizzling in the
dish. They should be charred around
the edges. Season with salt and a little
more pepper, if you like. Garnish with
oregano leaves and serve.

Energy 65Kcal/272kJ; Protein 2.1g; Carbohydrate 6.7g, of which sugars 4.9g; Fat 3.5g, of which saturates 0.6g; Cholesterol 0mg; Calcium 13mg; Fibre 2g; Sodium 14mg.

GREEN BEANS WITH TOMATOES ★

THIS TASTY, LOW-FAT RECIPE IS FULL OF THE FLAVOURS OF SUMMER. IT RELIES ON FIRST-CLASS INGREDIENTS, SO USE ONLY THE BEST RIPE PLUM TOMATOES AND GREEN BEANS THAT YOU CAN BUY.

SERVES FOUR

INGREDIENTS
- 15ml/1 tbsp olive oil
- 1 large onion, thinly sliced
- 2 garlic cloves, finely chopped
- 6 large ripe plum tomatoes, skinned, seeded and coarsely chopped
- 150ml/¼ pint/⅔ cup dry white wine
- 450g/1lb green beans, sliced in half lengthways
- 16 pitted black olives
- 10ml/2 tsp lemon juice
- salt and ground black pepper

COOK'S TIP
Green beans need little preparation, and now that many are grown without the string, you simply trim either end.

1 Heat the oil in a large, non-stick frying pan, then add the onion and garlic. Cook over a medium heat for about 5 minutes, until the onion has softened but not browned, stirring frequently, and reducing the heat, if necessary.

2 Add the tomatoes, white wine, green beans, olives and lemon juice, and cook over a gentle heat for a further 20 minutes, until the sauce has thickened and the beans are tender, stirring occasionally. Season to taste with salt and pepper and serve immediately.

Energy 130Kcal/543kJ; Protein 3.9g; Carbohydrate 12.4g, of which sugars 10.3g; Fat 5g, of which saturates 0.8g; Cholesterol 0mg; Calcium 73mg; Fibre 5g; Sodium 242mg.

MARINATED MUSHROOMS ★

A TOUCH OF SHERRY GIVES THIS LOW-FAT VEGETARIAN SIDE DISH A DELICATE PIQUANCY. SERVE WITH PLENTY OF CRUSTY BREAD TO MOP UP THE VELVETY JUICES.

SERVES FOUR

INGREDIENTS

15ml/1 tbsp olive oil
1 small onion, very finely chopped
1 garlic clove, finely chopped
15ml/1 tbsp tomato purée (paste)
50ml/2fl oz/¼ cup amontillado sherry
50ml/2fl oz/¼ cup water
2 cloves
225g/8oz/3 cups button (white)
  mushrooms, trimmed
salt and ground black pepper
chopped fresh parsley, to garnish

VARIATION

In Spain, wild mushrooms, known as *setas*, are served in this way.

1 Heat the oil in a non-stick pan. Add the onion and garlic and cook until soft. Stir in the tomato purée, sherry, water, cloves and seasoning. Bring to the boil, then reduce the heat, cover and simmer gently for 45 minutes, adding more water if it becomes too dry.

2 Add the mushrooms to the pan, then cover and simmer for about 5 minutes. Remove the pan from the heat and allow to cool, still covered. Chill in the refrigerator overnight. Serve the mushrooms cold, sprinkled with the chopped fresh parsley.

Energy 59Kcal/242kJ; Protein 1.5g; Carbohydrate 2.9g, of which sugars 2.2g; Fat 3.1g, of which saturates 0.5g; Cholesterol 0mg; Calcium 12mg; Fibre 1.1g; Sodium 14mg.

ORANGE CANDIED SWEET POTATOES ★

DICED SWEET POTATOES ARE TOSSED IN A SPICY SYRUP, THEN OVEN-BAKED, TO CREATE THIS SOFT TEXTURED SIDE DISH, IDEAL ACCOMPANIED WITH A STEAMED GREEN VEGETABLE.

SERVES EIGHT

INGREDIENTS
900g/2lb sweet potatoes
250ml/8fl oz/1 cup orange juice
50ml/2fl oz/¼ cup maple syrup
5ml/1 tsp grated fresh root ginger
7.5ml/1½ tsp ground cinnamon
6.5ml/1¼ tsp ground cardamom
2.5ml/½ tsp salt
ground black pepper
orange segments and ground
    cinnamon, to garnish

COOK'S TIP
This popular American dish is traditionally served at Thanksgiving and Christmas. Serve with extra orange segments to make it really special.

1 Preheat the oven to 180°C/350°F/Gas 4. Peel and dice the potatoes into squares, then steam them for 5 minutes.

2 Meanwhile, stir the remaining ingredients together. Spread out on to a non-stick shallow baking tin (pan).

3 Scatter the potatoes over the baking tin, then bake for 1 hour, until they are tender and well coated in the spicy syrup, stirring every 15 minutes.

4 Serve garnished with orange segments and ground cinnamon.

Energy 40Kcal/169kJ; Protein 0.3g; Carbohydrate 10.1g, of which sugars 8.3g; Fat 0.1g, of which saturates 0g; Cholesterol 0mg; Calcium 7mg; Fibre 0.3g; Sodium 147mg.

Beetroot Salad <u>with</u> Oranges ★

THE COMBINATION OF SWEET BEETROOT, ZESTY ORANGE AND WARM CINNAMON IN THIS LOW-FAT SALAD IS SURPRISINGLY TASTY, AND PROVIDES A LOVELY BURST OF COLOUR IN A WINTER BUFFET SPREAD.

SERVES SIX

INGREDIENTS

    675g/1½lb beetroot (beets), steamed
      or boiled, then peeled
    1 orange, peeled and sliced
    30ml/2 tbsp orange flower water
    15ml/1 tbsp caster (superfine) sugar
    5ml/1 tsp ground cinnamon
    salt and ground black pepper

1 Quarter the cooked beetroot, then slice the quarters. Arrange the beetroot on a plate with the orange slices, or gently toss them together in a bowl.

2 Gently heat the orange flower water with the sugar in a small pan, then stir in the cinnamon and season to taste.

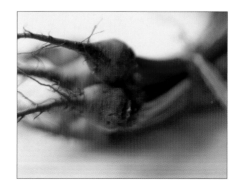

3 Pour the sweet mixture over the beetroot and orange salad, cool, then chill in the refrigerator for at least 1 hour before serving.

COOK'S TIP
You can use freshly steamed or pre-cooked beetroot. To cook raw beets, always leave the skin on, and trim off only the tops of the leaf stalks. Cook in a pan of boiling water or steam over rapidly boiling water for 1–2 hours, depending on size. Small beetroots are tender in about 1 hour, medium roots take 1–1½ hours, and larger roots can take up to 2 hours.

Energy 58Kcal/247kJ; Protein 2.2g; Carbohydrate 12.9g, of which sugars 12.2g; Fat 0.1g, of which saturates 0g; Cholesterol 0mg; Calcium 33mg; Fibre 2.5g; Sodium 75mg.

BEETROOT AND POTATO SALAD ★

THIS IS A BRIGHTLY COLOURED LOW-FAT VEGETARIAN SALAD WITH A LOVELY TEXTURE. THE SWEETNESS OF THE BEETROOT CONTRASTS PERFECTLY WITH THE TANGY DRESSING.

SERVES FOUR

INGREDIENTS
   4 medium beetroot (beets)
   4 potatoes, diced
   1 red onion, finely chopped
   150ml/¼ pint/⅔ cup low-fat natural
      (plain) yogurt
   10ml/2 tsp cider vinegar
   2 small sweet and sour cucumbers,
      finely chopped
   10ml/2 tsp creamed horseradish
   salt and ground black pepper
   fresh parsley sprigs, to garnish

COOK'S TIP
To save yourself time and energy, buy ready-cooked and peeled beetroot. They are readily available in many supermarkets.

1 Place the beetroot in a large pan with plenty of water. Bring to the boil, then reduce the heat and simmer for 40 minutes, or until tender.

2 Meanwhile, cook the potatoes in a separate pan of boiling water for 20 minutes, or until just tender.

3 When the beetroot are cooked, rinse and pull the skins off, chop into rough pieces and place in a bowl. Drain the potatoes and add to the bowl with the onion. Mix the yogurt, vinegar, cucumbers, horseradish and seasoning together. Reserve a little for garnish. Pour the rest over the salad. Toss, then garnish with parsley and the reserved dressing.

Energy 143Kcal/607kJ; Protein 5.5g; Carbohydrate 30.1g, of which sugars 10.7g; Fat 1g, of which saturates 0.3g; Cholesterol 1mg; Calcium 98mg; Fibre 2.9g; Sodium 106mg.

PERSIAN BAKED RICE ★

IN THIS PERSIAN-STYLE DISH, RICE IS COOKED SLOWLY OVER A LOW HEAT SO THAT A CRUST FORMS ON THE BOTTOM. THE MILD FLAVOURS OF SAFFRON AND ALMONDS GO PERFECTLY TOGETHER. THIS LIGHT DISH IS AN IDEAL ACCOMPANIMENT FOR VEGETARIAN CUTLETS OR SAUSAGES.

SERVES SIX

INGREDIENTS
  450g/1lb/2¼ cups basmati rice
  a good pinch of saffron threads
  15g/1oz/1 tbsp butter
  25g/1oz/¼ cup flaked
   (sliced) almonds
  salt and ground black pepper

COOK'S TIP
Saffron comes from a flower of the crocus family and is sold either as whole threads or strands, or in powdered form. Saffron threads should be soaked or steeped in a little warm or hot liquid, stock, milk or water, to infuse and disperse their flavour and colour, before adding the saffron and its liquid to dishes. Powdered saffron can be added directly to dishes. Saffron is expensive to buy but it adds a lovely orange hue and a subtle, aromatic flavour to dishes such as this one.

1 Cook the rice in a pan of salted boiling water for 5 minutes, then drain thoroughly. Meanwhile, put the saffron threads in a small bowl with 30ml/ 2 tbsp warm water and leave to infuse for at least 5 minutes.

2 Heat the butter in a large, non-stick pan and add the almonds. Cook over a medium heat for 2–3 minutes, or until golden, stirring occasionally. Add the rice and stir well, then stir in the saffron and its liquid, plus 1 litre/1¾ pints/ 4 cups water. Season with salt and pepper and cover with a tight-fitting lid.

3 Cook over a very low heat for 30 minutes, or until the rice is tender and a crust has formed on the bottom of the pan. Fork up the rice to mix in the crust before serving.

Energy 313Kcal/1309kJ; Protein 6.5g; Carbohydrate 60.2g, of which sugars 0.2g; Fat 4.8g, of which saturates 1.5g; Cholesterol 5mg; Calcium 25mg; Fibre 0.3g; Sodium 16mg.

THAI-SPICED RICE ★

THIS IS A LOVELY, SOFT, FLUFFY RICE DISH, PERFUMED WITH LIMES AND FRESH LEMON GRASS. AS WELL AS BEING A GOOD, LOW-FAT ACCOMPANIMENT FOR A FAMILY VEGETARIAN SUPPER, IT WOULD BE AN EXCELLENT CHOICE, IN DOUBLE OR EVEN TRIPLE THE QUANTITY, FOR A VEGETARIAN BUFFET TABLE.

SERVES FOUR

INGREDIENTS
2 limes
1 lemon grass stalk
225g/8oz/generous 1 cup long grain brown rice
15ml/1 tbsp olive oil
1 onion, chopped
2.5cm/1in piece fresh root ginger, finely chopped
7.5ml/1½ tsp coriander seeds
7.5ml/1½ tsp cumin seeds
750ml/1¼ pints/3 cups vegetable stock
60ml/4 tbsp chopped fresh coriander (cilantro)
1 spring onion (scallion) thinly sliced, and toasted coconut strips, to garnish
lime wedges, to serve

1 Thinly pare the limes using a zester or a fine grater, taking care to avoid cutting the bitter pith. Set aside the rind. Finely chop the lower portion of the lemon grass stalk and set aside.

2 Rinse the rice in plenty of cold water until the water runs clear. Tip it into a sieve (strainer) and drain thoroughly.

COOK'S TIP
You could substitute the finely grated rind of kaffir limes for an authentic Thai flavour, but you will need to use juicier Tahitian or Mexican limes for cutting into wedges to serve.

3 Heat the oil in a non-stick pan. Add the onion, ginger, spices, lemon grass and lime rind and cook over a gentle heat for about 3 minutes or until the onion is soft, stirring occasionally.

4 Add the drained rice and cook for 1 minute, stirring constantly, then pour in the stock and bring to the boil. Reduce the heat to very low and cover the pan with a tight-fitting lid. Cook gently for 30 minutes, then check the rice. If it is still crunchy, re-cover and leave for 3–5 minutes more. Remove the pan from the heat when done.

5 Stir in the fresh coriander, fluff up the grains, cover the pan again and leave for about 10 minutes. Transfer to a large serving dish or individual bowls, garnish with strips of spring onion and toasted coconut, and serve with plenty of lime wedges.

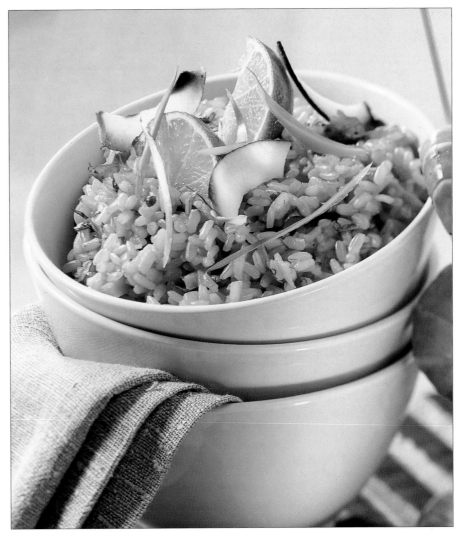

Energy 232Kcal/981kJ; Protein 4g; Carbohydrate 47g, of which sugars 1.7g; Fat 4.4g, of which saturates 0.8g; Cholesterol 0mg; Calcium 10mg; Fibre 1.3g; Sodium 2mg.

RED ONION, GARLIC AND LEMON RELISH ★

THIS POWERFUL LOW-FAT RELISH IS FLAVOURED WITH NORTH-AFRICAN SPICES AND PRESERVED LEMONS, AVAILABLE FROM DELICATESSENS OR FROM MIDDLE-EASTERN FOOD STORES.

3 Add a pinch of salt, lots of pepper and the sugar, and cook, uncovered, for 5 minutes. Soak the saffron threads in about 45ml/3 tbsp warm water for 5 minutes, then add to the onions, with the soaking water. Add the cinnamon stick, dried chillies, if using, and bay leaves. Stir in 30ml/2 tbsp of the sherry vinegar and the orange juice.

4 Cook over a low heat, uncovered, until the onions are very soft and most of the liquid has evaporated. Stir in the preserved lemon and cook gently for a further 5 minutes. Taste and adjust the seasoning, adding more salt, sugar and/or vinegar to taste.

5 Serve warm or cold, but not hot or chilled. The relish tastes best if it is allowed to stand for 24 hours.

SERVES SIX

INGREDIENTS
30ml/2 tbsp olive oil
3 large red onions, sliced
2 heads of garlic, separated into
  cloves and peeled
10ml/2 tsp coriander seeds, crushed
10ml/2 tsp light muscovado (brown)
  sugar, plus a little extra
pinch of saffron threads
5cm/2in piece cinnamon stick
2–3 small whole dried red
  chillies (optional)
2 fresh bay leaves
30–45ml/2–3 tbsp sherry vinegar
juice of ½ small orange
30ml/2 tbsp chopped
  preserved lemon
salt and ground black pepper

1 Heat the oil in a heavy pan. Add the onions and stir, then cover and reduce the heat to the lowest setting. Cook for 10–15 minutes, until the onions are soft, stirring occasionally.

2 Add the garlic cloves and coriander seeds (crushed but not finely ground). Cover and cook for 5–8 minutes, until soft.

VARIATION
To make a quick Lebanese onion relish, to serve 6, chop 500g/1¼lb ripe tomatoes and combine with 1 bunch of sliced spring onions (scallions). Crush 2 cloves of garlic with a large pinch of salt and gradually work in 15ml/1 tbsp lemon juice and 30ml/2 tbsp extra virgin olive oil. Toss the tomatoes and onions with the dressing and stir in a small bunch of chopped purslane or 30ml/2 tbsp of chopped marjoram or lemon thyme, then adjust the seasoning with salt, pepper, a pinch or two of sugar and maybe more lemon juice. Serve with a vegetarian grain salad made with bulgur wheat or couscous.

Energy 79Kcal/326kJ; Protein 1.3g; Carbohydrate 10.4g, of which sugars 8.1g; Fat 3.9g, of which saturates 0.5g; Cholesterol 0mg; Calcium 27mg; Fibre 1.4g; Sodium 4mg.

APPLE AND TOMATO CHUTNEY ★

THIS MELLOW, GOLDEN, SPICY CHUTNEY MAKES THE MOST OF FRESH AUTUMN PRODUCE. ANY TYPE OF WELL-FLAVOURED TOMATOES CAN BE USED SUCCESSFULLY IN THIS LOW-FAT VEGETARIAN RECIPE.

MAKES ABOUT 36 50G/2OZ SERVINGS

INGREDIENTS
  1.3kg/3lb cooking apples
  1.3kg/3lb tomatoes
  2 large onions
  2 garlic cloves
  250g/9oz/1½ cups pitted dried dates
  2 red (bell) peppers
  3 dried red chillies
  15ml/1 tbsp black peppercorns
  4 cardamom pods
  15ml/1 tbsp coriander seeds
  10ml/2 tsp cumin seeds
  10ml/2 tsp ground turmeric
  5ml/1 tsp sea salt
  600ml/1 pint/2½ cups distilled
    malt vinegar
  1kg/2¼lb/5¼ cups unrefined
    granulated sugar

3 Add the vinegar and sugar and bring to boil. Leave to simmer for 30 minutes; stir occasionally. Add the red pepper and cook for 30 minutes, stirring as the chutney becomes thick and pulpy.

4 Spoon the chutney into warm, dry, sterilized jars. Seal each jar with a waxed circle and cover with a tightly fitting cellophane top. Leave to cool, then label and store in a cool, dry place.

1 Peel, core and chop the apples. Peel and chop the tomatoes, onions and garlic. Quarter the dates. Core and seed the peppers, then cut into chunky pieces. Put all the prepared ingredients, except the red peppers, into a preserving pan.

2 Slit the chillies and set aside. Put the peppercorns and remaining spices into a mortar and roughly crush with a pestle. Add the chillies, spices and salt to the pan.

VARIATIONS
Use red onions or 8 shallots in place of standard onions. Use dried apricots or pears in place of dates.

Energy 151Kcal/644kJ; Protein 0.9g; Carbohydrate 39g, of which sugars 38.7g; Fat 0.2g, of which saturates 0g; Cholesterol 0mg; Calcium 25mg; Fibre 1.4g; Sodium 7mg.

SWEET TREATS

Desserts round off many meals perfectly and the recipes that follow are both delicous and low in fat. Choose from hot delights such as Apple and Blackcurrant Pancakes, Cassava Sweet, and Mango and Amaretti Strudel, or select from cool temptations including Mango Sorbet with Mango Sauce, Summer Berry Frozen Yogurt, and Jungle Fruits in Lemon Grass Syrup.

MANGO SORBET WITH MANGO SAUCE ★

THIS INDIAN SPECIALITY MAKES A VERY REFRESHING, LOW-FAT DESSERT. REMOVE FROM THE FREEZER 10 MINUTES BEFORE SERVING TO ALLOW IT TO SOFTEN AND RELEASE THE FULL FLAVOUR.

SERVES FOUR

INGREDIENTS
900g/2lb/5 cups mango pulp
2.5ml/½ tsp lemon juice
finely grated rind of 1 orange and
   1 lemon
4 egg whites
50g/2oz/¼ cup caster
   (superfine) sugar
120ml/4fl oz/½ cup low-fat Greek
   (US strained plain) yogurt
50g/2oz/½ cup icing
   (confectioners') sugar

1 In a large, chilled bowl that can safely be used in the freezer, mix half of the mango pulp with the lemon juice and the grated orange and lemon rinds.

COOK'S TIP
Ripe mangoes should yield when gently pressed. The colour of a mango is no guide to ripeness as the skin colour varies from one variety to another. A green mango can be as ripe as a bright red one.

2 Beat the egg whites in a separate grease-free bowl until soft peaks form, then fold into the mango mixture, with the caster sugar. Cover and freeze for at least 1 hour.

3 Remove the sorbet from the freezer and beat well. Transfer to an ice-cream container, and freeze until solid.

4 Lightly whisk the yogurt with the icing sugar and the remaining mango pulp. Spoon into a bowl and chill for 24 hours. Scoop out individual servings of sorbet and cover each with mango sauce.

Energy 206Kcal/881kJ; Protein 6.1g; Carbohydrate 47.1g, of which sugars 46.4g; Fat 0.8g, of which saturates 0.4g; Cholesterol 0mg; Calcium 92mg; Fibre 5.9g; Sodium 91mg.

LYCHEE AND ELDERFLOWER SORBET ★

THE TASTE OF ELDERFLOWERS IS WELL-KNOWN FOR BRINGING OUT THE FLAVOUR OF GOOSEBERRIES, BUT IT ALSO COMPLEMENTS LYCHEES WONDERFULLY, AS WITH THIS TEMPTING DESSERT.

SERVES FOUR

INGREDIENTS
  175g/6oz/generous ¾ cup caster
    (superfine) sugar
  400ml/14fl oz/1⅔ cups water
  500g/1¼ lb fresh lychees, peeled
    and stoned
  15ml/1 tbsp undiluted
    elderflower cordial
  dessert biscuits, to serve (optional)

1 Heat the sugar and water in a pan until the sugar has dissolved. Boil for 5 minutes, then add the lychees. Reduce the heat and simmer for 7 minutes. Remove from the heat and allow to cool.

2 Process the lychees and syrup in a blender or food processor to form a purée. Place a sieve (strainer) over a bowl. Pour the purée into it and press through with a wooden spoon.

3 Stir the elderflower cordial into the strained purée, then pour the mixture into a shallow freezerproof container. Freeze for approximately 2 hours, or until ice crystals start to form around the edges.

4 Remove the sorbet from the freezer and process briefly in a blender or food processor to break up the crystals. Repeat this freezing and processing procedure twice more, then freeze until firm.

5 Transfer the sorbet to the fridge for 10 minutes to soften slightly before serving in scoops. Serve with dessert biscuits, if you like.

COOK'S TIP
Ripe lychees have a prickly shell which can be reddish-brown, deep pink or white in colour, depending on the variety. The pearly white aromatic flesh of lychees tastes sweet yet slightly acidic.

Energy 249Kcal/1064kJ; Protein 1.4g; Carbohydrate 64.7g, of which sugars 64.7g; Fat 0.1g, of which saturates 0g; Cholesterol 0mg; Calcium 31mg; Fibre 0.9g; Sodium 4mg.

SUMMER BERRY FROZEN YOGURT ★

ANY COMBINATION OF SUMMER FRUITS WILL WORK WELL FOR THIS EXTREMELY LOW-FAT DESSERT, AS LONG AS THEY ARE FROZEN, BECAUSE THIS HELPS TO CREATE A COOL CHUNKY TEXTURE. WHOLE FRESH FROZEN BERRIES MAKE AN ATTRACTIVE DECORATION AND ARE TASTY IN THEIR OWN RIGHT.

SERVES SIX

INGREDIENTS
350g/12oz/3 cups frozen mixed
summer fruits
200g/7oz/scant 1 cup low-fat Greek
(US strained plain) yogurt
25g/1oz/¼ cup icing
(confectioners') sugar

COOK'S TIP
Packets of frozen mixed summer fruits or summer berries are available in many supermarkets, and are ideal for this recipe.

VARIATION
To make a rich and creamy ice cream, use double (heavy) cream in place of the yogurt. It's a lot less healthy and contains a much higher calorie and fat content, but it's delicious for an occasional treat.

1 Put all the ingredients into a blender or food processor and process until combined but still quite chunky. Spoon the mixture into six 150ml/¼ pint/⅔ cup ramekin dishes.

2 Cover each dish with clear film (plastic wrap) and place in the freezer for about 2 hours, or until firm.

3 To turn out the frozen yogurts, dip the dishes briefly in hot water, then invert them on to small serving plates. Tap the base of the dishes and the yogurts should come out. Serve immediately.

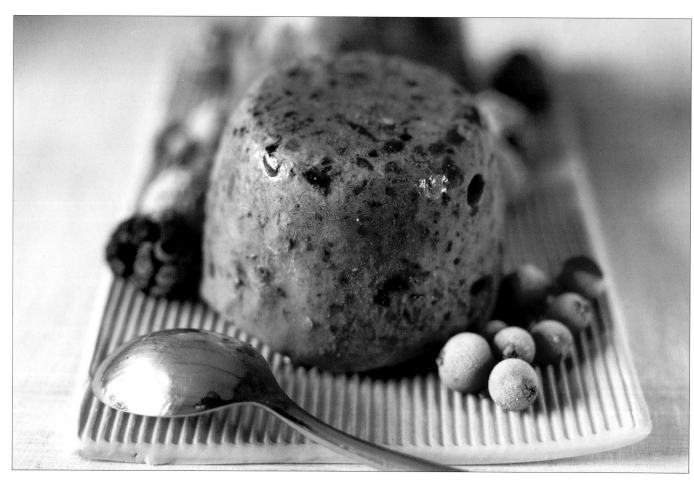

Energy 51Kcal/215kJ; Protein 2.2g; Carbohydrate 10.4g, of which sugars 10.4g; Fat 0.4g, of which saturates 0.2g; Cholesterol 0mg; Calcium 75mg; Fibre 0.7g; Sodium 32mg.

JUNGLE FRUITS IN LEMON GRASS SYRUP ★

THIS EXOTIC AND REFRESHING VIRTUALLY FAT-FREE FRUIT SALAD CAN BE MADE WITH ANY COMBINATION OF TROPICAL FRUITS — JUST GO FOR A GOOD BALANCE OF COLOUR, FLAVOUR AND TEXTURE. YOU CAN ALSO FLAVOUR THE SYRUP WITH GINGER RATHER THAN LEMON GRASS, IF YOU LIKE.

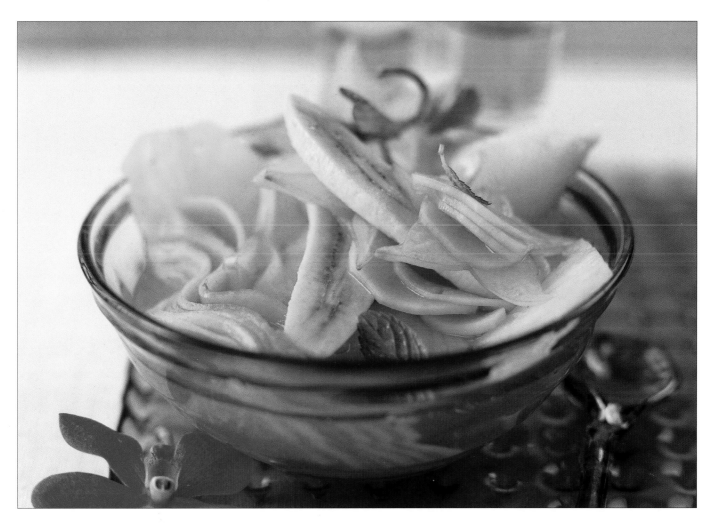

SERVES SIX

INGREDIENTS

1 firm papaya
1 small pineapple
2 small star fruit (carambola),
   sliced into stars
400g/14oz can preserved
   lychees or 12 fresh lychees,
   peeled and stoned
2 firm yellow or green bananas,
   peeled and cut diagonally
   into slices

For the syrup
115g/4oz/generous ½ cup caster
   (superfine) sugar
2 lemon grass stalks, bruised

1 To make the syrup, put 225ml/7½fl oz/scant 1 cup water into a heavy pan with the sugar and bruised lemon grass stalks. Bring the liquid to the boil, stirring constantly until the sugar has dissolved, then reduce the heat and simmer for 10–15 minutes. Remove the pan from the heat and leave to cool.

2 Prepare the fruit. Peel and halve the papaya, remove the seeds and slice the flesh crossways. Peel the pineapple and slice it into rounds. Remove the core and cut each round in half.

3 Put all the prepared fruit into a bowl. Pour the syrup, including the lemon grass stalks, over the fruit and toss lightly to combine.

4 Cover and chill for at least 6 hours, or overnight, to allow the flavours to mingle. Remove and discard the lemon grass stalks before serving.

Energy 199Kcal/849kJ; Protein 1.6g; Carbohydrate 50.3g, of which sugars 49.7g; Fat 0.4g, of which saturates 0g; Cholesterol 0mg; Calcium 49mg; Fibre 3.5g; Sodium 8mg.

PISTACHIO AND ROSE WATER ORANGES ★

THIS LIGHT AND CITRUSY DESSERT COMBINES, ALONG WITH PISTACHIO NUTS, TWO FAVOURITE MIDDLE EASTERN INGREDIENTS. IT IS DELIGHTFULLY FRAGRANT AND REFRESHING.

SERVES FOUR

INGREDIENTS
    4 large oranges
    30ml/2 tbsp rose water
    30ml/2 tbsp shelled pistachio nuts,
        roughly chopped

VARIATION
Use hazelnuts if you don't have pistachio nuts.

COOK'S TIP
Rose-scented sugar is delicious sprinkled over fresh fruit salads. Wash and thoroughly dry a handful of rose petals and place in a sealed container filled with caster (superfine) sugar for 2–3 days. Remove and discard the petals before using the sugar.

1 Slice the top and bottom off one of the oranges to expose the flesh. Using a small serrated knife, slice down between the pith and the flesh, working round the orange, to remove all the peel and pith. Slice the orange into six rounds, reserving any juice. Repeat with the remaining oranges.

2 Arrange the orange rounds on a serving dish. Mix the reserved juice with the rose water and drizzle over the oranges. Cover the dish with clear film (plastic wrap) and chill for about 30 minutes. Sprinkle the chopped pistachio nuts over the oranges to serve.

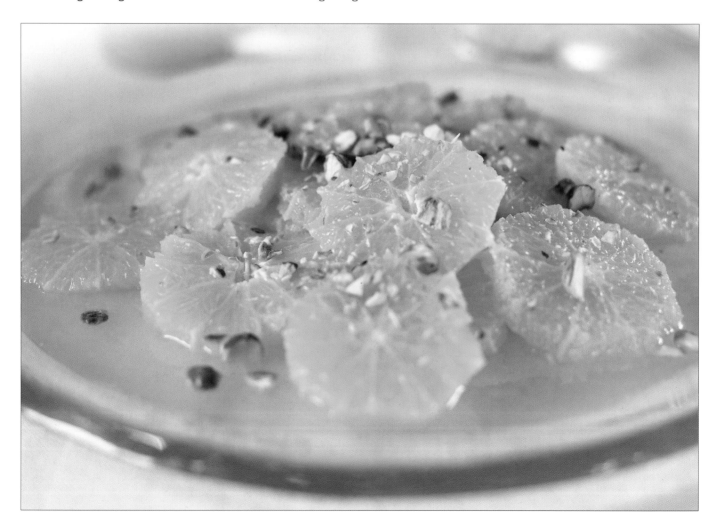

Energy 123Kcal/518kJ; Protein 3.7g; Carbohydrate 18.5g, of which sugars 18.3g; Fat 4.4g, of which saturates 0.6g; Cholesterol 0mg; Calcium 107mg; Fibre 4g; Sodium 50mg.

BLUSHING PEARS ★

PEARS POACHED IN ROSÉ WINE AND SWEET SPICES ABSORB ALL THE SUBTLE FLAVOURS AND TURN A SOFT PINK COLOUR, TO CREATE THIS ALLURING VIRTUALLY FAT-FREE DESSERT.

SERVES SIX

INGREDIENTS
6 firm eating pears
300ml/½ pint/1¼ cups rosé wine
150ml/¼ pint/⅔ cup cranberry or clear apple juice
a strip of thinly pared orange rind
1 cinnamon stick
4 whole cloves
1 bay leaf
75ml/5 tbsp caster (superfine) sugar
extra small bay leaves, to decorate

1 Thinly peel the pears with a sharp knife or vegetable peeler, leaving the stalks attached.

2 Pour the wine and cranberry or apple juice into a large, heavy pan. Add the orange rind, cinnamon stick, cloves, bay leaf and sugar.

COOK'S TIP
Check the pears by piercing with a skewer or sharp knife towards the end of the poaching time, because some may cook more quickly than others.

3 Heat gently until the sugar has dissolved, stirring constantly. Add the pears and stand them upright in the pan. Pour in enough cold water to barely cover them. Cover and cook gently for 20–30 minutes, or until just tender, turning and basting occasionally.

4 Using a slotted spoon, gently lift the pears out of the syrup and transfer them to a serving dish.

5 Bring the syrup to the boil, then boil it rapidly for 10–15 minutes, or until it has reduced by half.

6 Strain the syrup, then pour it over the pears. Serve hot or well-chilled, decorated with small bay leaves.

VARIATION
Use 6 firm, fresh peaches or nectarines in place of pears.

Energy 154Kcal/652kJ; Protein 0.6g; Carbohydrate 31.8g, of which sugars 31.8g; Fat 0.2g, of which saturates 0g; Cholesterol 0mg; Calcium 31mg; Fibre 3.3g; Sodium 8mg.

APPLE AND BLACKCURRANT PANCAKES ★

THESE TASTY, LIGHT PANCAKES ARE MADE WITH A WHOLEWHEAT BATTER AND ARE FILLED WITH A FRESH ZESTY BERRY FRUIT MIXTURE. HALF-FAT CRÈME FRAÎCHE TOPS OFF THIS TEMPTING DESSERT.

MAKES TEN PANCAKES

INGREDIENTS
115g/4oz/1 cup plain wholemeal
(whole-wheat) flour
300ml/½ pint/1¼ cups
skimmed milk
1 egg, beaten
30ml/2 tbsp sunflower oil
half-fat crème fraîche, to serve
(optional)
toasted nuts or sesame seeds, for
sprinkling (optional)
For the filling
450g/1lb cooking apples
225g/8oz blackcurrants
30–45ml/2–3 tbsp water
30ml/2 tbsp demerara (raw) sugar

COOK'S TIP
If you wish, substitute other combinations of fruit such as pears and blueberries for apples and blackcurrants.

1 To make the pancake batter, put the flour in a mixing bowl and make a well in the centre.

2 Add a little of the milk with the egg and 15ml/1 tbsp of the oil. Beat the flour into the liquid, then gradually beat in the remaining milk, keeping the batter smooth and free from lumps. Cover the batter and chill it while you prepare the filling.

3 Quarter, peel and core the apples. Slice them into a pan, then add the blackcurrants and water. Cook over a gentle heat for 10–15 minutes until the fruit is soft. Stir in enough demerara sugar to sweeten.

4 Meanwhile, lightly grease a non-stick frying pan with just a smear of the remaining oil. Heat the pan, whisk the batter, then pour about 30ml/2 tbsp of the batter into the pan, swirl it around to cover the base of the pan evenly and cook for about 1 minute until golden underneath. Flip the pancake over with a palette knife or metal spatula and cook the other side until golden. Put a sheet of baking parchment on a plate and keep hot while cooking the remaining pancakes.

5 Fill the pancakes with the apple and blackcurrant mixture and roll them up. Serve with a small dollop of crème fraîche, if using, and sprinkle with nuts or sesame seeds, if you like.

Energy 96Kcal/409kJ; Protein 3.5g; Carbohydrate 17.3g, of which sugars 10.2g; Fat 2g, of which saturates 0.4g; Cholesterol 20mg; Calcium 61mg; Fibre 2.6g; Sodium 22mg.

CASSAVA SWEET ★

SWEET AND STICKY, THIS LOW-FAT SNACK IS MORE LIKE AN INDIAN HELVA THAN A DESSERT. THIS RECIPE CAN ALSO BE MADE USING SWEET POTATOES OR YAMS IN PLACE OF THE CASSAVA.

SERVES SIX TO EIGHT

INGREDIENTS
  15g/½oz/1 tbsp butter, for greasing
  350ml/12fl oz/1½ cups coconut milk
  115g/4oz/generous ½ cup palm sugar
  2.5ml/½ tsp ground aniseed
  a pinch of salt
  675g/1½lb cassava root, peeled
    and grated

1 Preheat the oven to 190°C/375°F/ Gas 5. Grease an ovenproof baking dish with the butter. In a bowl, whisk the coconut milk with the sugar, aniseed and salt, until the sugar has dissolved.

2 Beat the grated cassava root into the coconut mixture, then pour it into the baking dish.

3 Bake in the oven for about 1 hour, or until nicely golden on top. Leave the dessert to cool in the dish before serving.

COOK'S TIPS
• Cassava is a tropical plant (originally from Brazil where it is called manioc), cultivated for its starchy roots. It looks somewhat similar to the yam, with a tough brown, often waxy skin, and creamy white or yellow hard flesh. The root's flavour spoils in a day or so, even if kept unskinned and under refrigeration. The skinned root must be kept under water until it is ready to be cooked.
• To prepare the cassava for grating, use a sharp knife to slit the whole length of the root and then carefully peel off the skin. Simply grate the peeled root using a coarse grater.

Energy 176Kcal/752kJ; Protein 1.5g; Carbohydrate 41g, of which sugars 17.8g; Fat 1.9g, of which saturates 1.2g; Cholesterol 4mg; Calcium 33mg; Fibre 1.1g; Sodium 62mg.

MANGO AND AMARETTI STRUDEL ★

FRESH MANGO AND CRUSHED AMARETTI WRAPPED IN WAFER-THIN FILO PASTRY MAKE A SPECIAL LOW-FAT TREAT THAT IS EQUALLY DELICIOUS MADE WITH FRESH APRICOTS OR PLUMS.

SERVES 4

INGREDIENTS
  1 large mango
  finely grated rind of 1 lemon
  2 amaretti
  25g/1oz/2 tbsp demerara (raw) sugar
  60ml/4 tbsp fresh wholemeal
   (whole-wheat) breadcrumbs
  2 sheets filo pastry, each 48 x 28cm/
   19 x 11in, thawed if frozen
  20g/¾oz/4 tsp non-hydrogenated soft
   margarine, melted
  15ml/1 tbsp chopped almonds
  icing (confectioners') sugar,
   for dusting

2 Crush the amaretti and mix them with the demerara sugar and breadcrumbs in a separate bowl.

4 Sprinkle the filo rectangle with the amaretti mixture, leaving a 5cm/2in border on each long side. Arrange the mango cubes over the top.

1 Preheat the oven to 190°C/375°F/ Gas 5. Lightly grease a large baking sheet and set aside. Halve, stone and peel the mango (see Cook's Tip). Cut the flesh into cubes, then place them in a bowl, and sprinkle with grated lemon rind. Set aside.

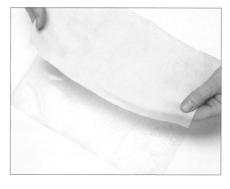

3 Lay one sheet of filo pastry on a flat surface and brush with a quarter of the melted margarine. Top with the second sheet of filo, brush with one-third of the remaining margarine, then fold both sheets over, if necessary, to make a rectangle measuring about 28 x 23cm/ 11 x 9in. Brush with half the remaining margarine.

COOK'S TIP
The easiest way to prepare a mango is to cut horizontally through the fruit, keeping the knife blade close to the stone. Repeat on the other side of the stone and peel off the skin. Remove the remaining skin and flesh from around the stone.

VARIATIONS
Use the finely grated rind of 1 lime or 1 small orange in place of lemon rind. Use chopped (shelled) pistachio nuts or hazelnuts in place of almonds.

5 Roll up the filo from one of the long sides like a Swiss roll (jelly roll). Lift the strudel on to the baking sheet making sure that the seam is underneath. Brush with the remaining melted margarine and sprinkle evenly with the chopped almonds.

6 Bake in the oven for 20–25 minutes or until golden brown, then transfer to a chopping board. Dust with sifted icing sugar, slice diagonally and serve warm.

Energy 190Kcal/803kJ; Protein 3.4g; Carbohydrate 35.2g, of which sugars 13.2g; Fat 4.9g, of which saturates 0.2g; Cholesterol 0mg; Calcium 48mg; Fibre 1.7g; Sodium 164mg.

BAKES AND BREADS

*It's hard to resist the delicious aroma of freshly
baked bread and bakes wafting through
your kitchen, and you can enjoy many of these
home-baked delights as part of a healthy low-fat
vegetarian eating plan. Included here is a selection
of tasty bakes such as Chocolate and Banana
Brownies, and Fresh Raspberry Muffins, as well as
satisfying breads from all over the world, like
Soda Bread and Pitta Bread.*

CHOCOLATE AND BANANA BROWNIES ★

NUTS TRADITIONALLY GIVE BROWNIES THEIR CHEWY TEXTURE. HERE OAT BRAN IS USED INSTEAD, CREATING A MOIST, MOREISH, YET HEALTHY ALTERNATIVE.

MAKES NINE BROWNIES

INGREDIENTS

75ml/5 tbsp reduced-fat
   cocoa powder
15ml/1 tbsp caster (superfine) sugar
75ml/5 tbsp skimmed milk
3 large bananas, peeled and mashed
215g/7½oz/scant 1 cup soft light
   brown sugar
5ml/1 tsp vanilla extract
5 egg whites
75g/3oz/⅔ cup self-raising
   (self-rising) flour
75g/3oz/¾ cup oat bran
15ml/1 tbsp icing (confectioners')
   sugar, for dusting

1 Preheat the oven to 180°C/350°F/ Gas 4. Line a 20cm/8in square cake tin (pan) with baking parchment. Set aside.

2 Blend the cocoa powder and caster sugar with the skimmed milk in a mixing bowl. Add the mashed bananas, soft light brown sugar and vanilla extract and mix well.

3 In a separate bowl, lightly beat the egg whites with a fork. Add the chocolate mixture and continue to beat well. Sift the flour over the mixture and fold in with the oat bran until well mixed. Pour evenly into the prepared tin.

4 Bake in the oven for 40 minutes or until firm. Cool in the tin for 10 minutes, then turn out on to a wire rack. Cut into squares and lightly dust with sifted icing sugar before serving.

COOK'S TIPS

• Store these brownies in an airtight container for a day before eating – they improve with keeping.
• You'll find reduced-fat cocoa powder in health food shops. If you can't find it, ordinary cocoa powder will work just as well, but, of course, the fat content will be higher!

Energy 200Kcal/846kJ; Protein 7g; Carbohydrate 37.2g, of which sugars 29.2g; Fat 3.6g, of which saturates 1.3g; Cholesterol 64mg; Calcium 61mg; Fibre 3.9g; Sodium 118mg.

FRESH RASPBERRY MUFFINS ★

THESE FRUITY, AMERICAN-STYLE MUFFINS ARE MADE USING BAKING POWDER AND LOW-FAT BUTTERMILK, GIVING THEM A LIGHT AND SPONGY TEXTURE.

MAKES TEN TO TWELVE

INGREDIENTS

   275g/10oz/scant 2½ cups plain
     (all-purpose) flour
   15ml/1 tbsp baking powder
   115g/4oz/generous ½ cup caster
     (superfine) sugar
   1 egg, beaten
   250ml/8fl oz/1 cup buttermilk
   60ml/4 tbsp sunflower oil
   150g/5oz/scant 1 cup fresh raspberries

1 Preheat the oven to 200°C/400°F/ Gas 6. Arrange 12 paper muffin cases in a deep muffin tin (pan). Sift the flour and baking powder into a mixing bowl, stir in the sugar, then make a well in the centre.

2 Mix the egg, buttermilk and oil together in a separate bowl, then pour it into the flour mixture and mix gently but quickly.

VARIATION
If fresh raspberries are not available, use frozen small raspberries (not defrosted) instead.

3 Add the raspberries and lightly fold in with a metal spoon. Spoon the mixture into the paper cases, dividing it evenly between each one.

4 Bake the muffins in the oven for 20–25 minutes until golden brown and firm in the middle. Transfer to a wire rack and serve warm or cold.

Energy 165Kcal/696kJ; Protein 3.6g; Carbohydrate 29.3g, of which sugars 11.9g; Fat 4.5g, of which saturates 0.6g; Cholesterol 17mg; Calcium 68mg; Fibre 1g; Sodium 17mg.

OATY CRISPS ★

THESE LIGHT OAT BISCUITS ARE VERY CRISP, CRUNCHY AND EXTREMELY MOREISH — IDEAL TO SERVE WITH MORNING OR AFTERNOON TEA OR COFFEE, OR SIMPLY AS A SNACK ON THEIR OWN.

<u>MAKES EIGHTEEN OATY CRISPS</u>

INGREDIENTS
   175g/6oz/1¾ cups rolled oats
   75g/3oz/½ cup light muscovado
      (brown) sugar
   1 egg, beaten
   60ml/4 tbsp sunflower oil
   30ml/2 tbsp malt extract

COOK'S TIP
To give these biscuits (cookies) a coarser texture, substitute jumbo oats for some or all of the rolled oats. Once cool, store the biscuits in an airtight container to keep them as crisp and fresh as possible.

VARIATIONS
Add 5–7.5ml/1–1½ tsp ground cinnamon or mixed spice with the oats, if you like. Add the finely grated rind of 1 lemon or 1 small orange with the oil, if you like.

1 Preheat the oven to 190°C/375°F/ Gas 5. Lightly grease two baking sheets and set aside. Mix the rolled oats and sugar in a bowl, breaking up any lumps in the sugar. Add the egg, sunflower oil and malt extract, mix well, then leave to stand for 15 minutes.

2 Using a teaspoon, place small heaps of the mixture well apart on the prepared baking sheets. Press the heaps into 7.5cm/3in rounds with the back of a dampened fork.

3 Bake the biscuits in the oven for 10–15 minutes, or until golden brown. Leave them to cool for 1 minute, then remove with a palette knife or metal spatula and cool on a wire rack.

Energy 86Kcal/364kJ; Protein 1.6g; Carbohydrate 12.8g, of which sugars 5.7g; Fat 3.6g, of which saturates 0.4g; Cholesterol 11mg; Calcium 9mg; Fibre 0.7g; Sodium 12mg.

DROP SCONES ★

ALSO KNOWN AS PIKELETS, THESE POPULAR LITTLE LOW-FAT DROP SCONES ARE DELICIOUS SERVED WARM, SPREAD WITH A LITTLE JAM, FRUIT PURÉE OR HONEY.

MAKES EIGHTEEN DROP SCONES

INGREDIENTS
225g/8oz/2 cups self-raising
  (self-rising) flour
2.5ml/½ tsp salt
15ml/1 tbsp caster (superfine) sugar
1 egg, beaten
300ml/½ pint/1¼ cups skimmed milk
15–30ml/1–2 tbsp sunflower oil

COOK'S TIP
For savoury drop scones, add 2 chopped spring onions (scallions) and 15ml/1 tbsp of grated fresh Parmesan cheese to the batter. Serve with cottage cheese.

1 Preheat a griddle or heavy frying pan until hot. Sift the flour and salt into a mixing bowl.

2 Stir in the sugar, then make a well in the centre. Add the egg and half the milk, then gradually incorporate the surrounding flour to make a smooth batter. Beat in the remaining milk.

3 Lightly oil the griddle or pan. Drop tablespoons of batter on to the surface, leaving them until they bubble on the surface and the bubbles begin to burst.

4 Turn the drop scones over with a palette knife or metal spatula and cook until the underside is golden brown. Keep the cooked drop scones warm and moist by wrapping them in a clean cotton napkin while cooking others.

Energy 59Kcal/252kJ; Protein 2g; Carbohydrate 11.1g, of which sugars 1.8g; Fat 1.1g, of which saturates 0.2g; Cholesterol 11mg; Calcium 66mg; Fibre 0.4g; Sodium 56mg.

FRUITED MALT LOAF ★

THIS IS A RICH AND STICKY MALT LOAF THAT IS LOW IN FAT AND IDEAL FOR VEGETARIANS.
IF IT LASTS LONG ENOUGH TO GO STALE, TRY TOASTING IT FOR A DELICIOUS TEATIME TREAT.

SERVES EIGHT

INGREDIENTS
  150ml/¼ pint/⅔ cup lukewarm
    skimmed milk
  5ml/1 tsp active dried yeast
  a pinch of caster (superfine) sugar
  350g/12oz/3 cups plain
    (all-purpose) flour
  1.5ml/¼ tsp salt
  30ml/2 tbsp light muscovado
    (brown) sugar
  175g/6oz/generous 1 cup sultanas
    (golden raisins)
  15ml/1 tbsp sunflower oil
  45ml/3 tbsp malt extract
For the glaze
  30ml/2 tbsp caster (superfine) sugar
  30ml/2 tbsp water

1 Place the milk in a bowl. Sprinkle the yeast on top and add the sugar. Leave for 30 minutes until frothy. Sift the flour and salt into a mixing bowl, stir in the muscovado sugar and sultanas, and make a well in the centre.

2 Add the yeast mixture with the oil and malt extract. Gradually incorporate the flour and mix to a soft dough, adding a little extra milk, if necessary.

3 Turn on to a floured surface and knead for about 5 minutes until smooth and elastic. Grease a 450g/1lb loaf tin (pan).

4 Shape the dough and place it in the prepared tin. Cover with a damp dish towel and leave to rise in a warm place for 1–2 hours or until well risen. Preheat the oven to 190°C/375°F/Gas 5.

5 Bake the loaf in the oven for 30–35 minutes, or until it sounds hollow when it is tapped underneath.

6 Meanwhile, prepare the glaze by dissolving the sugar in the water in a small pan. Bring to the boil, stirring, then reduce the heat and simmer for 1 minute. Place the loaf on a wire rack and brush with the glaze while still hot. Leave the loaf to cool before serving.

COOK'S TIP
Sultanas are basically dried grapes and are packed with nutrients including iron. They are low-fat but with natural sugars.

Energy 260Kcal/1103kJ; Protein 5.3g; Carbohydrate 58.6g, of which sugars 25.3g; Fat 2.1g, of which saturates 0.3g; Cholesterol 1mg; Calcium 97mg; Fibre 1.8g; Sodium 38mg.

APRICOT SPONGE BARS ★

THESE LOW-FAT SPONGE FINGERS ARE DELICIOUS AT TEATIME — THE APRICOTS WILL KEEP THE BARS MOIST FOR SEVERAL DAYS AT LEAST AND THEY ARE BEST KEPT IN A COOL, DRY PLACE.

MAKES EIGHTEEN

INGREDIENTS
225g/8oz/2 cups self-raising
  (self-rising) flour
115g/4oz/½ cup soft light
  brown sugar
50g/2oz/⅓ cup semolina
175g/6oz/¾ cup ready-to-eat dried
  apricots, chopped
30ml/2 tbsp clear honey
30ml/2 tbsp malt extract
2 eggs, beaten
60ml/4 tbsp skimmed milk
60ml/4 tbsp sunflower oil
a few drops of almond extract
30ml/2 tbsp flaked (sliced) almonds

1 Preheat the oven to 160°C/325°F/Gas 3. Lightly grease and then line an 18 x 28cm/7 x 11in baking tin (pan). Set aside.

2 Sift the flour into a mixing bowl, then stir in the sugar, semolina and apricots. Make a well in the centre and add the honey, malt extract, eggs, milk, oil and almond extract. Mix the ingredients together until smooth and well mixed.

3 Spoon the mixture into the prepared tin, spreading it evenly to the edges, then sprinkle the flaked almonds over the top.

COOK'S TIPS
Use a sharp knife to cut the cooled cake into even bars or slices. Use a pair of kitchen scissors to snip the apricots into small pieces.

4 Bake in the oven for 30–35 minutes, or until the centre springs back when lightly pressed. Remove from the tin and turn on to a wire rack to cool. Cut into 18 slices to serve.

COOK'S TIP
If you don't have pre-soaked (ready-to-eat) dried apricots, just chop ordinary dried apricots, soak them in boiling water for 1 hour, then drain well and add to the mixture.

VARIATIONS
Use self-raising (self-rising) wholemeal (whole-wheat) flour in place of white flour. Use ready-to-eat dried pears or peaches, or raisins or sultanas (golden raisins) in place of apricots.

Energy 134Kcal/566kJ; Protein 2.7g; Carbohydrate 24.8g, of which sugars 13.2g; Fat 3.3g, of which saturates 0.5g; Cholesterol 21mg; Calcium 36mg; Fibre 1.1g; Sodium 16mg.

SPICED PEAR AND SULTANA TEABREAD ★

THIS IS AN IDEAL TEABREAD TO MAKE WHEN PEARS ARE PLENTIFUL — AN EXCELLENT USE FOR WINDFALLS AND IT CREATES A TASTY, LOW-FAT SNACK OR SWEET TREAT.

SERVES EIGHT

INGREDIENTS
25g/1oz/¼ cup rolled oats
50g/2oz/¼ cup light muscovado (brown) sugar
30ml/2 tbsp pear or apple juice
30ml/2 tbsp sunflower oil
1 large or 2 small eating pears
115g/4oz/1 cup self-raising (self-rising) flour
115g/4oz/scant 1cup sultanas (golden raisins)
2.5ml/½ tsp baking powder
10ml/2 tsp mixed spice
1 egg, beaten

VARIATION
Use eating apple(s) in place of pear(s).

1 Preheat the oven to 180°C/350°F/ Gas 4. Grease and line a 450g/1lb loaf tin (pan) with baking parchment. Put the oats in a bowl with the sugar, then pour over the pear or apple juice and oil, mix well and leave to stand for 15 minutes.

2 Quarter, core and coarsely grate the pear(s). Add to the oat mixture with the flour, sultanas, baking powder, mixed spice and egg, then mix together thoroughly.

3 Spoon the mixture into the prepared loaf tin and level the surface. Bake in the oven for 50–60 minutes, or until a skewer inserted into the centre comes out clean.

4 Turn out the teabread on to a wire rack and peel off the lining paper. Leave to cool completely. Serve in slices.

Energy 176Kcal/743kJ; Protein 3g; Carbohydrate 34.1g, of which sugars 20.8g; Fat 4g, of which saturates 0.6g; Cholesterol 24mg; Calcium 40mg; Fibre 1.8g; Sodium 20mg.

BANANA AND GINGERBREAD SLICES ★

THESE LOW-FAT SLICES ARE VERY QUICK TO MAKE AND ARE DELICIOUSLY MOIST BECAUSE OF THE ADDITION OF MASHED BANANAS TO COMPLEMENT THE GINGER.

MAKES TWENTY SLICES

INGREDIENTS
275g/10oz/scant 2½ cups plain
  (all-purpose) flour
20ml/4 tsp ground ginger
10ml/2 tsp mixed spice
5ml/1 tsp bicarbonate of soda
  (baking soda)
115g/4oz/½ cup soft light
  brown sugar
60ml/4 tbsp sunflower oil
30ml/2 tbsp molasses or black treacle
30ml/2 tbsp malt extract
2 eggs, beaten
60ml/4 tbsp orange juice
3 bananas
115g/4oz/scant 1 cup raisins

1 Preheat the oven to 180°C/350°F/ Gas 4. Lightly grease and line an 18 x 28cm/7 x 11in baking tin (pan). Set aside.

2 Sift the flour into a bowl with the ground spices and bicarbonate of soda. Stir in the sugar, mixing well.

VARIATION
To make Spiced Honey and Banana Slices: omit the ground ginger and add another 5ml/1 tsp mixed spice; omit the malt extract and the molasses or black treacle and add 60ml/4 tbsp strong-flavoured clear honey instead; and replace the raisins with either sultanas (golden raisins), or coarsely chopped ready-to-eat dried apricots, or semi-dried pineapple. If you choose to use the pineapple, then you could also replace the orange juice with pineapple juice.

3 Make a well in the centre, add the oil, molasses or black treacle, malt extract, eggs and orange juice and mix together thoroughly.

4 Peel and mash the bananas, add them to the bowl with the raisins and mix together well.

5 Pour the mixture evenly into the prepared tin and bake in the oven for about 35–40 minutes, or until the centre of the cake springs back when lightly pressed.

6 Leave the cake to cool in the tin for 5 minutes, then turn out on to a wire rack and leave to cool completely. Cut into 20 slices to serve.

Energy 133Kcal/563kJ; Protein 2.3g; Carbohydrate 25.9g, of which sugars 15.2g; Fat 3g, of which saturates 0.5g; Cholesterol 19mg; Calcium 37mg; Fibre 0.7g; Sodium 18mg.

PITTA BREAD ★

*LOW IN FAT, PITTA BREAD IS FUN TO MAKE, AND LOOKS ALL THE BETTER FOR A LITTLE WOBBLINESS
AROUND THE EDGES. IT ADDS SO MUCH BODY WHEN YOU EAT WITH LOW-FAT SOUPS AND STEWS.*

MAKES TWELVE PITTA BREAD

INGREDIENTS
  25g/1oz fresh yeast
  500g/1¼lb/5 cups unbleached strong
    white bread flour, or half strong
    white and half strong wholemeal
    (whole-wheat) bread flour
  15ml/1 tbsp sea salt
  15ml/1 tbsp olive oil
  250ml/8fl oz/1 cup water

1 Dissolve the yeast in 120ml/4fl oz/
½ cup warm water. Allow to stand for
10 minutes. Put the flour(s) and salt in
a large mixing bowl and stir in the yeast
mixture. Mix together the oil and water,
and stir enough of this liquid into the
flour mixture to make a stiff dough.

2 Place the dough in a lightly oiled
bowl, cover with a clean dish towel and
leave in a warm place for at least 30
minutes and up to 2 hours.

3 Knead the dough on a lightly floured
surface for 10 minutes, or until smooth.
Lightly oil the bowl again, place the
dough in it, cover once more and leave
to rise in a warm place for about 1 hour,
or until doubled in size.

4 Divide the dough into 12 equal
pieces. With lightly floured hands,
flatten each piece, then roll out into a
round measuring about 20cm/8in in
diameter and about 5mm–1cm/¼–½in
thick. Keep the rolled breads covered
with a clean dish towel.

5 Heat a large, heavy frying pan over a
medium-hot heat. When smoking hot,
gently lay one piece of flattened dough
in the pan and cook for 15–20 seconds.
Carefully turn it over and cook the
second side for about 1 minute.

6 When large bubbles start to form on
the bread, turn it over again. It should
puff up. Using a folded clean dish
towel, gently press on the bread where
the bubbles have formed. Cook for a
total of 3 minutes, then remove the
pitta from the pan. Repeat with the
remaining flattened dough pieces until
all the pittas have been cooked.

7 Wrap the pitta breads in a clean dish
towel, stacking them as each one is
cooked. Serve the pittas hot while they
are soft and moist.

VARIATION
To cook the breads in the oven, preheat
the oven to 220°C/425°F/Gas 7. Fill an
unglazed or partially glazed ovenproof
dish with hot water and place in the
bottom of the oven. Alternatively, soak
a handful of unglazed tiles in hot water
and arrange them in the bottom of the
oven. Use either a non-stick baking sheet
or a lightly oiled ordinary baking sheet
and heat in the oven for a few minutes.
Place two or three pieces of flattened
dough on to the hot baking sheet and
place in the hottest part of the oven.
Bake for 2–3 minutes. They should puff
up. Repeat with the remaining dough
until all the pittas have been cooked.

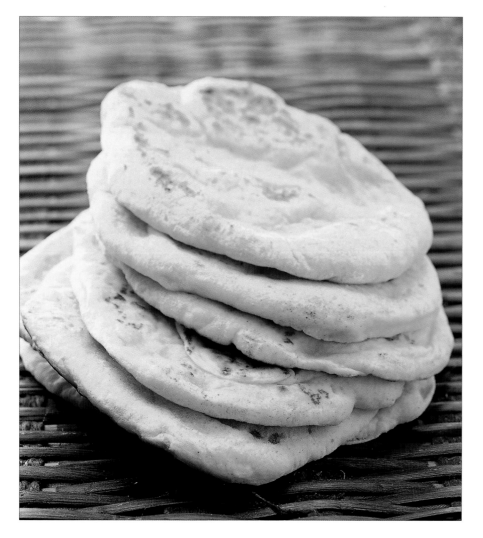

Energy 150Kcal/638kJ; Protein 3.9g; Carbohydrate 32.4g, of which sugars 0.6g; Fat 1.5g, of which saturates 0.2g; Cholesterol 0mg; Calcium 58mg; Fibre 1.3g; Sodium 165mg.

SODA BREAD ★

THIS DELICIOUS SODA BREAD RECIPE TAKES ONLY A FEW MINUTES TO MAKE AND NEEDS NO RISING OR PROVING. IF POSSIBLE, EAT SODA BREAD WHILE STILL WARM FROM THE OVEN AS IT DOES NOT KEEP WELL.

SERVES EIGHT

INGREDIENTS
   450g/1lb/4 cups plain (all-purpose)
     flour, plus extra for sprinkling
   5ml/1 tsp salt
   5ml/1 tsp bicarbonate of soda
     (baking soda)
   5ml/1 tsp cream of tartar
   350ml/12fl oz/1½ cups buttermilk

1 Preheat the oven to 220°C/425°F/ Gas 7. Flour a baking sheet and set aside. Sift all the dry ingredients into a mixing bowl and make a small well in the centre.

2 Add the buttermilk and mix quickly to form a soft dough. Turn on to a floured surface and knead lightly. Shape into a round about 18cm/7in in diameter and place on the baking sheet.

VARIATION
Use plain (all-purpose) wholemeal (whole-wheat) flour in place of some or all of the white flour.

3 Cut a deep cross in the top of the loaf and sprinkle with a little flour. Bake in the oven for about 25 to 30 minutes, then transfer the soda bread to a wire rack to cool down. Best served still warm in slices or wedges.

COOK'S TIP
Soda bread needs a light hand. The ingredients should be bound together quickly in the bowl and kneaded very briefly. The aim is to get rid of the largest cracks, as the dough will become tough if it is handled for too long.

COOK'S TIP
Buttermilk is high in lactic acid, and when, in recipes such as this one, it is mixed with an alkali such as bicarbonate of soda (baking soda), the chemical reaction that results produces a gas called carbonic acid. This has the effect of aerating the dough and making it much lighter. Sour cream can be used in place of buttermilk, as it is also acidic.

Energy 206Kcal/875kJ; Protein 6.8g; Carbohydrate 45.6g, of which sugars 2.8g; Fat 0.9g, of which saturates 0.2g; Cholesterol 2mg; Calcium 132mg; Fibre 1.7g; Sodium 267mg.

CHAPATIS ★

THESE CHEWY, UNLEAVENED BREADS ARE EATEN THROUGHOUT NORTHERN INDIA. THEY ARE IDEAL SERVED AS AN ACCOMPANIMENT TO LOW-FAT SPICY VEGETARIAN DISHES. CHAPATIS ARE BEST WHEN MADE AT HOME BY HAND RATHER THAN SHOP-BOUGHT.

MAKES SIX CHAPATIS

INGREDIENTS
175g/6oz/1½ cups Atta or plain
  (all-purpose) wholemeal
  (whole-wheat) flour
2.5ml/½ tsp sea salt
about 120ml/4fl oz/½ cup water
5ml/1 tsp sunflower oil
a little melted ghee, butter or
  non-hydrogenated margarine, for
  brushing (optional)

COOK'S TIP
• If using a food processor to make the dough, place the flour and salt in the processor and pulse to blend. Slowly add the water until a soft dough forms.

1 Sift the flour and salt into a large mixing bowl. Add the water and mix to a soft dough using your hand or a round-bladed knife. Knead in the oil, then turn the dough out on to a lightly floured surface.

2 Knead for 5–6 minutes until smooth. Place the dough in a lightly oiled bowl, cover with a damp dish towel and leave to rest for 30 minutes. Turn out on to a floured surface. Divide the dough into six equal pieces. Shape each piece into a ball.

3 Press each ball of dough into a larger round with the palm of your hand, then roll into a 13cm/5in round. Stack, layered between clear film (plastic wrap), to keep moist.

4 Heat a griddle or heavy frying pan over a medium heat for a few minutes until hot. Take one chapati, brush off any excess flour, and place on the griddle. Cook for 30–60 seconds, or until the top begins to bubble and white specks appear on the underside.

5 Turn the chapati over using a metal spatula and cook for a further 30 seconds. Remove from the pan and keep warm, layered between a folded dish towel, while cooking the remaining chapatis. If you like, the chapatis can be brushed lightly with melted ghee or butter immediately after cooking. Serve warm.

COOK'S TIPS
• *Atta* or *ata* is a very fine wholemeal (whole-wheat) flour, which is only found in Indian stores and supermarkets. It is sometimes simply labelled chapati flour.
• Atta can also be used for making rotis and other Indian flat breads.

Energy 99Kcal/422kJ; Protein 3.7g; Carbohydrate 20g, of which sugars 0.5g; Fat 1.1g, of which saturates 0.2g; Cholesterol 0mg; Calcium 38mg; Fibre 1.9g; Sodium 165mg.

SPRING ONION FLATBREADS ★

OVEN-BAKED FLATBREAD IS A STAPLE FOOD FROM INDIA TO NORTH AFRICA AND THE CAUCASUS. USE THESE DELICOUSLY SPICY FLATBREADS AS SOON AS THEY'RE COOKED TO WRAP AROUND CHARGRILLED VEGETABLES AND CHUNKY VEGETABLE SALADS, OR SERVE WITH TASTY VEGETARIAN DIPS SUCH AS HUMMUS.

MAKES SIXTEEN FLATBREADS

INGREDIENTS
    450g/1lb/4 cups strong white bread
    flour, plus extra for dusting
    5ml/1 tsp salt
    7g/¼oz packet easy-blend (rapid-rise)
    dried yeast
    4 spring onions (scallions),
    finely chopped

1 Place the flour in a large mixing bowl and stir in the salt, yeast and spring onions. Make a well in the centre and pour in about 300ml/½ pint/1¼ cups lukewarm water. Mix to form a soft, but not sticky, dough.

2 Turn out the dough on to a floured work surface and knead for about 5 minutes, until smooth.

3 Put the dough back in the bowl, cover with a damp dish towel and leave to rise in a warm place until doubled in size.

4 Knock back (punch down) the dough to get rid of any excess air, then turn it out on to a floured work surface or board. Divide the dough into 16 equal pieces and roll each piece into a smooth ball. Roll out each ball to flatten it to a 13cm/5in round.

5 Heat a large, heavy frying pan until hot. Dust off any excess flour from one dough round and cook for 1 minute, until slightly browned in parts, then flip over and cook for a further 30 seconds. Repeat with the remaining dough rounds.

VARIATION
To make garlic flatbreads, use 2 finely chopped garlic cloves in place of the spring onions (scallions).

Energy 97Kcal/410kJ; Protein 2.7g; Carbohydrate 21.9g, of which sugars 0.5g; Fat 0.4g, of which saturates 0.1g; Cholesterol 0mg; Calcium 40mg; Fibre 0.9g; Sodium 124mg.

INDEX